THE THEATRE OF THE
HOLOCAUST

THE THEATRE OF THE
HOLOCAUST

FOUR PLAYS

edited and with an introduction by
ROBERT SKLOOT

RESORT 76   Shimon Wincelberg

THRONE OF STRAW   Harold and Edith Lieberman

THE CANNIBALS   George Tabori

WHO WILL CARRY THE WORD?   Charlotte Delbo

The University of Wisconsin Press

Published 1982

The University of Wisconsin Press
114 North Murray Street
Madison, Wisconsin 53715

The University of Wisconsin Press, Ltd.
1 Gower Street
London WC1E 6HA, England

First printing

Printed in the United States of America

For LC CIP information see the colophon

ISBN 0–299–09070–1 cloth; 0–299–09074–4 paper

Resort 76 © 1981 Shimon Wincelberg, originally published as *The Windows of Heaven* © 1962 Shimon Wincelberg, and originally produced by the Royal Dramatic Theatre, Stockholm, Sweden. All inquiries concerning performance should be sent to Eisenbach-Greene, Inc., 760 North La Cienega Boulevard, Los Angeles, California 90069.

Throne of Straw © 1972 Harold and Edith Lieberman, © 1982 Harold Lieberman. *Throne of Straw* was originally produced by Dorothy Sinclair. All inquiries concerning performance should be sent to Harold Lieberman, 520 South Burnside Avenue, Los Angeles, California 90036.

The Cannibals © 1967, 1968 George Tabori. All inquiries concerning performance should be sent to Bertha Case, 345 West 58th Street, New York, New York 10019.

Who Will Carry the Word? © 1982 Charlotte Delbo, originally published in French, *Qui rapportera ces paroles?* © 1974 by Editions Pierre Jean Oswald. All inquiries concerning performance should be sent to Charlotte Delbo, 33 Rue Lacépède, 75005 Paris, France.

For JoAnn, Sarah Kate, and Julia Rose

Contents

Acknowledgments

I should like to express my gratitude for the encouragement and assistance I received in putting together this anthology, especially to Mendel Kohansky, Edie Naveh, Alan Lettofsky, Judy Sidran and Brian Keeling.

THE THEATRE OF THE
HOLOCAUST

Introduction

The usually quiet unfolding of human history is sometimes interrupted by events of shattering and lasting effect on the lives of whole peoples. In the twentieth century the world has seen more than a few such events. A case could be made, for example, that the exploration of the solar system in the 1960s and 1970s, in a benign way, qualifies as such an event because it forced people to revise the understanding they have of themselves and their relationship to the world around them. Less to be celebrated, but no less influential, was the Great Depression of the 1930s; a still more painful and unsightly mark was left on the world's order and its people by the First World War. During their course and in their aftermath, such events, by causing nations and peoples to rethink the central questions of existence, have been the inspiration for the imaginative literature of every age, as history is retold and re-experienced in song and story, poem and play.

Among the events of recent Western history that today reside in our consciousness, none is more disturbing than the Holocaust. More than any other event of our time, the Holocaust has caused entire nations and peoples to revise understandings of themselves by provoking disquieting and continuing inquiries of the most moral kind. It has forced individuals to reassess their knowledge of the human species, a reassessment which has been deepened and intensified by the large body of testimony and witness which those who were personally touched by the Holocaust have produced. Along with this work, which has appeared in remarkable profusion, has come the recent outpouring of political novels, television spectaculars, coffee table picture books, church sermons, university courses, literary essays, theatre pieces, hip journalism, and porno-

3

graphic films on the Holocaust theme, clear proof of how strongly the subject has taken up residence in our contemporary consciousness.

This anthology attempts to assess the relationship of the Holocaust to the drama of our time, to describe its character and evaluate its importance. By bringing to the reading public four remarkable plays belonging to what I have called "the Theatre of the Holocaust," I hope to call even greater attention to a body of work which has assumed a notable place in today's theatre.[1] Taken together, the four plays represent the scope and breadth of their special genre. They achieve their effects through diverse styles and artistic strategies corresponding to each author's differing aesthetic inclinations and ethical assumptions; but whether taken individually or together, they present a compelling picture which can not and should not be ignored.

As a prelude to the plays themselves, it will be helpful to discuss in some detail the historical events to which the plays are a response, and the artistic difficulties inherent in treating those events. Only after placing the plays in an historical and aesthetic context can the nature of their achievement be fully recognized and the ethical conclusions they draw be fairly evaluated.

All four plays—Shimon Wincelberg's *Resort 76,* Harold and Edith Lieberman's *Throne of Straw,* George Tabori's *The Cannibals,* and Charlotte Delbo's *Who Will Carry The Word?*—have received professional productions in the United States or Europe, but all deserve the greater recognition which their accessibility in one volume will afford them; gathering them in one place where they can be thematically related and theatrically contrasted will, I believe, enhance their individual reputations and stimulate other stage productions of them—which is the only way these (or any) plays can be fully brought to life. Their rich theatricality and exemplary integrity clearly set them apart from other less perceptive and more exploitative pieces to which they are superficially related

---

1. This designation excludes the several examples of plays written or performed in the ghettos and concentration camps.

by theme. In presenting these plays to the reading public, I hope to further stimulate discussion of the great historical, social, aesthetic, and ethical questions which the Holocaust raises. In seeking answers to those questions we place ourselves in the company of an ever-increasing part of our generation which is struggling to come to terms with that awful time, only recently past, which has scarred our present consciousness and caused us to be, for better or worse, forever different from the way we once were.

1. THE HOLOCAUST AND HISTORY

The Holocaust, originally a Greek word meaning "burnt whole," has been taken in our century to refer to the historical period which coincides with the rise of Nazi Germany in 1933 and extends to its demise in 1945. But it is particularly applied to those years between 1939 and 1945 when Nazi persecution of ethnic minorities and other "undesirables," especially Jews, achieved an unprecedented efficiency and hitherto unimaginable brutality. In the work of modern historians, in the testimony of the pitifully few survivors of these historical events, and even in the impeccable records the Germans themselves kept, we can read the details of what it was like to live under the merciless tyranny of a Germany determined to bring under its domination all of Europe and much of the rest of the world besides. We can also read about the resistance to the Germans by individuals and groups, for this is also part of the Holocaust story.

The historical facts are easily summarized. After six years of "preparations," the German government was finally ready to implement what came to be called in its debased bureaucratic language "the final solution to the Jewish question," as well as to purge Europe of all other citizens unsympathetic to its regime. The preliminary stage included repressive legislation (the Nuremberg Laws of 1935 making Jews second-class citizens), economic oppression (removing Jews from all businesses and professions and confiscating their property), social deprivation (expelling all Jewish children from German schools), public humiliation (ordering Jews to wear the Star of David or, on hands and knees, to scrub side-walks), and physical degradation (beating up Jews and other per-secuted people or deporting them as stateless persons to other in-hospitable places). Before and during those years, German citizens were subjected to viciously anti-Semitic propaganda in which Jews were labeled as subhuman criminals or likened to nonhuman dis-ease-causing insects; it was a kind of racism which touched a re-sponsive nerve in many of the national and ethnic populations of Europe. Through such ubiquitous psychological and cultural con-ditioning, the barbarous measures that were either being taken or being planned against the Jews became increasingly acceptable. By 1937, the first concentration camps on German soil, of which Da-chau and Buchenwald were to become the most notorious, were established; by that year no Jew in any country of central Europe could have been considered safe.

In the short period of some six and a half years, the 2,000-year-old Ger-man-Jewish community, numbering half a million in 1933 (including for-eign and stateless Jews), was uprooted and reduced to a group of some 220,000 outlaws who could expect nothing but continued persecution and harassment, and finally deportation to death.[2]

The worst was soon to come. With the rest of the world offering little more than lip service in support of the oppressed peoples (the Evian Conference of 1938 produced no commitment for assisting the thousands of new refugees), Germany, together with its allies and its sympathizers, correctly assumed that the rest of the world would do little or nothing to resist their inhuman policies. In fact, emigration from Europe to the United States, Palestine, or else-where became *more* difficult during this period, although several hundred thousand Jews did manage to escape in this way. At the Wannsee Conference in January, 1942, a month after America's en-try into the war, the Germans explicitly called for the country-by-country extermination of the Jews of Europe.

Thus the destructive force of the Holocaust was felt most harshly

---

2. "Holocaust," *Encyclopaedia Judaica* (Jerusalem: Keter Publishing House, 1971), 8:839.

and tragically by the Jews; in persecuting them Hitler saw an advantageous method of spreading the pernicious doctrine of Aryan (German) superiority while finding a useful outlet for German racism, violence, and greed. Among millions of civilians anti-Semitic activity became a part-time avocation, and the actual destruction of Jews became the full-time occupation of a large percentage of this number. The magnitude and virulence of anti-Jewish feeling reached such proportions that hatred of Jews and fear of them became a national obsession entirely superseding whatever tangible political or economic benefit might have been derived from their persecution. The story of the sufferings of the Jews and other persecuted groups (political dissenters, religious believers, homosexuals, and gypsies) makes for the most horrifying reading in all the writing of the events of this period. In speaking of the Holocaust we speak most particularly of the life and death of the helpless populations who were systematically and relentlessly pursued until the greater portion of them succumbed to a sadistic strategy wholly dedicated to removing them and the memory of them from the world.

Persecution had always played a central part in the history of the Jews, but never before had it been attempted on such a massive scale with such diabolical efficiency. November 9–10, 1938, *Kristallnacht* ("The Night of Broken Glass"), when 191 synagogues were destroyed and thousands of people assaulted throughout Germany, has become the most often-cited example of the systematic and widespread brutalization the Jews endured before the invasion of Poland less than a year later, when the hostilities of World War Two officially began. Overwhelmed by an adversary whose arrogance was encouraged by the "free" world's indifference and whose power was increased by its victims' cultural biases, religious beliefs, psychological necessities, demographic conditions, and economic hardships, the persecuted peoples met their appointment with a horrifying destiny.

Mass murder occurred both at random and with strict organization, in rural areas and in population centers. It was not unusual for special squads of German soldiers to gather together the entire

Jewish population of a town and shoot them all. It was even more common for Jews to be taken to regional centers for incarceration in ghettos where they would face slow starvation or death by disease under the most squalid and degrading conditions. (Also usual was the Jews' attempt to continue religious and cultural activities even under those conditions.) By 1942, convoys of railway cattlecars were regularly taking the Jews of Europe to concentration camps where most were killed outright and a few met a slower death as slave laborers. The most hideous examples of these camps were built by the Germans in eastern Poland for the sole purpose of exterminating Jews: Treblinka, Sobibor, Maidanek, Belzec, Chelmno. At Auschwitz, the most notorious of the camps, two million people were murdered between 1941 and 1944.

After the mass executions, which were usually accomplished with poison gas ("zyklon B"), the bodies were incinerated in giant crematories; much has been written about the overpowering stench of burning flesh which settled over the small Polish town of Oświęcim (Auschwitz) and environs. By 1944, with the German defeat in sight, the trains with their doomed human cargo kept rolling toward their destinations, often at the expense of military necessity; and even in the final months of the war, thousands more perished in the forced death marches around central Europe as the Germans tried, with no hope of success, to evade the advancing Allied armies. The final toll is almost impossible to comprehend: in the six years which encompass the war in Europe, at least eleven million civilians died, a figure which includes an estimated six million Jews, one out of three in the world, of whom one and one-half million were children.

In 1945, after a rapid rise and an even faster decline, the Third Reich which Hitler had proclaimed would last a thousand years came to its end. But most important for the purposes of this volume, in 1945 the concentration camps where millions had perished were opened to public view, and the world was suddenly confronted with evidence of an event which was unlike anything known or imagined until that time (although many of the facts of that condition were publicly reported for months or years before).

In the sunken eyes and broken bodies of the few surviving victims of such terrifying brutality, in the pictures of once-living human beings bulldozed into hill-sized mounds or lime-filled pits, and in the images of the frightened, often smug murderers, appeared some new human truth which could not be ignored even if it could not be immediately understood. The implications of that evidence, according to one of the major historians of the Holocaust, are shattering: "From this moment, fundamental assumptions about our civilization have no longer stood unchallenged, for while the occurrence is past, the phenomenon remains."[3]

Since 1945, with history, autobiography, fiction, poetry, and drama as a guide and a reminder, the world slowly and painfully has had to come to grips with unparalleled human depravity and human suffering and has had to try to find a meaning in them. The Holocaust has many legacies—political, cultural, psychological, theological—but the heart of its heritage is the continuing moral inquiry into the meaning of the events of that time.

Simply as a fact and as a precedent, it [the Holocaust] mocks our desire to affirm life's goodness and undermines our hope that never again will human beings gather in such vast and well-ordered numbers to commit mass murder. It stands as proof of the human potential for radical evil and therefore also as a prophecy of our possible future.[4]

We pursue this inquiry because something began during the Holocaust just as surely as something ended, and we are seekers of understanding in the territory defined by those events of 1933–45.

Anyone who wishes can now obtain a clear historical account of the Holocaust, the large picture as well as many of the details. What is far more difficult is to make sense of those events so that we can achieve some sort of meaningful relationship with history; for although there is truth to be found in the ashes of this experience, searching for this truth usually leads to emotional frustration

3. Raul Hilberg, *The Destruction of the European Jews* (New York: Quadrangle Books, 1961), p. 760.

4. Terence Des Pres, introduction to J. F. Steiner, *Treblinka*, 2d ed. (New York: New American Library, 1979), p. x.

and intellectual uncertainty. The questions come easily: How could these horrifying events occur in one of the most civilized and advanced nations of the world? Why did most of the free world remain aloof to the plight of the Jews and other persecuted minorities? How did the victims of persecution react to their conditions? The outlines of the answers can by now be discerned. But the answers to more personal inquiries are painfully elusive: Had we been involved in the events of this time, how would we have behaved? What relationship do we share with the victims and with the perpetrators of the Holocaust? What are the implications for post-Holocaust religion and the nature of faith? What is goodness and what is evil, and how can we recognize them in others and in ourselves?

I suggest that when answers are sought to these and other disturbing questions, it is likely that we will come closer to finding them with the assistance of those artists who have gone ahead of us into this once-unimaginable landscape. The plays in this volume re-create the Holocaust world and show us what it was like to be alive in those dark years. And it is to the artistic difficulties inherent in this imaginative activity that we must now turn our attention.

2. THE HOLOCAUST IN LITERATURE

One cultural fact of our age is that the imaginative literature on the subject of the Holocaust continues to proliferate at an astonishing rate. Fiction, autobiography, poetry, and drama about the Holocaust experience, and criticism of those forms, appear with an insistent regularity confirming one evaluation that "its presence in memory has not only lasted but . . . has grown in force and authority."[5] Despite the repugnant images of "Hell made immanent" (in George Steiner's phrase), despite the volatility of the subject matter and the ambiguity of many of the conclusions which can be drawn from it, the temptation to withdraw from involvement is strongly resisted.

5. Des Pres, introduction to *Treblinka*, p. x.

One reason for this is that many artists see their pursuit of the subject as an inherently moral one; they believe that standing aside from the Holocaust or keeping silent about it is simply not a permissible choice. They accept the challenge of the Holocaust's victims, who frequently and fervently urged that the truth of those events, or at least the facts about them, be conveyed to future generations. Elie Wiesel, one of the best and most articulate of these artists, and a survivor of Auschwitz as well, has found that his own work is motivated by a "profound conviction": "Anyone who does not actively, constantly engage in remembering and in making others remember is an accomplice of the enemy. Conversely, whoever opposes the enemy must take the side of his victims and communicate their tales, tales of solitude and despair, tales of silence and defiance." [6]

Here, *on moral grounds,* Wiesel (although he has not been entirely consistent in this kind of statement) is counseling against choosing silence. The contrary opinion is most forcefully stated by the English critic George Steiner who, following the lead of the German sociologist T. W. Adorno, and despite his own perceptive and moving prose on the subject, has foreseen the collapse of the imagination when confronted with the Holocaust as historical fact. [7]

Through such debate, we can distinguish three major and interconnected questions concerning the relationship of artists to the Holocaust. First, is it possible for the Holocaust to be dealt with in works of art? Second, if it can be dealt with, will the experience be cheapened, trivialized, or exploited in the treatment it is given? And third, what moral responsibility do artists have in taking up the Holocaust theme? As might be expected, the answers are complicated, controversial, and highly debatable.

The most thoughtful consideration of these questions is found in

6. Elie Wiesel, "The Holocaust as Literary Inspiration," in *Dimensions of the Holocaust* (Evanston, Ill.: Northwestern University Press, 1967), p. 16.

7. George Steiner, *In Bluebeard's Castle* (New Haven: Yale University Press, 1971).

Lawrence Langer's important study, *The Holocaust and the Literary Imagination*. At the beginning of his work he poses his own inquiry: "How should art—how *can* art—represent the inexpressibly inhuman suffering of the victims, without doing an injustice to that suffering?"[8] Langer is writing about artistic endeavor falsifying the experience it tries to depict by giving it a shape and intelligibility it never in fact possessed. He is concerned that because the Holocaust was a time of chaos and madness, a structured artistic re-creation of that experience, beginning with the process of selecting what part or aspect of the experience to treat, might distort and even deny the very nature of what life at that time was like. As a result, the audience might receive a kind of aesthetic satisfaction which betrays the historical reality or distracts attention from the ethical implications of the Holocaust.

After a long and forceful discussion of this issue, Langer concludes that the "principle of aesthetic stylization" does not, in fact, permit a distracting and destructive kind of pleasure, and he supplies a number of examples of nondramatic literature to prove his point. He shows how in the work of great artists, the evil in the Holocaust experience can be transcended and the horror transformed to produce something which engages us in a humane and compelling way. In propounding what he calls an "aesthetics of atrocity," Langer argues that "the task of the artist is to find a style and a form to present the atmosphere or landscape of atrocity, to make it compelling, to coax the reader into credulity—and ultimately, complicity."[9]

It is clear that the artists of this generation, great and otherwise, have generally rejected the way of silence and taken up Langer's statement of mission, with varying degrees of success. Setting aside examples of commercial exploitation of the Holocaust, and, sadly, there are many of them, we can conclude that artists reject silence; they write or paint or sing about the Holocaust because they are

---

8. Lawrence L. Langer, *The Holocaust and the Literary Imagination* (New Haven: Yale University Press, 1975), p. 1.

9. Ibid., p. 22.

attracted by something which can touch us to the core and they accept the challenge of making it accessible to the imagination in order to so touch us. They reject silence or stillness or darkness because they feel the need to respond to the survivors' call and bear witness to the degradation the victims endured and, sometimes, with great courage, overcame. They seek to retell the story and thereby make the murdered live again, if only in the imagination; they want to pay what Terence Des Pres calls in his excellent book, *The Survivor,* the "debt to the dead." [10] No other historical event of our time has forced upon artists this kind and magnitude of moral obligation: ". . . it is simply not possible to sympathize by indulging in silence, for to do so is to court madness or death. At just those points where, through some abiding and still operative reflex of language, silence converts once more into words—even into words *about* silence—Holocaust Literature is born." [11]

A situation such as this accounts in part for the passionate and volatile responses to artistic treatments of the Holocaust. Because of the complexity of the historical factors, and because the events of those years touch upon so many moral issues, the Holocaust has become a seemingly inexhaustible source of meaning for millions of people, although the meaning perceived depends on each person's personal circumstances. In truth, shattering events, like those mentioned earlier in this essay, always produce multiple, often contradictory understandings. One's outlook will be affected by whether one is a Jew or a Christian (or neither), a German, Russian, Pole, Israeli, or American, a survivor or child of a survivor, a politician, a veteran, a homosexual, etc. It is therefore not surprising that the Holocaust has been taken up by differing artists to articulate a host of differing perspectives on the human condition. But the important fact is that the Holocaust experience contains issues to which *all* groups respond.

10. Terence Des Pres, *The Survivor: An Anatomy of Life in the Death Camps* (New York: Oxford University Press, 1976), p. 39.
11. Alvin H. Rosenfeld, "The Problematics of Holocaust Literature," in *Confronting the Holocaust: The Impact of Elie Wiesel* (Bloomington: Indiana University Press, 1978), p. 2.

In general, playwrights of the Theatre of the Holocaust are motivated by five objectives, often simultaneously pursued: 1) to pay homage to the victims, if not as individuals then as a group; 2) to educate audiences to the facts of history; 3) to produce an emotional response to those facts; 4) to raise certain moral questions for audiences to discuss and reflect upon; and 5) to draw a lesson from the events re-created. What makes their work different from attempts to deal with other tragic themes, war for example, is their conviction that the Holocaust was a *unique* historical (and theological, political, and social) event, an event unlike anything else in the long and often tragic story of Western civilization.

The question of the uniqueness of the Holocaust is a controversial one. On one hand are those who argue that the attempted extermination of the Jews and other "unwanted" groups was merely another chapter in humanity's dark record, although an action which was carried out with an uncommon efficiency. Advocates of this viewpoint find parallels with other historical events. The Nazi objective of keeping pure the "master race" was political as well as racial; the camps and ghettos, we are reminded, did produce war materiel. The Holocaust, so this argument runs, differs in scale but not in essence from other genocidal activity.[12]

On the other hand are the larger number of survivors and observers who regard the Holocaust as the seminal contemporary event in both Jewish and world history, an event against which our present morality may be measured, and our future predicted. The historian Nora Levin has written: "In Nazi Germany, mass murder became a civic virtue. In the years from 1933 to 1945 there was a quantum leap in the history of human destructiveness. . . . The Holocaust challenges us to reverse this process, if we can, to regain our humanity and restore the old taboos or live in a world with models for unlimited evil."[13] Levin and many others argue that

12. See Paul Robinson's remarks in his review of Bruno Bettelheim's *Surviving*, in *The New York Times Book Review*, April 29, 1979, pp. 7, 63.

13. "Reflections on the Holocaust," an address to the Ethical Culture Society, October 16, 1977. For a statement of why the Holocaust is unique, see "Holocaust," *Encyclopaedia Judaica*, 8:832–906.

when considered *in its totality* the Holocaust is without historical parallel; the fanatical barbarity, the technological efficiency, the virulent political and racial ideology, the world's insensitivity, and the virtual inconceivability of the size of the human slaughter, when taken together, describe an event unlike any other before or since. In this second view, the Holocaust, by altering the course of human history, raises profound and dire implications for the future of the entire world.

In accepting the Holocaust as unique, historians, artists, and audiences are greeted by another problem: the danger in metaphorical or analogical discussion. For if the Holocaust is a unique event, what it is compared to or symbolized by can be chosen only with the greatest sensitivity and depicted with the greatest precision. An inapt comparison could degrade the victims' suffering or courage, or diminish the respect due them. On the simplest level we see this problem in the often indiscriminate use of the term Holocaust itself, to refer to the consequences of floods, fires, riots, road accidents, multiple suicides, or bankruptcies. In the highly charged atmosphere which often surrounds depictions or discussions of the Holocaust (especially when survivors are present), responsible artists attempt the task of definition with an extreme consciousness of risk, for an inappropriate analogy or a failure of language is liable to expose the artist to accusations of falsification, trivialization, insensitivity, hypocrisy, or betrayal—aesthetic criticism on moral grounds.[14] Protecting against the debasement of language is the job of every artist, but artists of the Holocaust must exercise a special kind of vigilance so that the full horrifying power of the word is preserved.

14. In her study of Holocaust literature, Sidra DeKoven Ezrahi writes: "Even the most vivid presentation of concrete detail and specificity, the most palpable reconstruction of Holocaust reality, is blunted by the fact that there is no analogue in human experience." *By Words Alone* (Chicago: University of Chicago Press, 1980), p. 3.

Rosenfeld concludes, *"there are no metaphors for Auschwitz, just as Auschwitz is not a metaphor for anything else."* *Confronting the Holocaust*, p. 19. Des Pres' assertion is no less categorical, if differently focused: "It [life in the camps] was the world itself, albeit a world such as we know through art and dream only. And here

The search for a style and a form for the Holocaust experience, with all the challenges, responsibilities, and risks it entails, is yet more difficult in the theatre, because of all the arts theatre is the most public and the most *real*. By presenting verbal and visual action in a perpetual present moment, the theatre creates an experience which *lives* before other people; performed by live actors during a time shared with an audience, a live performance has an impact and effectiveness which is immediate and powerful. While other art forms presuppose a more passive relationship between the art object and the audience, the theatre's temporal and physical nature evokes immediate and intense interaction, permitting less evasion by encouraging greater subjective involvement. In this way history is made to live again in the most palpable of ways.

Another critical problem confronting playwrights who wish to deal with the Holocaust centers on the use of realism, a late nineteenth-century theatrical form which is still most common in contemporary drama. Born out of an attraction to rationalism and materialism, a belief in social progress, an urge to correct societal abuse of the unfortunate, and readiness to exploit the popular fascination with theatrical replication, realism succeeded extraordinarily well so long as it lodged itself in drawing rooms and preoccupied itself with the salutary possibilities of a scientifically regulated future and the evils of social misconduct. During the generation of its greatest success (1880–1914), realistic playwrights were often able scenically and textually to describe contemporary affairs in a complex vision of "life as it is lived." This characteristic became realism's legacy to the movies and television, the appearance of which did much to relieve theatre of the arbitrary standard of truth to life by which it had come to be judged.

Dramatic realism never lacked for critics, and the theatrical

---

especially we must not be misled by our reliance on metaphor: the survivor is not a metaphor, not an emblem, but an *example*." *The Survivor*, p. 208.

One play which might serve for all such demeaning and irresponsible usages of the Holocaust as metaphor is Myrna Lamb's *Scyklon Z*, especially its final scene, "In the Shadow of the Crematoria," where the Holocaust is used as a hook upon which to hang a brief and insubstantial look at one aspect of sexual liberation. In *The Mod Donna and Scyklon Z*. (New York, 1971).

movements which followed it in our century attacked realism with vigor and conviction, usually on the grounds that it presented not more truth, but considerably less. And when we remember that realism, philosophically and formally, was predicated on objectivity and rationalism, it becomes increasingly clear why some artists and critics reject as inappropriate any realistic treatment of the most hope-defying and irrational event of modern times. Thus we are returned to Langer's argument, or a similar one by Susan Sontag: "To simulate atrocities convincingly is to risk making the audience passive, reinforcing witless stereotypes, confirming distance, and creating meretricious fascination. . . . Like its simulation as fiction, the display of atrocity in the form of photographic evidence risks being tacitly pornographic." [15]

Still, realism in the theatre is not so easily dismissed, if only because the dangers of abstraction are also considerable. Also, the presence of the live actor always makes realistic demands on the playwright. Whatever the approach taken by the dramatist, a commitment to *some kind* of stage reality must be made from the earliest moments of conception; the playwright must decide what picture of the world of the Holocaust is to be visually presented and spatially concretized in the production of his or her script. But since the world of the ghettos and concentration camps is impossible to duplicate on the stage, the writer on the Holocaust is caught in a dilemma: how to give stage images their full burden of meaning without making them unrecognizable through abstraction or untruthful through replication. In reaction to just this situation, criticism of the Theatre of the Holocaust often makes two opposite arguments: that a realistic approach is a falsification of the subject and that an abstract approach is a betrayal of it. In truth, there is no single correct style for the Theatre of the Holocaust, and we should be cautious of those who insist on only one kind of treatment.

In their search for the forms to achieve their individual objec-

---

15. Susan Sontag, "Eye of the Storm," *New York Review of Books*, January 21, 1980, p. 36. This is an excerpt of a review of Han-Jürgen Syberberg's *Hitler: A Film from Germany*.

tives, it is not surprising that playwrights of the Theatre of the Holocaust have employed a wide range of dramatic modes. Peter Weiss's *The Investigation* attempts a documentary style, Nellie Sachs's *Eli* is an extended poem in dramatic form, Erwin Sylvanus's *Dr. Korczak and the Children,* one of the best plays on the Holocaust theme, makes use of Pirandellian techniques, and George Tabori's *The Cannibals,* included in this volume, presents a surreal, nightmarish world where the actors assume the presences not only of victims, but of oppressors, insects, idiots, and even God.

It is true, however, that many other Holocaust plays retain a realistic base, because that is what people know best; audiences accept the form most readily because it is most "lifelike." Although the tension which develops between acceptance of the form and simultaneous revulsion with the content is likely to be intellectually unsettling and emotionally unendurable, the opposite strategy of deliberately distorting reality in an attempt to present the theme more accurately runs another sort of risk: losing sight of the "facts," and, with them, of the Holocaust's historical uniqueness.

In responding to this problem, playwrights have often tried to create believable environments by "softening" the depiction of ghetto or camp life; one method is to exclude or reduce the appearance of the Nazi oppressors and instead to focus on their victims. The dramatization of Anne Frank's *Diary* does without the Germans as actual stage presences; similarly, Shimon Wincelberg's *Resort 76* and Charlotte Delbo's *Who Will Carry the Word?* avoid actually showing the Nazis on stage. In Harold and Edith Lieberman's *Throne of Straw,* we see a German officer in the first scene, but only his civilian factotum thereafter; the central conflicts of the play occur among the Jewish victims. Arthur Miller's *Incident At Vichy* does not graphically picture the horrors of the Holocaust but rather implies them through events in the waiting room of the Vichy police station where the detainees' deportation and destruction is prefigured and symbolized (as when the silent, elderly Jew is cruelly separated from his most prized and only possession, a feather pillow, which is torn apart on stage).

Among other better-known Holocaust plays, Rolf Hochhuth's

The Deputy, about the Catholic Church's response to the destruction of European Jewry, comes close to an actual depiction of the brutality of the Holocaust experience, especially in the concentration camp setting of act 5. But Hochhuth uses abstraction in his story too, distorting and allegorizing historical fact. So does Jean-Paul Sartre in *The Condemned of Altona*, which tells of a corrupt and decadent German family working out its war guilt. Sartre's is one of the few plays of importance which appear to relate the "German side" of the Holocaust story; however, as the playwright later admitted, *Altona* wasn't about the Holocaust at all, but about the war between France and Algeria a decade after the Holocaust.[16] (Here is a fine example of the problem of the "diminishing analogy," cited earlier.) Both these plays are stylistic hybrids internally at odds with themselves. The same can be said of Martin Sherman's *Bent*, which deals with the problems of homosexuals in Nazi Germany, and of Robert Shaw's *The Man in the Glass Booth*, a story about a man who is both a Nazi and a Jew, which seems to care more for theatrical shock than intellectual coherency. Ultimately, these four playwrights (Hochhuth, Sartre, Sherman, and Shaw) fall short of the artistic success they seek for two reasons: they are unable to satisfyingly integrate their various styles, and they tend toward sensationalism by reducing and exploiting the Holocaust in order to favor their own religious, national, sexual, or psychological commitments.

Nevertheless, although the specific points of view of the playwrights vary considerably in the Theatre of the Holocaust, the point of departure is always the same: the historical event itself. It is important to realize how strongly the playwrights of this group rely not only on history but on the *idea* of history to give their imaginative creations an additional measure of stature, conviction, and even, for some, respectability. Thus, Hochhuth published an extensive and meticulous historical essay to accompany his massive play about Pope Pius XII, in order to give it more credibility and

16. Jean-Paul Sartre, "The Condemned of Altona," in *Sartre on Theater*, ed. Contat and Rybalka (New York: Pantheon Books, 1976), pp. 253–308.

himself more ready evidence to call to *The Deputy*'s defense in case it was attacked (which it was). Sartre published interviews and essays separately from his plays and made historical points to anticipate and counteract audience ambivalence or hostility toward the Gerlach family. The protagonist of Shaw's psychological fantasy, the schizophrenic Goldman-Dorff, is clearly modeled on the figure of Adolf Eichmann, Hitler's chief assistant in charge of extermination of the Jews. Erwin Sylvanus focuses on one of the Holocaust's most celebrated heroes, Janusz Korczak, the Polish orphanage director who *chose* to go to his death along with "his children"; in this short play Sylvanus continually shatters the realistic description of character and the realistic use of space so that our confrontation with Korczak's "history" will be more powerful. Anne Frank, of course, was among the most famous victims of the Holocaust, and her simple story has achieved universal recognition.

Of the plays in this volume, both *Throne of Straw* and *Resort 76* explicitly draw upon the lives of Jews in the ghetto of Lodz, Poland, under the harsh rule of Mordechai Chaim Rumkowski to whom the Germans delegated certain administrative powers. The Liebermans contrast the last years of Rumkowski's life with the last years of the fictional but representative Wolf family in order to convey their moral understanding of Rumkowski's notorious career. In *The Cannibals,* George Tabori's characters, two survivors and the sons of those who perished in one of the barracks of a concentration camp, create through sound effects and vaudeville turns the world of the Holocaust as Tabori sees it; our knowing that the play is dedicated to the memory of Tabori's father Cornelius, "a small eater" who died in Auschwitz, gives his characters greater power over us. And Charlotte Delbo, one of the few playwrights who was a survivor of the camps, although striving for anonymity for her individual characters, lets us know in her book *Le convoi du 24 Janvier* (1965) that their history is real: of the 230 women in her group who were deported to Auschwitz, only forty-nine lived to see their liberation.

The creative efforts of all the playwrights reflect many different

play: 1) the story of the theft of the cat (which is thought to be valuable enough to be exchanged for bread and a "safe" job), 2) the story of the engineer Blaustain and his pregnant wife Esther, 3) the story of Anya and the partisans, 4) the story of the "outsider" Krause, an ordinary and pathetic German considered by the others to be a Nazi apologist, and 5) the story of the boy Beryl and his teacher Schnur. Each story contains a description of characters caught in a moment when an action must be taken which has enormous ethical implications. Should the cat be exchanged, eaten, or set free? Should the expected child be allowed birth? Should Blaustain abandon his wife and join his sister Anya and the partisans? Should Krause be accepted or rejected? Should Beryl continue to believe in God? Each question demands the making of a moral decision to find its answer; each action supports or denies the possibility of courage, responsibility, friendship, freedom, honesty, trust, love, or faith in the most extreme and deadly circumstances.

It is left to Schnur, by profession a slaughterer but by inclination a teacher, to deliver the play's most dramatic moral message. With the imminent arrival of the Nazis who are coming to kill him for running a Jewish "school," he administers his final lesson to his young pupil who has been physically battered and emotionally broken by the Germans.

BERYL: . . . I want to eat, I want to be warm, I want to kill, I want to be like *them!*

SCHNUR: Like them? Without the knowledge of being made in His image? A beast of prey, without shame, without conscience, living for no higher pleasure than the smell of blood?

BERYL: Why not? What makes us better than they?

SCHNUR: Because you are a man! A man, and not an animal.

According to Schnur, spiritual aspiration and humane behavior are what distinguish a human being from the beasts and, in this case, the Jews from the Germans; the great challenge is to retain these qualities even in an environment of violence, bestiality, and senseless suffering. To Blaustain's anguished cry, "I don't want responsibilities!" Schnur replies firmly: "What makes you think you have a choice?"

This is a truly existential creed, one which steals meaning out of the void and imposes reason on a world which insistently denies purpose and defies understanding. Schnur's faith gives others courage if not hope. Blaustain and Esther decide to allow the birth of their child, although they cannot assure its survival, after Schnur recalls the ancient Jewish creed: "He who saves one life is as though he had saved an entire world." Thus a man trained as a slaughterer possesses the most refined reverence for life, and he would gladly trade his own life rather than be forced to participate in the taking of another's. The final symbolic action of the play is the release of the cat to "freedom" in the ghetto, to "tell the other animals . . . what it was like to be a Jew." In taking this action despite their need, these degraded and long-suffering people reject becoming murderers of any form of life; they disavow such slaughter not because they are "deaf-mutes, imbeciles or children," but because they are human beings.

There are many similarities between *Resort 76* and Harold and Edith Lieberman's *Throne of Straw,* first produced in 1973. Both plays are set in Lodz, the city in central Poland which was known as "The Manchester of the East" because of its huge textile industry, although *Resort* never identifies its location, as such. Both describe the terror of living in the ghetto established by the Nazis and administered by a Jewish Council (*Judenrat*) and a Jewish police force. In Wincelberg's play the chairman of the Council is only passingly referred to (as the "Emperor"); in *Throne of Straw* he is the protagonist, the historical figure Mordechai Chaim Rumkowski. The two plays are concerned with the choices which must be made in order to increase the chances of survival of comrades, loved ones, or self; both plays assemble a wide variety of characters who serve to represent the differing ways in which the ghetto inhabitants reacted to their conditions. Between these two groups of victims, several characters are strikingly alike: Yankele and Yablonka serve as comic figures; Israel and Schnur perish with their faith more or less intact, and serve as models for the young; Rosa and Miriam in *Throne,* more fully than the briefly seen figure of Anya the partisan in *Resort,* show us a picture of physical resistance which the play-

wrights include as an option available to the victims of the Holocaust.

The plays cover much common thematic ground. Both touch on
the most controversial and upsetting subject in Holocaust literature, Jews who betray other Jews, but whereas *Resort 76* only refers to the Blue Police, the Liebermans make the actions of Gabriel
and Rabinowitz (and of their boss Rumkowski) a major focus of
the moral debate at the center of *Throne of Straw*. They explore as
their central theme the place morality has in human action, and
describe (often with great humor) the tragic results which follow
from acting in a world where usual moral standards no longer apply; they seek to find the answer to a frequently asked question
concerning the possibility and usefulness of individual acts of resistance to oppression when nothing less than human life is at stake;
they recognize that even the *contemplation* of moral action in these
conditions can increase the danger to oneself and to others. Both
inquire into the conditions under which a life of decency and integrity can be maintained, and without which life has no meaning
at all.

But these two plays also diverge in important ways, revealing
something of the range of approach that is found in the Theatre of
the Holocaust. The noteworthy aspect of *Throne of Straw* is its
incorporation of Epic (or Brechtian) stage techniques to put distance between the audience and the characters. Brecht, the greatest
German playwright-theorist of this century (and himself a refugee
from the Nazis), challenged the realistic theatre with one of his
own devising. He despised popular realistic staging, which he contemptuously called "culinary," for its entertaining deceptions and
politically paralyzing effects. In opposition to it he developed a type
of theatre which would always insist on its reality *as theatre;* for
Brecht the true test of a play's greatness thereby became not how
faithfully it duplicated external reality but how close it came to
stirring up social protest.

At the heart of Epic Theatre's technique is the explicit desire of
forcing the spectator to draw back from emotional involvement at
strategic moments in the play, to *alienate* the audience by making

the familiar strange through some aspect of staging (*Verfremdungs-effekt*). It is the utilization of this Epic strategy which so distinguishes *Throne of Straw* from *Resort 76*.[19] A list of its Brechtian aspects includes: the possible use of slides or projections to specify a larger historical reality; the narrator figure (Yankele) who comments on the action of the characters, often poetically; the use of satirical music to undercut audience involvement with the characters and further objectify the action; the rapid alternation of many scenes of dissimilar rhythms and tones; the rejection of "realistic" stage pictures; and the direct appeal to the audience to intellectually assert itself when wrestling with some of the ethical issues the Holocaust raises.

These staging techniques make *Throne of Straw* very different in effect on an audience from the realistic, more traditional *Resort 76*, despite the thematic similarities between the two plays. The place where that difference is most clearly drawn is in the plays' final moments. *Resort 76* is content to leave its audience emotionally involved in the action it describes; the audience departs the theatre appreciative of the small—if temporary—victory of the forces which affirm life over the horrors of meaningless death. Despite Beryl's beating, Krause's suicide, and Schnur's removal, there is an air of reckless gaiety about these squalid surroundings when the cat is released to a freedom its owners can never know. The last words we hear in *Throne of Straw*, however, are directed *at the audience* by the half-mad Yankele, who warns his hearers about the dangers of jumping to conclusions concerning the terrible events they have just seen.

> I take this passion play from place to place
> And please while it's with you
> Don't feed me your dinner table morals about how
> They should have behaved;
> Only say what you would have done.

19. Brecht confronted the Holocaust from his own experience of the rise of Hitler and its effect on the Germans. His most lasting effort on this subject is his short play *The Jewish Wife*, an excellent study of bravery and cowardice.

A final question until I return:
Since shrouds have no pockets
And ashes no permanent home
Where will you keep them [the victims]?

This final question is asked directly of the audience while the house lights are on them; the Liebermans conclude their play by turning the moral inquiry back to us.[20]

Yankele's question is made the more pointed and logical because the readers of the play have been informed (as the audience might be in a program note) of the historical truth of the play's action; in their "Note on Historical Accuracy" the playwrights acknowledge that theirs is "not a work of history," but say that they "have made every effort to remain true to the major events and characters of the Lodz Ghetto during the years of the Holocaust." (Rumkowski's speech in act 2, scene 6 is, in fact, his actual words.) Epic staging techniques make the objective historical facts a frame for the dramatic action. When Yankele breaks through the "frame" of the action, he is able to force an emotional distance between the audience and the story; under Yankele's aggressive interrogation the audience, like all the play's characters, must make a moral judgment—a choice—about what the play's implications are. When this happens, the spectators are made into survivors in the way Des Pres has described:

Survivors do not bear witness to guilt, neither theirs nor ours, but to objective conditions of evil. In the literature of survival we find an image of things so grim, so heartbreaking, so starkly unbearable, that inevitably the survivor's scream begins to be our own. When this happens the role of spectator is no longer enough.[21]

It is the Liebermans' wish that the spectators, once they become survivors, should have no option but to explore their feelings and

20. See Robert Skloot, "Directing the Holocaust Play," *Theatre Journal* (December, 1979), 526–40, for a fuller discussion of the 1978 production of *Throne of Straw*.

21. Des Pres, *The Survivor*, p. 54.

reinterpret their moral understanding of issues raised by contact with a work of art.

The decision to behave morally under extreme stress, and then to confront the consequences of that behavior, are the themes George Tabori has taken up in his play *The Cannibals*.[22] Himself an eastern European and the son of a father who perished in Auschwitz, Tabori uses a cast consisting of the sons of the camp inhabitants, two survivors, and an S.S. guard to explore the questions of good and evil, of faith and loss of faith. His play is both unusual and daring, and, in its special use of certain popular acting techniques, highly theatrical and thoroughly nonrealistic.

In a headnote, Tabori describes his play as "being the extraordinary tale of a dinner party as told by the sons of those who attended the feast and the two survivors by whose courtesy the facts are known." His unwritten premise is found in the unanimous testimony of survivors to the great amount of time they passed in discussions and obsessive visions of food. He takes this phenomenon to its limit by imagining and dramatizing the decisions made by camp inmates who are faced with the choice of cannibalism or annihilation.[23] By this means Tabori is able to explore the crucial moral questions concerning the behavior of the Holocaust's victims; he also extends his political and cultural frame of reference to include the moral responsibility of Christians for the degradation and decimation of the Jews and others who were on the Nazis' agenda for extermination.

In performance, *The Cannibals* asks the audience to accept an unusual relationship with the characters; in watching the play we need not fear for the lives of the characters because they are incapable of dying, that is, most of the people of the play are shown to be acting out the circumstances surrounding the deaths of their fathers and not themselves. By assuming their fathers' identities,

22. Published first in *The American Place Theatre: Plays*, ed. Richard Schotter (New York: Dell Books, 1973). The play was premiered at the American Place Theatre, New York, November 3, 1968.

23. There is little evidence for believing that cannibalism was often practiced in the camps, but that cannibalism was contemplated is surely not beyond imagining.

they are twice removed from us: they are not only actors in a play, but characters (sons) assuming the roles of others (their fathers) in a play within a play. This enables us to witness without confusion characters in the play (Puffi and the Ramaseder Kid) dying and coming back to life. Further, because the headnote and scene 1 tell us that the people are either survivors (Heltai and Hirschler) or the surviving sons of victims who have gathered to retell a horrible story, our concern is focused not on the outcome of the story but rather on how the story's action will be achieved and on the events which led up to life and death in "the white room." Tabori skillfully employs a Brechtian technique to force the audience away from "suspense" and toward an intellectual investigation of social and moral issues. (It is true we cannot know whether Heltai and Hirschler are accurate in the facts they have recounted to the others; we accept their version since it remains uncontradicted and because the two seem to have no selfish motive in relating it. But they are a rather grotesquely unsympathetic pair.)

The alternation of each man from his identity as father to his identity as son (to say nothing of "acting" the parts of God, women, animals, idiots, infants, and insects, among others) is highly theatrical and often deeply moving, as when Haas reveals his father's homosexuality (scene 8), Glatz discusses his father's betrayal of friends (scene 11), and Uncle despairs that he will never be able to understand his father's actions (scene 12). When these discoveries are made, the actors playing the fathers *turn to the audience* to become the actors playing the sons, and these extraordinary shifts in identity temporarily force a distance between the play and us, another example of Brechtian technique which Tabori exploits superbly. (The audience is engaged directly at other times, for highly theatrical effect, as at the end of scene 10 when the characters fall to their knees and advance on the audience as they scrub the floor before "dinner.") In fact, the play as a whole is propelled along by these individual revelations and confessions; when there are no more of them, the "sons" absorb themselves once again into the identities of their "fathers," and the play is over.

But Tabori adds one final and stunning twist to *The Cannibals*.

At the conclusion of scene 11, each prisoner of the play has decided *not* to eat the soup which contains the boiled bits of Puffi's body; each has made a moral choice to "oppose this abomination till my dying breath," as Uncle swore previously in the play. But the arrival of S.S. Schreckinger changes their situation; correctly assuming that the cooking pot contains "the fat man," he demands that they either eat or be gassed immediately. The earlier voluntary (if agonized) rejection of cannibalism receives one last challenge from "the Angel of Death" himself, to the accompaniment of a jolly polka played by the camp orchestra. Only Heltai and Hirschler accept the meal, and as a direct consequence live to tell the story to the sons of those who declined (who then tell it to us). Importantly, the two who do eat have neither sons to carry on after them, nor fathers worthy of mention. When the others remove their clothes and exit naked to their deaths, Tabori presses home his exploration of the ethical dimension of the behavior of those who survived *and* of those who perished by asking us to attempt certain distinctions: Which of them was brave and which cowardly? Who was barbaric and who civilized? Which action was life-affirming and which life-denying?

Throughout the play, the arguments for and against cannibalism in particular and all killing in general are presented in the exchanges between Uncle (whose name is given as Cornelius at one point, the name of the playwright's father) and Klaub, the medical student. Their positions are maintained with passion and eloquence, especially in "The Trial" (scene 12), where the debate is further extended to a discussion of the Jew in society. Uncle is reviled and humiliated by the others, but the sight of his degraded and vulnerable form arouses compassion in his tormentors, and they take him up, dress and warm him, and reject the human banquet they have prepared. It is left to the vicious anti-Semite Schreckinger to stand for all the "dear brethren in Christ," whose religious ritual and historical practice have caused them to destroy their own souls at the same time that they devour their victims. In his last long monologue with himself—acting as his father *and* son—Schreckinger reveals his own fear, anger, confusion, and hate in the presence of that reviled race which resists humiliation and despair with a persistence he cannot explain and with a grace he cannot comprehend.

In its use of the nonverbal techniques of contemporary improvisational/group-theatre practice, *The Cannibals* manages to achieve moments of high poetic stature. In one sense, the play is about the power language possesses to articulate the stories of the often anonymous but tragically real millions who were lost in the Holocaust. The survivors' mission to give voice to the Holocaust experience is possible to fulfill in the hands of playwrights (and poets and novelists) like Tabori, who have the courage to walk the road to the doors of death and the imagination to create, and skill to describe, a window of morality in the dark chamber of total denial.

Charlotte Delbo's *Who Will Carry The Word?* (*Qui rapportera ces paroles?*) was written in 1966 and first performed in 1974.[24] Like *The Cannibals,* it attempts to describe what many Holocaust plays avoid: the life in the concentration camps *at the time it was lived.* Delbo, like Bryks, whose novella was the basis for Wincelberg's dramatization, was a survivor of Auschwitz; her play carries the weight of authenticity mediated through an austere poetic imagination. The title of her play reveals her obsession with the role of witness and survivor. Her concern with who will be alive to report the Holocaust experience and who, having endured it, can continue to report it, is seen in the diminishing number of characters in her play; the diminishing number also reflects how few actual survivors are alive today (in 1981 most are over fifty-five) and, by implication, the increasing number of people everywhere who would prefer ignorance to knowledge and confusion or evasion to truth.[25] There is an implicit rebuke in her title as well as a warning:

24. Originally published in Paris by Editions Pierre Jean Oswald, 1974. The play premiered at the Cyrano Théâtre, March 14, 1974, directed by Francois Darbon.

25. Hamida Bosmajian concludes her book *Metaphors of Evil: Contemporary German Literature and the Shadow of Nazism* (Iowa City: University of Iowa Press, 1979) with the same somber conclusion: "As the living memory of the Holocaust will pass, the surfaces of written records or photographic images and the sites of a concentration camp itself will rigidify, will become historical scar tissue impervious

we ignore the events of the Holocaust at our peril. Langer, in discussing Delbo's memoir *None of Us Will Return*, writes: "We endure the worst but are always surprised by the unthinkable. For this reason, one will never move beyond atrocity until the unthinkable enters the deepest recesses of human consciousness."[26]

There are twenty-three women in the cast of Delbo's play. Most of them are given names and ages in the list of characters; but for crucial reasons, Delbo provides them with little else in the way of distinguishing characteristics. In fact, she otherwise insists on near anonymity for them. In a definite way, this makes the play harsher, even crueler, than the other three in this volume, because the condition of the women is so extreme: even their human individuality has been stolen from them. In her introductory note she specifies *"the faces do not count"* and *"the costumes do not count,"* that is, they do not contribute to individualizing the characters. The identity of these women is that of a crowd, and they take on an importance directly related to their bulk or mass. (This was Euripides' objective in creating the chorus in *The Trojan Women*.)

Delbo's intention is to award these women stature *as a group,* to record through their initial presence and subsequent absence how many thousands perished and, by the end of the play when only Françoise and Denise remain, how few survived. The other reason for her decision to stage *Who Will Carry the Word?* in this fashion was to show us how close to death these women were, even when they were alive. That is, the line between the living and the dead in the concentration camps was often invisible; Langer writes of Delbo's description of "the extraordinary sensation of some victims of atrocity of being dead while still alive,"[27] and Delbo depicts such conditions with the utmost economy, simplicity, and suggestiveness.

Understanding the ravages of physical and psychological deprivation these women suffered, audiences are both shamed and

---

to the memory of pain. This is no genuine healing but is an inevitability of human reality." (P. 228.)

26. Lawrence L. Langer, *The Age of Atrocity* (Boston: Beacon Press, 1978), p. 211.

27. Ibid., p. 214.

strengthened; it is undeniably true that under such conditions life was barely possible, and only then by virtue of incredible stamina, unaccountable chance, and, most important, the extraordinary heroism of countless unknown individuals. (I believe it important that these women are political prisoners, as Delbo herself was, and thus not susceptible to the additional degradation which the Jews suffered as a result of their racial history; that is, these women brought with them a background of rebellion and noncompliance rather than one of accommodation and endurance.[28] And yet of this play's women, hardly one in ten survives!) So even in this play we see dramatized the possibility of *choice;* Françoise raises the issue in the first scene in her conversation with Claire, where Claire struggles to convince Françoise that suicide is cowardly and irresponsible and that taking one's life is not really a choice at all.

FRANÇOISE: Forget your formulas; here they aren't worth anything. It's [Suicide's] the only right I have left, the only choice. The last free act.
CLAIRE: There are no free acts here. No choices like that.
FRANÇOISE: Oh yes. I have a choice. I have a choice, between becoming a cadaver which will have suffered for only eight days, which will still be clean enough to look at, and one which will have suffered fifteen days, which will be horrible to look at.
CLAIRE: You have nothing left. No such choices, nothing. You are not free to do it. You don't have the right to take your life.
FRANÇOISE: And why don't I have the right?
CLAIRE: A fighter doesn't commit suicide.

For Delbo, as for so many other survivors, the mission of the fighter is to return and "render an account to the others."

Unburdening herself and rendering the account requires that Delbo courageously describe the camp experience itself, that is, her own experience. Through carefully articulated abstract staging, she overcomes the awesome aesthetic problems of her subject and ac-

28. Edward Alexander explores this Jewish tendency in the first chapter ("The Incredibility of the Holocaust") of his analysis of Holocaust literature, *The Resonance of Dust* (Columbus: Ohio State University Press, 1979). He writes: "I want to suggest that the inability of the victims themselves to credit the threat and then the actuality of destruction was a function not only of human psychology and the mad inventiveness of the Germans but of Jewish History and Jewish sensibility." (P. 3.)

complishes the goal which Langer sees as extremely difficult but eminently desirable.

The paradox of the Holocaust *for the artist* is its exclusiveness, the total absence of any shared basis of experience that would simplify the imagination's quest for a means of converting it into universally available terms—to find, in short, in the events of the Holocaust the kind of immediacy of impression, of direct communication, that one senses in the acidity of a lemon or the feel of wool.[29]

Delbo discards literal realism and indicates how to suggest the venue where the action of her play takes place. (One of her two requests for an Epic device, Françoise's address to the audience at the end of act 2, causes an unwarranted stylistic confusion, although the concluding remarks to the audience, because the "play" is over, make an effective epilogue.) A bare inclined plane serves as the exterior compound; action downstage suggests the interior of the barracks. Spotlights, sirens, and the gestures of the actors complete the stage effects which impress on the audience the barren and brutal environment of the concentration camp. No actual violence is seen; as in ancient Greek tragedy, it is retold by characters onstage with a grim explicitness sometimes followed by an image of terrible consequence, as when Claire's body is left on stage at the end of act 1, scene 4.[30] Ultimately, all of Delbo's images, and her dialogue as well, serve a single purpose. She takes from the Holocaust experience the idea of obligation; what she gives to us is a lamentation which demands that we understand what happened and unceasingly report it. For Delbo, the Holocaust is our permanent burden and we must carry the word of it everywhere.

---

29. Langer, *The Holocaust and the Literary Imagination*, p. 289.

30. In fact, all four plays in this volume rely heavily on sound effects to indicate the threatening and hostile reality outside the usually crowded but isolated spaces these doomed figures inhabit. Thus motorcades, churchbells, and a gramophone are heard often in *Resort*, and the factory whistle, artillery, and railway noises in *Throne*. In *The Cannibals*, the Loudspeakers (which are included in the cast of characters) provide sound effects, information, and music, and the sirens and shots of the camp punctuate Delbo's play. A director needs to pay close attention to the effect of these stage devices.

4. THE FUTURE AND ITS POSSIBILITIES

The four plays in this volume, in their separate and distinct ways, place us in close touch with a world which ended only a generation ago. As representative plays of the Theatre of the Holocaust they accomplish multiple objectives: to educate us to the history of that time, to move us with the stories of the perished millions, to raise crucial moral questions for us to ponder, to demonstrate the human action that can be taken in times of extreme stress and how it can be evaluated, and to suggest ways in which the darkest hours of our night-filled century can be kept from descending again. Concerning this last objective the plays' *practical* effect must be seen as less than successful, reason enough, perhaps, for bringing them together in order to stimulate new stage productions and compel greater attention to their concerns. Though the value and significance of theatre should not be judged solely, if at all, on the fulfillment of its social objectives, making these plays accessible surely answers some deeply felt need of our generation.

In telling their stories, the playwrights utilize differing theatrical forms to present similar, even identical issues. One such issue, their concern with the moral dimension of human choice, contains several other subsidiary concerns: the loss of faith, the denial of God, the meaning of suffering, the nature of evil, and the possibility for good. Choice, however, implies an essentially personal action, and none of these playwrights is satisfied with discussing the implications of individual effort only. They, and others like them (Miller, Hochhuth, Sylvanus), take their common concern one step further, externalizing it and transforming it into the idea of *responsibility*. They explore not merely the meaning of our actions on ourselves, but the effect our actions have on others.

Schnur's advice to Beryl and Blaustain, the example Israel sets for David, Miriam's pleas to Rumkowski, and the efforts of Delbo's characters to warn one another and stay alive *and help others stay alive,* all suggest courses of action that have some chance, however small, of defeating—or at least temporarily staying—the destructive force in the worlds depicted by these plays. These actions plainly have significance as examples of humane behavior; but they take on special urgency and heightened meaning because of the magnitude of the evil they defy.

Tabori's play is the most cynical in conception of the four, sympathizing with the abstainers from the human banquet who accepted their deaths in the gas chambers, but finally doubting how "normal" morality can be of any use to survival. In the Blaustains' decision to have their child in *Resort 76*, in the rebellion of Miriam and Rosa against Rumkowski and of Israel's sacrifice in *Throne*, in the majority's rejection of Schreckinger's order in *The Cannibals*, in Gina's refusal to assist in the extermination of children in *Who Will Carry the Word?* we see decisions which point to the affirmation of a single ethical principle: that at the very least, *we must never participate in doing the work of the forces of inhumanity*. Indisputably, the four plays deny the assertion of Tabori's S.S. guard that "there is a Fuehrer in the asshole of the best of us."

To be sure, other examples of Holocaust literature are not so reckless (or perhaps so foolish) in their discovery of a moral splinter in the shattered glass of the Holocaust experience, but the vision of these four plays takes on a greater sharpness for the picture of those people who, in Des Pres' phrase, keep "steady in their humanness." Broken and horribly abused, tempted to cross the only line which has meaning and gives meaning to them, they are shown as both ordinary in their humanity and exceptional in their morality. Our seeing them in action allows their behavior to become included in the schedule of options available to us in a time of (and often in spite of) the most extreme physical degradation and spiritual loss. In doing so, these plays have effectively addressed, in both artistic and moral terms, what may be the central moral issue of the Holocaust.[31]

31. Some years ago A. Alvarez discerned a similar strategy in Jorge Semprun's Holocaust novel *The Long Voyage*, of which he wrote: "What Semprun is doing, in short, is exploring the possibilities of human behavior in inhuman circumstances. . . . He is trying to demonstrate imaginatively that from the absence itself of morality a morality can emerge." From "The Literature of the Holocaust," in *Beyond All This Fiddle* (London: Allen Lane, Penguin Press, 1968), p. 31.

To do nothing, to keep silent, is an option rejected by these play-wrights (and others like them) who struggle to make sense of the Holocaust experience and to draw from it some kind of truth which, whatever shape it takes, can inform our present and future lives. They know that within the Holocaust experience lie the most troubling questions we can raise about ourselves and others, about whole nations and peoples. In the theatre they create a world which is more intense and more *real* than the world most of us know; through their plays we can have contact with times and places it is good never to have experienced but terrible never to understand. They cause us to remember the many who, in choosing silence, may have prepared for and even encouraged the Holocaust; they ask us to remember the few who, in choosing to resist, often in ways which during "normal" times never would have been identified as resistance, acted in a way that is worthy of emulation.

We hope that the conditions of life which existed for the many and the few a generation ago are ones we and others shall never have to face. But if we should see that time approaching again, the playwrights of the Theatre of the Holocaust remind us that there *are* choices to be made during those times, and they show us how we can be better prepared to make the right ones.

Robert Skloot
Madison and Jerusalem

Spring, 1981

Shimon Wincelberg

RESORT 76

based on the novella
A CAT IN THE GHETTO
by Rachmil Bryks

CAST OF CHARACTERS
In Order of Appearance

YABLONKA, 30–60 years old, a mountebank.
KRAUSE, 40–50 years old, an outsider.
SCHNUR, 40–60 years old, a slaughterer.
BERYL, 13–15 years old, his pupil.
BLAUSTAIN, 35–45 years old, an engineer.
ESTHER, 30 years old, his pregnant wife.
HAUPTMANN, 60 years old, a retired officer.
HUPERT, 45 years old, a charlatan.
MADAME HERSHKOVITCH, 40 years old, a charwoman.
ANYA, 20–30 years old, Blaustain's sister.

All characters are fictitious or dead. Any similarity to actual events is regretted.

SETTING

The action takes place in and around the living quarters of "Resort 76," a small factory for the salvage of textile wastes. The locale is one of the the Rehabilitation Zones[1] of an occupied country in eastern Europe. The time is during the Second World War. The season is winter.

Act 1	Sunday afternoon
Act 2	Sunday evening
Act 3	Monday morning

1. Rehabilitation Zones: a sardonic euphemism for territory which the Nazis captured and ruthlessly controlled. The area referred to in the play is the city Lodz in central Poland.

RESORT 76

ACT 1

Fade up on the damaged horizon of an industrial city. Drooping electric wires, gap-toothed housetops and factory chimneys, a sullen, sunless sky.

Sounds: Some sour, derisive strains on a harmonica. Windborne snatches of more distant noises, blending, overlapping: the dying wail of an air-raid siren ... the labored chug of a railroad engine ... a jaunty old Prussian marching song ... vibrations of a heavy truck ... slivers of wind knifing through the bones. In contrast, the harmonica, close by, sounds morbidly cheerful.

Fade up on a snow-encrusted brick wall chipped and scarred by bullets and shell fragments. A tall, baroque iron gate decorated by a clumsy sign:

RESORT 76
Salvage of Textile Wastes
No Trespassing

Behind the wall, the upper story of a small, cracked, fire-smudged factory building. The wall is barnacled with announcements and decrees of the Military Government in curt, gothic black on white, forbidding all the usual things. The only poster legible to us reads:

WORK IS FREEDOM

As the light firms into the foggy grayness of a winter afternoon, enter YABLONKA, *a small, bent, hook-nosed man with a wild, wiry shock of red hair and the large, staring, shrewd, hooded eyes and nutcracker jaws of a Punch puppet. He is dressed somewhat less adequately than a scarecrow, an effect enhanced by the amounts of straw and newspaper he has stuffed in his clothing. Unaccountably, his clothes, his hair, his very skin are stained with garish patches of dye. He walks on his wooden-soled shoes like a man furtively kicking dirt into his open grave. He wears a battered tin mess kit slung around his waist by a string. His skin, where the dye-stains permit, is transparent, as though it enclosed little more than bones and water. He stops, shivering, runny-nosed, to admire one of the newer posters.*

Another gust of wind. YABLONKA *shivers, pockets the harmonica. He glances shyly, furtively about him. Then, with one swift pickpocket's movement, he rips off a corner of a poster and stuffs it greedily under his vest for warmth. Another guilty glance over his shoulder. Then he tears off a smaller piece and explosively empties his nose into it. Seeing no one about, he gets down on all fours searching keenly amidst the holes and rubble on the ground.*

YABLONKA: Here, kitty, kitty, kitty, kitty . . . puss, puss, puss . . .
    (But now, with a melodramatic gesture of alarm, he sees someone approaching. At once he straightens up and executes a little pantomime of excruciating casualness, as he resumes blowing into his harmonica.
        KRAUSE, *the man who enters, is upright, stocky, blond, pink-cheeked, middle-aged, dressed in a Tyrolean-type hat and leather coat. Also a shirt, tie, socks, leather shoes with laces, and no doubt even underwear. He is carrying a small suitcase, an umbrella and a thermos flask. He is unbearably tired and depressed, but too proud to show it.)*
KRAUSE: Here, you . . . old fellow?
    (YABLONKA, as though just made aware of him, turns and executes a servile little bow.)
KRAUSE: How do I get to this address? *(He hands YABLONKA an official-looking document.)*
YABLONKA: "Resort 76" . . . Hmmmm . . . *(He darts KRAUSE a suspicious look, backs off adroitly until the sign for Resort 76 is*

*hidden behind his back. Then squints, examines the document
from all angles, scratches his head.)*
YABLONKA *(half under his breath):* Amkho . . .?[2]
KRAUSE. What?
YABLONKA *(shakes his head):* Amkho?
KRAUSE: What the devil are you talking about?

(YABLONKA *assumes a feebleminded posture.* KRAUSE *snatches
back his document, picks up his suitcase, ready to keep on
looking.* YABLONKA, *however, adroitly recovers the paper, examines it once more, as though some new factor had just been
added.)*
YABLONKA *(with sudden intelligence):* Ah . . . You are looking for
Resort 76 . . . The carpet factory. You've come to make an inspection? Believe me, sir, you'll find everything in perfect order. Why trouble yourself? *(He tries to put a comradely arm
about* KRAUSE's *shoulder and lead him back in the direction he
came from.* KRAUSE, *repelled by his odor, brushes him off, angrily recovers his document, glares at the street.)*
KRAUSE: "Order"? I've never seen such chaos, such total lack of
civic pride.
YABLONKA: I know exactly what you mean.
KRAUSE: After all, this place hasn't been properly bombed in over
a year now, has it?
YABLONKA: What can we do? We're not an important enough tar-
get anymore.
*(KRAUSE lifts one of his feet out of the gummy filth which coats
the street.)*
KRAUSE: Look at this! As though gypsies were living here. What
city is this, anyway?
YABLONKA *(shrugs):* I've wondered about that myself. *(He looks
indignantly at his own muddy shoes.)*
KRAUSE: Now which way do I go?

---

2. *Amkho:* literally "your people" (Hebrew), this term is used idiomatically by
Yablonka to ask Krause if he is Jewish.

YABLONKA: For what?

KRAUSE: Resort 76!

YABLONKA: You're sure that's where you want to go?

(KRAUSE *glances uneasily at his document.*)

KRAUSE: Positive.

YABLONKA (*an endearing smile*): You've come to the right party. Go down this street. No. Yes. All the way to the end . . . (*an apologetic smile*). That is, up to the barbed wire. Then you turn right . . . No, *left*. Go through the courtyard, over the fence, then down the next street, again all the way to the end . . .

(KRAUSE *listens dazedly. But* YABLONKA *appears suddenly to have lost interest.*)

KRAUSE: Yes? And then?

YABLONKA (*shrugs*): You go back the way you came.

KRAUSE: Thank you so much for your very kind help. (*He is ready to move on.*)

YABLONKA: Uh, sir? . . . You didn't happen to notice anywhere . . . a little pussycat? (*He starts to give an expert impersonation of one.*)

KRAUSE (*suddenly sympathetic*): Why? Did you lose one?

YABLONKA (*suddenly angry*): Lose one? What do you take me for— a criminal? Don't you know the law: "Ownership of a four-legged animal"?

(*He indicates the appropriate poster, does a two-second parody of a firing squad; and, very insulted, turns away.* KRAUSE *shakes his head, is about to move off. At once,* YABLONKA *is back at his side with a conciliatory smile.*)

You wouldn't like to buy some sweet saccharin? Ten for a dollar?

KRAUSE: Certainly not. I don't even use sugar. Ruins the taste of the coffee. All that sweetening. No wonder you people all have diabetes.

YABLONKA: Coffee! (*Touches* KRAUSE's *suitcase.*) You have some coffee in there you want to sell? Sixty-five dollars a pound. Or you'd rather have Swiss francs?

KRAUSE: Are you trying to involve me in a black market transaction?

YABLONKA *(eagerly):* Oh, yes. Please.

KRAUSE: Do you know what would happen if I called a policeman?

YABLONKA *(sadly):* He would arrest both of us. Or maybe just you. There's no money to be made out of *me* . . . Maybe you would like to buy a patch?

KRAUSE: A "patch"?

(YABLONKA flashes the star-shaped yellow patch he wears under his coat. KRAUSE glares at him narrow-eyed.)

YABLONKA *(friendly as a puppy):* Last week I heard somebody say, for a joke, our neighborhood has begun to look like Hollywood in America. Wherever you turn, you see a star.

(KRAUSE refuses to laugh. Increasingly tired, frightened and peevish, he tries to move on. YABLONKA clings to his arm.)

Handmade, two for a dollar, guaranteed not to shrink.

KRAUSE: Will you leave me alone, you old idiot?

YABLONKA *(gently):* Sir, I may be an idiot, but I'm not old. There's some uncertainty about my age, because I had a brother who looked just like me, and to this day even I am not sure which one of us was shot during the roundup. It could be *I'm* the one who's dead, and my mother didn't have the heart to tell me.

(His triumphant cackle is cut short by the sound of a train whistle. YABLONKA listens, coiled up with anxiety, until it has faded. Holds up a yellow cloth star.) Four for a dollar, quick, before the police grab you for being "improperly dressed."

KRAUSE *(sadly):* You people would do anything for money, wouldn't you? *(He tries once more to move off.)*

YABLONKA *(a sweet smile):* Yes, sir *(indicates KRAUSE's suitcase).* Maybe you have some potato peels in there you'd like to sell?

KRAUSE: What?

YABLONKA: Marmalade? Coffee grounds? No? Egg shells? Or maybe a cat, a little pussycat? I'd pay two hundred marks for a live cat, cold cash, no bargaining.

KRAUSE: You will excuse me, I'm sure. *(With a final glance of uneasiness, he hurries off.)*

YABLONKA: Or seventy-five for a dead one, if it's still fresh. *(No answer.* YABLONKA *waits until* KRAUSE *is out of sight, then ambles off in the opposite direction, bent over, gesturing with his fingers as though proffering some delicacy.)*
Here, kitty, kitty, kitty . . . puss, puss, puss . . .
(In the distance, the sudden banging of church bells.

Fade out. Fade up on a warehouse loft, converted, by means of wood, cardboard, wire, string and pieces of cloth, into a row of "apartments"—each of them a cubicle accommodating little more than a bed of some sort—and a common living room. The windows look out upon the huddled roofs and chimneys of a bomb-scarred industrial city. The room holds a table, covered with a tattered lace tablecloth, a bench, an assortment of chairs; a tall, ornate mahogany cupboard, and numerous flimsy or improvised chests and suitcases, elaborately locked. Also a dead grandfather clock, a washtub, a small, hidden bookshelf, the corpse of a bicycle, and a baby carriage filled with soil which bears a number of sullen, colorless plants. The window ledges are covered with flower pots and improvised planters, some of which also have begun to yield a sickly gray leaf here and there. The walls slant toward each other to conform with the angle of the roof.

*As the echo of the church bell gives way to the bell signaling the end of the eight-to-six shift, the door leading to the factory ["Arbeitsresort"] downstairs flies open and for a moment fills the room with clouds of vile, multicolored fumes. The shadowy figures of four workers coming off the daylight shift file tiredly into the room to wash, stretch, lie down, drink water, etc. One of them [*HAUPTMANN*] disappears into his cubicle. Another [*BLAUSTAIN*] checks the blacked-out windows before turning on the light. The other two [*SCHNUR and* BERYL*] head straight for the bench on which they study. Except for the garish spectrum of indelible dye-stains on people's hands, faces, hair, clothes, there is not a touch of color anywhere. The walls, the sky, the furniture, the people, the vegetation [as far as the*

*latter two can be told apart] all are in shades of muddy gray,
lightened only by an occasional touch of soot-black and tinges
of phosphorescent green.*

*An old-fashioned horn gramophone is intoning the conclu-
sion of a sentimental Polish-Yiddish folk song of the 1930s.
There is an oven, both for heat and for cooking, built of old
bricks, a sheet of tin, a stove-pipe. At the moment it is cold for
lack of fuel. Downstage, a little balcony or outside gallery may
afford an occasional moment of privacy to a maximum of two
people at a time.*

*ENGINEER BLAUSTAIN draws aside the curtain to one of the
cubicles and is relieved to find his wife, ESTHER, asleep. He
checks her pulse, then sits down at the table, huddled over a
scrap of brown paper, on which he is writing, or trying to
write, with a one-inch stub of pencil, whose point he keeps
licking vainly for inspiration. From time to time, he stares,
annoyed at the two workers now sitting in a corner, audibly
studying from a large, tattered folio. They are: SCHNUR, a
bearded, broad-shouldered man in his fifties, whose peacetime
occupations were religious tutoring and the slaughter of cattle,
both professions currently obsolete and illegal. He wears a
threadbare black coat held together by safety pins, a cylindri-
cal black visored cap, and a pair of wooden-soled boots. His
pupil is BERYL, a slender, fidgety boy, with immense shining
eyes set in a frighteningly adult face, pasty, wrinkled, and occasionally cynical as that of a midget. His hands, as though
independent of his brain, are occupied with making a bird out
of bits of wood, wire and cloth. He is dressed in loose adult
castoffs and wooden shoes.)*

SCHNUR: Now again . . . "All may slaughter . . ."

BERYL *(sing-song):* "All may slaughter, and their slaughtering is
acceptable . . ." *(stops, looks up).* Animals only, or people,
too?

SCHNUR *(gently):* Don't talk about things you don't understand.
Go on. By heart. *(He puts his hand over the page.)*

BERYL *(trying to remember):* "All may slaughter, except a deaf-mute, an imbecile and a . . ."

(Behind one of the curtains, ESTHER BLAUSTAIN *moans in her sleep.* BLAUSTAIN *instantly hurries over.* ESTHER *is a handsome, skeletal young woman, whose pregnancy barely shows. She is covered with a torn, blood-stained quilt.)*

BLAUSTAIN: Did you call me?

ESTHER: Is it time yet?

BLAUSTAIN: Another half hour. You want some water?

ESTHER *(an apologetic but radiant smile):* I think I would rather have a boiled egg, with a little butter mixed into the yolk . . . That's how Mama used to make it for me.

BLAUSTAIN: Nothing else?

ESTHER *(clutches his hand):* You are not angry?

(For a moment he seems ready to explode. But he controls himself, shakes his head, covers her. She is already sleeping again. BLAUSTAIN *gives her a troubled look, returns to his seat.)*

BERYL: "Except a deaf-mute, an imbecile, and a child." Why?

SCHNUR: Why? Because, don't you see, a knife handled in igno-rance can cause pain.[3]

BERYL: So much fuss over spilling a little blood! . . . No wonder *they* think we're peculiar.

BLAUSTAIN *(gently):* Schnur . . .

SCHNUR: Now comes the question . . .

BLAUSTAIN: *Schnur . . .*

(HAUPTMANN emerges from his cubicle. A man of sixty, square-shouldered, pathologically neat, dressed in the remnants of a World War One officer's dress uniform, one hand rigid in a black leather glove. His face is bloodless, his eyes focused in the distance. After a moment, glancing about him as though faintly surprised at the company in which he finds himself, he

---

3. By Jewish law, the ritual slaughter has to be achieved with as little pain as possible to the animal.

*withdraws again, removes one of his clean, lusterless cavalry
boots and shines it ferociously with a rag. At the same time,*
SCHNUR *looks up at* BLAUSTAIN *with his shy, stubborn, un-
worldly smile.* BERYL *at once takes advantage of the distraction by "flying" his toy bird over to the window and wistfully
looking out.)*

SCHNUR: Yes, Engineer Blaustain?

BLAUSTAIN: Can't you see he doesn't *want* to study?

SCHNUR: Of course.

BLAUSTAIN: Then why are you torturing him?

SCHNUR: Why should he want to study? No one ever taught him
    that, to live in this world, you need a map.

BLAUSTAIN: *This* is a map of the world out *there?*

SCHNUR *(a diffident shrug):* I don't fully understand it myself. But
    imagine how many worlds the Almighty must have created
    and nullified before He allowed this one to stand.

BLAUSTAIN: Speaking as an engineer, I think He was satisfied a little
    too soon.

SCHNUR: Beryl, sit down. *(*BERYL *reluctantly complies.)* The ques-
    tion is, what if they did slaughter already, without permission,
    but did it properly? Can we or can we not eat the meat?

BLAUSTAIN: Dammit, Schnur, can't you teach him something else?
    You're making me sick! You know the last time I saw a piece
    of fresh meat? *(Low.)* I mean, meat from an animal.
    *(*ESTHER *has sat up, watching him fearfully from behind her
    curtain.)*

SCHNUR: What can I do? It's the only book we have on his level of
    understanding . . . True, at his age, *I* was only up to the Laws
    of Damages, the Laws of Sacrifices, the Laws of Divorce . . .

BLAUSTAIN: The "Laws of Divorce!" To a thirteen-year-old! He
    doesn't even know what a woman *smells* like.

BERYL: Yes, I do. A woman smells like . . . fresh buttermilk.

BLAUSTAIN: Why don't you teach him something *sensible*, some-
    thing a normal boy can use—like smuggling, or forgery, or
    how to cut a policeman's throat?

SCHNUR *(shrugs):* Things like that a boy can pick up in the street *without* learning. But, if it upsets you, maybe I can dig up a copy of the volume of "Civil Damages." A little elementary for his age, but just to pass the time . . .

BLAUSTAIN: You still have *books?*

SCHNUR: I buried some in a milk can behind the children's cemetery. Tonight, after curfew, I'll slip out and . . .

BLAUSTAIN: You want to get shot?

BERYL: *I'll* go.

SCHNUR: No! We'll study without a book. What are the Four Foundations of Civil Liability? The ox's hoof; the pit left uncovered; the tooth of a grazing animal; and . . . you know the fourth one?

BLAUSTAIN: My God! You can sit there and split hairs about damages by an ox's hoof, in a building that has an unexploded hundred-pound bomb sitting in the basement?

(A man has entered from the street. Brisk, preoccupied, like a boss arriving late for work. This is HUPERT, *a man whose elegant, fur-collared overcoat is held together only by the tenacity of its lining.)*

HUPERT: Another bomb? This place is getting dangerous.

BLAUSTAIN: The same old one.

HUPERT: You had me worried.

(He warms his hands luxuriously over the stove, until he touches it and realizes it's cold.)

Hear the latest? I got it last night on the shortwave, from Stockholm.

BLAUSTAIN: Hupert, do you really *have* a radio?

HUPERT: I will not dignify that question.

HAUPTMANN: Any news from America?

HUPERT: This is directly from Washington. Both sides are crippled by a shortage of aviation fuel. You hear?

SCHNUR: You mean they might have to stop fighting?

HUPERT: Are you crazy? They've reached an *agreement* through the Red Cross. How to save fuel and still do the same amount of damage . . . From now on, Russian planes will bomb Moscow, and German planes will bomb Berlin.

*(*BLAUSTAIN *turns his back on him.)*

BERYL: And who will bomb *us?*

BLAUSTAIN: They'll take turns.

(ESTHER *suddenly begins to choke from a lung-tearing cough.*
BLAUSTAIN, *for a moment, buries his head on the table, unable
to face her.* HUPERT *gallantly scuttles over to* ESTHER'S *cubicle.)*

HUPERT: Madame Blaustain! *(He inclines with an elephantine
flourish to kiss her hand, then playfully pretends to examine
her inflated belly.)* And how's the little monkey in your belly
coming along? Started kicking yet?

ESTHER *(shakes her head):* He probably thinks if he keeps quiet, I'll
let him stay till the war is over.

HUPERT: Ha-ha, he knows when he's well off, the little parasite. A
pity he can't take in boarders, eh? *(He tickles her belly until
she feebly shrieks with laughter.)*

HUPERT: Chick, chick, chick. Ha-ha. Soon you'll be laundering his
diapers in the River Jordan, and wishing you were back here,
with paved streets and cabarets and automatic plumbing, and
no mosquitoes gorging on your blood.

*(He imitates a mosquito buzzing, trying to alight on some in-
delicate place, while* ESTHER *giggles herself into exhaustion.)*
Some people don't know when they're well off.

BLAUSTAIN: Hupert, will you leave her alone?

*(HUPERT takes BLAUSTAIN's unwilling arm, and leads him over
to a corner, his gold teeth flashing in a seductive smile.)*

HUPERT: You know what day *I* am living for? Right after the war,
I am going to make a *film* about all this. (BLAUSTAIN *stares at
him, unmoving.)* Can you think of a more dramatic subject?
Look around you. It has everything. Romance, conflict, heroism, laughter, suspense . . .

BLAUSTAIN *(irritably):* Conflict? What conflict? Idiot, where do you
see conflict?

HUPERT *(nudges him):* I've still got my eyes open for a skillful
dramatist to work with me on the scenario. An opportunity
for some neglected poet to make a worldwide reputation for
himself with one stroke. Eh? I suppose you're wondering what
I'm leading up to. Well, not to beat around the bush—it's *you*
I've got my eye on, mister. You hear what I called you? "Mis-

ter," like an American. You are speechless. Never mind. When I am done teaching you the disciplines of cinematic technique—montage, close-up, slow motion, focus, subtitle, box office—a whole new career will open up for you. I have the story all worked out in my head. A young, passionate, beautiful Aryan woman, so utterly devoted to her husband, she follows him voluntarily into the ghetto, and . . . *(bereavement chokes his voice; but after a moment he forces a ghastly smile of benevolence).* Well? What do you think of the idea? Eh? Fully copyrighted, of course. First thing in the morning, I'll speak to my attorney about having us transformed into a corporation of limited liability. That means we not only cease as individuals, but all personal responsibility ceases with us.

(BLAUSTAIN glances almost involuntarily at ESTHER's cubicle.) How about it? *(He captures BLAUSTAIN's hand. BLAUSTAIN wearily permits him to pump it.)* Do you speak English? You must learn English at once. In Hollywood, *everyone* speaks English. "I, You, He, She, It, Ve, You, Zey. Time is money. Fair play. Knock-out. Herbert Hoover. Foxtrot. No Irish need apply. The cat sat on the mat. I pledge allegiance to the flag. How do you do? Reach for the sky. Son of a bitch. What is dee way to the lavatory?" We'll go into production the minute the war is over. Confidentially, it can't last more than another month or two. Both sides are bleeding to death economically. Even *with* American financing.

BLAUSTAIN: Hupert, do you know where you'll be when the war is over? The same place as the rest of us . . . *(he points at the ground)* . . . with grass growing out of your cheeks.

HUPERT: I am thinking of calling it, "She Died for Her Love." An effective title, no?

(Overcome by a surge of grief, he turns away, wipes his eyes. Simultaneously, SCHNUR has finished combing his lopsided beard and turns his attention back to BERYL, who is fidgeting like any other boy who'd rather be outside playing.)

SCHNUR: Now, listen . . .

BERYL *(almost involuntarily):* Why should I? You're not my father.

(SCHNUR *looks at him steadily for a moment. Then, abruptly, in a sing-song—*)

SCHNUR: "*If* an ox gored a cow who had just given birth . . ."

(*The rest is drowned out by a sharp rap on the door. Everyone freezes.* HUPERT *exchanges a glance of terror with the others and dives under one of the beds, his feet remaining plainly visible under the too-short curtain. Another impatient knock.* BLAUSTAIN *rises grimly, goes over to the baby carriage, roots around among the dirt, and draws out a small automatic pistol wrapped in oil paper. He unwraps it, shoves it into his waistband, buttons his jacket to cover it and, with a heavy, reluctant tread, goes to the door.*)

BLAUSTAIN: Who is it?

VOICE: Is this Resort 76?

BLAUSTAIN: Yes.

VOICE Well, open up, will you?

(BLAUSTAIN *casts a worried look toward* SCHNUR, *who has just finished hiding the book under his mattress and locking* BERYL *in the cupboard. He pulls back the bolt and opens the door.* KRAUSE *enters, clean, vigorous, self-possessed, glares at* BLAUSTAIN, *and looks about him with open disapproval.* BLAUSTAIN'S *nervousness makes him, despite his height, look almost diminutive beside* KRAUSE.)

KRAUSE: Which one of you is . . . (*consults paper*) . . . Engineer Blaustain?

BLAUSTAIN: I am.

(KRAUSE *hands him a sheet of paper, draws himself up for a formal introduction which stops just short of heel-clicking.*)

KRAUSE: Krause. I was sent by the Housing Authority. (*Looks uneasily about him.*) I've been assigned an apartment in this building.

(BLAUSTAIN, *having read the note, relaxes visibly.* SCHNUR *re-opens the door to the cupboard.* BERYL *stares at* KRAUSE *as though he were some strange creature from another planet.* HUPERT *creeps back out from under the bed, and silently, behind* KRAUSE'S *back, proceeds to recover homburg, briefcase and dignity.*)

BLAUSTAIN *(amused):* An "apartment." This note is dated two p.m. It took you four hours to find us?

KRAUSE *(mops his brow):* Some fool of a cripple I met in the street sent me on a wild goose chase toward the other end of town. Twice I almost got shot by our own soldiers . . .

(All stare at him peculiarly at that last phrase.)

BLAUSTAIN *(softly):* Our *own* soldiers?

KRAUSE: And then he tried to sell me some saccharin into the bargain.

HUPERT *(sharply):* How much?

(His sudden appearance gives KRAUSE a visible start.)

KRAUSE: Huh? . . . What's it to *you?* . . . Ten for a dollar, I think . . .

HUPERT: Yablonka. I hope you didn't buy. *My* price is eighteen for a dollar, chemically pure, made in Sweden, may I die this minute if I'm telling a lie.

(He rummages in his briefcase. SCHNUR starts to help BERYL out of the cramped cupboard.)

KRAUSE: I'd like to know what the devil you people take me for! I've never seen an American dollar in my life.

(HUPERT instantly produces a ragged, patched-up dollar bill. KRAUSE turns pale.)

I suppose you realize there are strict penalties for this sort of thing? Up to five years at hard labor.

HUPERT: In a real prison? Are you sure? Five years of regular meals? Show me where, I'll cut you in for half.

BLAUSTAIN: Wait a minute. What "sort of thing"?

KRAUSE: Possession of foreign currency. Especially of an enemy country. A neighbor of mine only last month got sent to a suicide battalion, just because my wife happened to mention to the milkman . . .

(The others look at him, aghast.)

HUPERT *(waves the dollar bill):* This . . . this is an "enemy" country?

KRAUSE: I suppose it is news to you people there is even a war going on. That our Motherland at this moment is fighting a crusade, single-handedly, to preserve European civilization from the black barbarians of the Western world.

(HUPERT instantly palms the dollar bill.)

HUPERT: You didn't see a thing!

(He vanishes. SCHNUR, behind KRAUSE's back, sadly shakes his head. BLAUSTAIN goes over to KRAUSE, looks squarely into his face.)

BLAUSTAIN: Herr Krause. May I ask you a very personal question?

KRAUSE: Certainly not. I barely know you.

BLAUSTAIN: I wasn't thinking of asking you to take down your pants. But . . . why are you here?

KRAUSE: I thought you'd get around to that. Well, I'm not of *your* persuasion, if that's what you're after . . .

BLAUSTAIN: Then, to what do we owe the honor?

KRAUSE *(shrugs irritably):* Some sort of bureaucratic mix-up, I suppose. Hard to avoid that sort of thing in time of war. But it should all be straightened out in a day or two. Meanwhile, I'm to report to you for some sort of work assignment.

(BLAUSTAIN takes the document. In the distance, church bells; KRAUSE turns sharply toward the window, listening with unbearable nostalgia.)

BLAUSTAIN: A chemist. Good. We can use you.

KRAUSE: Well, actually, I'm only a druggist . . . that is, I was a clerk in a pharmacy . . . I tried to explain to them at the Housing Bureau, that if they could find me employment in my own field . . . chemical warfare, poison gas, that sort of thing, I'd be of a lot more value to the War Effort. *(Sadly.)* Of course, I don't suppose you people care much about helping the War Effort.

(In the distance, the whistle of a passing train. All but KRAUSE freeze and follow it with their ears.)

BLAUSTAIN: Ah, but you're quite wrong. We care very much. As long as we turn out a useful and attractive item at a reasonable cost per unit, we stay in business.

KRAUSE *(sadly):* "Business as usual" . . . young men of all nations cheerfully laying down their lives on every battlefield of the civilized world . . . but the profits must go on. Well, what are you making here, anyway? Parisian frocks?

BLAUSTAIN: This season we are specializing in high-grade Oriental rugs. Would you like to see?

KRAUSE: Rugs? Out of what?

BLAUSTAIN *(shrugs):* Whatever comes on hand. Right now we seem to be well supplied with old clothes. Here, have a look.

(He takes him to an iron door downstage, opens it, adroitly dodges a thick cloud of yellow vapor, and through it, points at the factory below. KRAUSE *flinches back, tears in his eyes, coughing as though poisoned. None of the others are affected in the slightest.)*

That pot over there, on the right, is to boil out the blood-stains . . .

KRAUSE: Blood! How do old clothes get blood on them?

BLAUSTAIN *(shrugs):* How else would they become old clothes? Then they are shredded up into fibers, which are then dyed, over there . . .

(The emerging cloud of vapor abruptly turns red. KRAUSE *snaps back with another burst of coughing.)*

BLAUSTAIN: . . . and carefully rewoven into the finest grade Persian rugs.

HUPERT *(belligerently):* I would defy any pure-blooded Persian to tell them from the real thing.

BLAUSTAIN: Our friend Hupert is planning to patent the process after the war . . . if he can solve the problem of how to cope with a sudden shortage of bloody clothing.

HUPERT: There'll be no shortage, don't you worry about that.

KRAUSE: A carpet factory! Now what the hell kind of a contribution to the War Effort do you call that?

BLAUSTAIN: Well, of course some of the other factories are luckier. One of them gets tons and tons of human hair and beards for stuffing mattresses . . .

HUPERT: A million times softer than horsehair. In fact, after the war, if I could patent the process . . .

BLAUSTAIN: . . . or shoes, to recondition into Army boots . . . Or carloads of teeth, to search for gold fillings . . . In fact, I understand back in the Mother Country they've even developed a formula for making soap out of human fat. Isn't that remarkable? Only . . . how do you suppose they *advertise* it?

KRAUSE *(subdued):* I'd like to see my apartment now, if you don't mind.

(He picks up his suitcase, starts for the door, stops, amazed, when he sees BLAUSTAIN *has simply whipped back the curtain on an empty cubicle. The others look at him, motionless, unsmiling, and it begins to sink in to* KRAUSE *that this is not a joke after all. He takes a step toward the cubicle, suspicious, as though another step would commit him to irrevocable acceptance of this indignity.)*

KRAUSE *(suddenly frightened):* This . . . ? You are quite certain there isn't some mistake?

*(*BLAUSTAIN *nods.* KRAUSE *enters the cubicle, examines it with distaste. He notes a piece of rope dangling from a pipe overhead. He tugs at it.)*

What's that for?

BLAUSTAIN: Whatever use you want to make of it. The person who lived there before you . . . uh . . . Well, *you* could use it for a lamp, it holds quite a bit of weight. *(Quietly.)* A hundred and fifteen pounds, to be exact.

*(*KRAUSE *stares at the rope, drops his suitcase, takes off his jacket and tie, and sinks tiredly onto his creaking, limping bed.)*

BERYL *(with pitying fascination, to* SCHNUR*):* He's tired? *Already?*

*(*KRAUSE *gets up and draws the curtain. The others resume their activities.* HUPERT *is passionately staring out of the window.* BLAUSTAIN *has lifted* ESTHER's *weightless body out of bed and deposited her behind the door of the toilet.* SCHNUR *gently takes* BERYL's *ear and guides his nose to the page.*

The door bursts open and YABLONKA *gleefully comes in.)*

YABLONKA: Hey, Blaustain, you must be getting important, they sent someone to spy on you, only I caught him outside and sent him off to the other end of town . . . By the time he finds his way, he'll have a dozen holes in him for being out after curfew.

(He stops, open-mouthed, aware of KRAUSE's *accusing presence in the entrance of his cubicle. Then turns to* BLAUSTAIN *in mutely gesturing horror, as though wondering whether it's too late still to warn him.)*

BLAUSTAIN: It's all right. He was sent here by mistake just like the rest of us.

KRAUSE: No, no, no. My case is altogether different. It's simply a matter of . . .

YABLONKA: No hard feelings? I'll let you have saccharin at the regular price. Fifteen for a dollar.

HUPERT: Eighteen!

YABLONKA *(automatically):* Twenty-one!

*(*KRAUSE *sharply draws his curtain, lies down again.* YABLONKA *slumps into a chair, breathing hard.)*

(To BLAUSTAIN:*)* They've closed down Resort 43. For "sabotage." Everybody's been put on the train. They didn't turn out enough boots. Too many people were stealing the leather to make goulash. So watch your step. I don't want us to be next . . . I *like* it here!

*(*HUPERT *has resumed looking out of the window.)*

HUPERT: Look at those damned little rascals down there. Playing with a corpse. Can't even tell if it's a man or a woman. Looks more like a dried fish.

(No one shows the slightest interest except SCHNUR, *who looks pained, and* BERYL, *who dashes over for a peek.)*

Now they're tickling its nose with a straw, to see if they can make it sneeze.

BLAUSTAIN *(shrugs):* What do you want? A child is a child, and a toy is a toy.

(He takes the automatic out of his belt, wraps it up, puts it back into the baby carriage under the soil, as HAUPTMANN *flings open his door as though about to attack someone. But all he does is go over to the shelf and select one of the books.)*

We hear the toilet being thunderously flushed, and BLAUSTAIN *goes in, fetches* ESTHER, *carries her back to bed.)*

ESTHER *(suddenly almost coy with overflowing affection):* Remember how Papa didn't want me to go with you? Because you were too . . . "worldly"?

BLAUSTAIN: I think he suspected you were not the absolutely first girl I had ever known.

ESTHER: If Papa could see me now . . .

BLAUSTAIN: He's better off where he is.

ESTHER: No, no. He'd be *happy* for me. That I have a husband like you to take care of me.

*(*BLAUSTAIN, *pained, tucks her in. She falls asleep at once.* HAUPTMANN, *with a cry of rage, comes forward, waving the book at* SCHNUR.)*

HAUPTMANN: I refuse to learn another word of English! Listen to this: "If you drink much from a bottle marked 'poison,' it is almost certain to disagree with you sooner or later." *(Looks up, outraged.)* The man is an idiot! What if a book like this fell into the hands of a child? *(Consults the title page.)* "Alitze in Vonderland." By Levis Carroll. Of course. An Englishman. *(Bitterly satirical.)* Yes, my lord. Tennis, anyone? Veddy good, sah. A cup of tea, my lord?

SCHNUR: Ah, for a glass of hot tea, with a fat yellow lemon floating on top, and two lumps of sugar . . . Ah . . . How easily the body is enslaved by self-indulgence.

(Overcome by the vision, he gets up to pour himself a glass of water, which he doctors with a piece of saccharin and a pinch of coffee grounds. At the same time, from ESTHER, *another burst of coughing. She awakens, choking for breath.* BLAUSTAIN *runs over.)*

ESTHER: I'm all right *(strokes his face)*. But look at *you*. Thin as a noodle. You never eat a proper meal, unless I nag you.

BLAUSTAIN *(forces a smile):* It's your fault.

ESTHER *(alarmed):* My fault?

BLAUSTAIN: You've spoiled me for anyone else's cooking.

ESTHER: You're such a good husband. I only wish I didn't . . . you know . . .

(*She gestures at her belly, as though apologizing either for the bulge or for its meagerness.* BLAUSTAIN *averts his face.* ESTHER *is choked by another burst of coughing.*

KRAUSE *throws open his curtain.*)

KRAUSE: Hadn't you better get that woman to a hospital, whoever she belongs to, before we *all* catch something?

BLAUSTAIN (*quietly*): She's not quite ripe for the hospital yet.

KRAUSE: Why not?

BLAUSTAIN: She's still alive. (*He goes over to check on the progress of the sickly yellow leaf being grown in the baby carriage, then takes a watering can from the window sill and impatiently sprinkles the leaves.*)

HUPERT (*throws open the window, yells out*): Get away from that corpse, you damned little snotnoses! (*He listens to their reply.*) What? (*Listens.*) Oh. (*Abashed, he shuts the window, explains to the others*): It's theirs.

(BLAUSTAIN *puts away the watering can and once more bends, like an anxious father, over the carriage when* KRAUSE, *from his cubicle, notices this.*)

KRAUSE: You have a *baby* in there? Now, really! A coughing woman is bad enough. But I can *not* sleep in one room with a crying infant. Really. This is too much. (*He snatches his coat off a hook, ready to leave.*)

BLAUSTAIN: Calm yourself, Herr Krause. There is no baby.

KRAUSE (*suspiciously, indicates baby carriage*): Then whose is that?

YABLONKA: Some people who didn't need it anymore.

KRAUSE: What, the carriage or the baby?

BLAUSTAIN (*shakes his head*): Both. The baby was classified as "unproductive." Like any other household pet. So it had to go.

KRAUSE: Go where?

BLAUSTAIN: Eh?

KRAUSE: Where did the baby go?

BLAUSTAIN: How can a baby "go" anywhere . . . ? All the Authorities can do is . . . dispose of it.

KRAUSE *(bitterly):* Very amusing, I'm sure.

(*He starts back toward his cubicle, but* BLAUSTAIN *remains with him, pushing the carriage.* YABLONKA *has taken a deck of cards out of his pocket and invited* SCHNUR, *who shakes his head. So, without enthusiasm, he settles for* HUPERT, *who snatches a pillow off the nearest bed and sits down on it like a man with piles. They begin at once to quarrel bitterly over the deal.*)

BLAUSTAIN: You see? A little earth, a drop of water, a handful of seeds, and there you are . . . a vegetable garden.

KRAUSE *(goes closer, looks down):* Vegetables? These things are *vegetables? (His hand lifts up one of the sickly grayish-yellow stalks, and drops it hastily as though he couldn't bear the way it felt. He rubs his hands against his trousers.)*

BLAUSTAIN *(proudly):* Radishes. You'd be amazed how easy it is to grow radishes.

KRAUSE *(angrily):* These look like no radish leaves I've ever seen.

(BLAUSTAIN *shrugs, gives them a long, troubled, affectionate look, as a kind father might look at a retarded child.* YA-BLONKA *and* HUPERT *hurry over to check.*)

BLAUSTAIN: Once upon a time we had cabbages, cucumbers, even onions. But they began to act like civilized nations. They ate each other alive. (*He tears off a leaf, divides it with his teeth, thoughtfully chews up one half, offers the remainder to* KRAUSE.)

KRAUSE: You don't think *that* gives you a balanced diet?

BLAUSTAIN: It doesn't?

KRAUSE: Where are your proteins, your fats, your calcium, your blood sugar, your twenty-two essential amino acids? Don't you realize, the most minute imbalance in the four basic humors of the organism is enough to overwhelm the delicate chemistry of the brain, inducing paranoia? Melancholia. Hysteria. Not to mention delusions of persecution.

HUPERT *(to* BLAUSTAIN*):* You see? There *is* a scientific explanation!

KRAUSE *(he bites into the leaf, chokes, spits it out):* Where do I get my ration book?

BLAUSTAIN: At the Opprovizatzia.[4]

KRAUSE *(looks at his watch):* Are they still open?

BLAUSTAIN: As in all civilized countries, the Ration Bureau is closed on Sundays. I hope you've brought some food with you.

KRAUSE: Oh, yes . . . My wife packed me a couple of sausages . . . *(He takes out a piece of blood sausage and bites into it.* YABLONKA, HUPERT *and* BLAUSTAIN *stare fascinatedly into his mouth, as the sweet blood drools down his chin.* HAUPTMANN *puts his head out, inhales deeply through his nose, then emerges with a rag and, with an equal amount of arrogance and shyness, mutely attempts to polish* KRAUSE's *shoes, as his way of begging for a bite of the sausage.* KRAUSE *irritably withdraws his feet.)*

HUPERT *(to* KRAUSE, *with the manner of a man making a lewd proposition):* You wouldn't consider *selling* a piece of that, would you? *(The eyes seem ready to fall out of his head with greed.)*

KRAUSE: *Sell* something my wife made for me with her own hands? She'd never forgive me. If you don't mind my saying so, that is exactly the trouble with you people. Reckon everything in terms of money. Crucify our Savior, and then expect the world to share their sausage with you.

(The door has opened behind him, and MADAME HERSHKOVITCH *enters. A charwoman, all in gray. The scarecrow dress she wears might have been made of the same coarse material with which she scrubs floors. She is about to rush over to* BLAUSTAIN, *trembling with excitement, but at the sight of* KRAUSE *eating, she stops, open-mouthed, rigid with shy covetousness.* BERYL, *too, has begun wistfully to inhale the aroma, until recalled to his studying by a nudge from* SCHNUR.

Suddenly irritated by the rude way HUPERT *is staring into his mouth,* KRAUSE *withdraws into his cubicle and turns his back. The three men look at each other in silence.* YABLONKA *shrugs and crawls into his cot, curls up and pulls the blanket*

---

4. Opprovizatzia: the food distribution center of the ghetto.

over his head. HUPERT *puts his briefcase on the table, rests his cheek on it, and dozes off.)*

MME. HERSHKOVITCH *(diffidently):* Engineer Blaustain, can I see you in private for a minute? *(She insists, almost a little flirtatiously, on dragging him out to the little balcony for privacy.* BLAUSTAIN *flinches for a moment at the raw, howling wind.)*

BLAUSTAIN: Madame Hershkovitch, if you want to borrow a piece of bread, I can tell you right now, the answer is no. I don't care *which* one of your children is dying.

MME. HERSHKOVITCH *(a belligerent smile):* Who's *asking* you for bread? I want to *give* you bread. *(Hoarsely.)* How would you like to have a two-pound loaf of bread, for nothing, just for lifting a finger?

BLAUSTAIN: Which finger? *(He's ready to go back inside. She clutches onto him.)*

MME. HERSHKOVITCH: Have you heard that the food supplies have become infested with rats and mice?

BLAUSTAIN: Thank you for the happy news. No wonder the bread lately has a slight taste of arsenic.

MME. HERSHKOVITCH: Fool. As long as we're needed, they can't *use* too much poison. The mice would mix it into the grain.

BLAUSTAIN: So?

*(*MME. HERSHKOVITCH *feels compelled to buttonhole him physically.* BLAUSTAIN *tries not to squirm at her breath. Inside,* YABLONKA *has his ear pressed to the door.)*

MME. HERSHKOVITCH: So they have to kill them some other way. And this is what I heard while I was scrubbing the stairs over at the Administration Building. Not officially, mind you, in case the Germans find out. But . . . anyone who will bring them a cat, a live cat to kill the mice, will get a job as a clerk at the Ration Board—with a four-pound loaf of bread as an advance on his wages . . .

*(*BLAUSTAIN *gives her a weary look, tries to go back inside.* YABLONKA *scurries away from the door.)*

BLAUSTAIN *(unimpressed):* So *that's* why everyone's been looking for a cat.

MME. HERSHKOVITCH: You don't believe it? I tell you, they're *desperate* for a cat.

BLAUSTAIN: Sure I believe it. I believed it last week, too. So what? Do I have a cat? Do you? Has anybody *seen* a cat in the last six months? And if you had a cat, what do you think your life would be worth?

MME. HERSHKOVITCH *(almost coquettishly):* Blaustain, I'm disappointed in you. A cultured person, instead of *insulting* a poor, helpless widow would say, "What is your proposition?" I'm taking my life in my hands talking to you.

(BLAUSTAIN, *catching on, at once glances furtively behind him and moves her away from the door.)*

BLAUSTAIN *(softly):* You mean *you* have a *cat?*

MME. HERSHKOVITCH *(suddenly angry):* What else would I have— an elephant?

BLAUSTAIN: Where?

(She drags him still further away from the door, and whispers into his ear with a hot intimacy which makes BLAUSTAIN *feel just a little squeamish.)*

MME. HERSHKOVITCH: I caught it early this morning, over at the children's cemetery. I chased it for three blocks, my heart was coming out of my mouth. It almost escaped under the barbed wire.

(BLAUSTAIN *is now as alert as a drowning man who suddenly sees a lifeboat. In his excitement, he almost puts an arm about* MME. HERSHKOVITCH's *shoulder. But, instantly suspicious again, he draws back once more.)*

BLAUSTAIN: Why are you telling this to *me? (Angry.)* Don't you know a thing like that has to be kept absolutely secret? You think you're living among saints?

MME. HERSHKOVITCH: That's why I came to David Blaustain. A man I *know* I can trust absolutely, with my life . . .

BLAUSTAIN *(suspicious):* For what? To keep the cat for you? Are you insane? To stay up all night and risk my life on top of it? Oh, no.

MME. HERSHKOVITCH: Look at me! Do I have to remind you who

I was? How many servants? Who ate at my table? And now. In one small room with fifteen other women. You don't need to tell *me* I'm not living among saints. They see me come in with a cat . . . even if I could stay up all night . . . one knock on the head with an iron bar . . . and then who would take care of my five innocent little worms? . . . You?

BLAUSTAIN *(angry):* I can't keep it here for you! I can't. Now leave me alone!

MME. HERSHKOVITCH: You have dozens of places in this building where you could lock up a cat for one night.

BLAUSTAIN: And what of the responsibility? If the police raided us? Or somebody broke in and stole it?

MME. HERSHKOVITCH *(a sweet, trusting smile):* I know you would guard it like it was your own child.

BLAUSTAIN: It's *not* my child! I don't *want* a child . . .

ESTHER *(sits up):* David? Where are you?

(YABLONKA hurries over to reassure her.)

BLAUSTAIN *(to MME. HERSHKOVITCH):* You expect me not to close an eye all night to guard *your* lousy cat?

(He is ready to go back inside. She drags at his arm.)

MME. HERSHKOVITCH: Not *my* cat. Our cat. *(Another nudge of intimacy.)* We'll be partners. Fifty-fifty. Like man and wife, ha-ha, look at him, he's blushing. *(She hooks her arm coquettishly into his. BLAUSTAIN tries to detach himself.)*

MME. HERSHKOVITCH *(a sudden wink):* Ask your wife. *She'll* tell you to do it.

BLAUSTAIN *(sharply):* What makes you say that?

MME. HERSHKOVITCH: Please . . . Herr Engineer. A person has eyes in her head.

(BLAUSTAIN glares at her like a man who feels himself black-mailed. The setting sun has turned blood-red.)

You've been trying to get Esther into the hospital, no? For an operation to remove a little "growth." Ha-ha. Don't blush. When it comes to *that*, we're *all* animals. Only the waiting list in the hospital is so long, by the time your wife's turn comes around, she'll be carrying her belly between her teeth. And *then* what'll her life be worth? One tickle with a bayonet, and pfft! She'll pop like a paper bag.

(BLAUSTAIN *covers his ears, tries to go back inside. She pulls him away from the door, almost breathing into his mouth, with what seems to him a grin of witch-like malevolence.*)

Or maybe you've already made plans to give her a French goodbye? Hah? Bought yourself a nice, clean Certificate of Baptism, and over the wall you go, eh? Like your sister. She got away all right, didn't she?

BLAUSTAIN *(angry):* How do I know?

MME. HERSHKOVITCH: Ah, but a sister is not a wife, and a wife is not a sister, is it? A wife is part of your flesh. Leave her stranded, and maybe one of their Army doctors . . . you know . . . a few little experiments, while she's still alive, hah?

(BLAUSTAIN *puts his hands around her throat to silence her. But the harder he squeezes, the more determined she is to tell him all about it.*)

But the wife of a man with a job at the Ration Board . . . she'd go in like a queen and come out like a virgin. Any *normal* man in your position, if I offered him fifty percent of a cat, he'd *marry* me! He'd wash my feet and drink the water.

ᵣ LAUSTAIN: All right, where is it? *(He is suddenly trembling with impatience. But first, she makes him shake on the deal.)*

MME. HERSHKOVITCH: Right down there, I put a garbage can over it. *(She leans over the balcony, starts to point, suddenly flinches back, shocked.)*

BLAUSTAIN: What's the matter?

MME. HERSHKOVITCH *(low):* There's someone . . . poking around among the cans . . . looking for food . . . Another minute, and he'll find the cat.

BLAUSTAIN: Call him over . . . quick . . . Here . . . throw him a piece of sugar . . . *(He reaches down into his pocket and hands her the sugar.)*

MME. HERSHKOVITCH *(leans over and beckons at someone below):* Psst . . . Little boy . . . over here!

(BLAUSTAIN *rushes out, crosses the loft, hurries down the*

stairs. The others look after him, puzzled. The sky and the room begin slowly to darken. MME. HERSHKOVITCH *looks greedily at the piece of sugar, cannot restrain herself from taking a lick before she throws it down. And at once hurries out after* BLAUSTAIN. *Offstage, the gentle sound of a church bell.)*

HUPERT: Where are they going?

YABLONKA *(confidential):* She has a cat.

HUPERT *(loud):* A *cat!* *(Almost in tears.)* Why didn't she come to *me?*

(He starts after them, at the door remembers his briefcase, comes back for it, rushes out.)

Madame Hershkovitch! Wait! *(Offstage.)* You haven't heard *my* offer.

(YABLONKA glances after him, grins, shakes his head. In BLAUSTAIN's cubicle, a hand fumbles for the curtain.)

ESTHER: David . . . ? David, where are you going? *(She tries to get up, but is too weak.)* David . . . ? If you want to go with another woman . . . you don't have to do it behind my back.

(SCHNUR and YABLONKA exchange a glance of pity and resignation. Outside, the clock on a steeple begins to strike the hour. Lights fade.)

ACT 2

Five minutes later. In the darkness, the scratchy wail of a tango on the large, old-fashioned phonograph about to run out of steam. Fade up on YABLONKA *sitting, half-asleep, in front of the music. He awakens as the record comes moaning to a halt.* SCHNUR *is giving* BERYL *a demonstration on the proper way to sharpen and test a ritual butcher knife.* YABLONKA *watches them sourly.* KRAUSE *is still sleeping.* ESTHER *is silent, except for an occasional small gasp of pain. Outside, a foot patrol marches past.* YABLONKA *winds up the gramophone once more, and puts on a raucous Polish military march.* HAUPTMANN *comes out of his cubicle, checks his pocket watch, then, shyly aped by* BERYL, *marches over to the balcony, snaps to attention, salutes. The others try politely not to watch— all except* KRAUSE *who, awakened by the music and the hobnailed boots pounding the cobblestones, comes out and watches him, puzzled.*

KRAUSE: That fellow. He looks like a military man. What is *he* doing here?

YABLONKA: Where else should he be?

KRAUSE: Doesn't he know, in times like these, his country needs every able-bodied man?

YABLONKA: He's a Yankee.

KRAUSE: A what?

SCHNUR: He had an American visa.

KRAUSE: Then what's he doing *here*?

SCHNUR: He wouldn't leave without his mother.

KRAUSE: And now?

YABLONKA: What?

KRAUSE: I suppose she's dead.

YABLONKA: Who?

KRAUSE: His mother.

YABLONKA: What is she to *you*?

KRAUSE: I mean, she died, I suppose?

70

YABLONKA: She was eighty-seven years old, what could she do in America, walk the streets?

KRAUSE *(shakes his head):* A cruel country, America. *I* wouldn't want to live there. *(He withdraws into his cell.)*

SCHNUR: Maybe cruel, but . . . interesting. They say that when you have to take an oath in court, they allow you to wear a hat. Maybe after the war, if they would let me in . . .

YABLONKA: You think you'd be any better off than you are right now? Don't tell me about America. In 1929, my Uncle Zahnvel came running back to Poland like his hair was on fire. He said the air was black with people jumping out of skyscrapers. *(Tears in his eyes.)* Me, you couldn't *pay* me to go.

SCHNUR: Still . . . don't people call it the "Land of the Free and the Home of the Brave"?

(BERYL has taken advantage of SCHNUR's momentary distraction by engaging in a fast bit of soccer practice with a cloth ball, dribbling it nimbly around the floor.)

YABLONKA: Sure. If you're a gangster. Only you think *that's* such an easy job to get? *(Shakes his head pessimistically.)* Fresh off the boat, they put you first on a special island, what they call a "Melting Pot." To make you into a "Yankee." Inside and out . . . Katzenellenbogen becomes Katz. Solomon becomes Sullivan. Rosenfeld becomes Roosevelt.

SCHNUR: I wonder if that's true.

YABLONKA: About Roosevelt? It still wouldn't do *you* any good.

SCHNUR: Why?

YABLONKA: You're not a member of his "union."

BERYL: What's that?

YABLONKA: They have two unions—Demokraten and Repooblikahner. You join one—the other fellows come and break your head.

SCHNUR: But at least you have a *choice.*

YABLONKA: A "choice"! You know who's the *real* President of America? *(A furtive glimpse over his shoulder.)* Al Caponey from Chicago. You don't buy from him the whiskey, you end up in a block of cement holding up a skyscraper. And if you *do*, Uncle Sam puts you in the clink and gives it to you with a rubber hose. This you call a choice?

(SCHNUR, *meanwhile, has recaptured* BERYL *and gently led him back by the ear.*)

SCHNUR: And yet, a man can be named Rosenfeld and still be elected President.

YABLONKA: Don't you know that was a special case?

SCHNUR: How?

YABLONKA (*confidential*): He's married to a *shiksa*.[5]

SCHNUR: I still believe, if he knew what's going on here, he would *do* something.

YABLONKA: Sure. He would warn them: Either stop it at once, or— I'll make another speech. (HAUPTMANN *throws open his door, glares at* YABLONKA, *and like a wooden cuckoo pops back in.*) Excuse me. I insulted his President. But what can *he* do? You think he hasn't got enough aggravation from the Indians? Sitting Bull. Geronimo. Paleface. Buffalo Bill.

SCHNUR (*mildly*): Still, after all this is over, if I could get a visa . . . I personally would be willing to take my chances.

YABLONKA: On being scalped alive? Not me . . . At least here you know where you stand.

(He puts on another record, a gentle folk song, listens to it intently for a moment, does not immediately notice when the needle gets stuck in a groove and, suddenly irritated by the grating, monotonous, cheerful noise, knocks the arm off the record.

HAUPTMANN bursts out, enraged, holding an open book.)

HAUPTMANN: Calumnies! Ignorant, idle gossip! Listen to this: "I have been assured by a very knowing American of my acquaintance in London, that a young healthy child well nursed is at a year old a most delicious, nourishing and wholesome

---

5. *Shiksa:* a yiddish word for a gentile woman.

food, whether stewed, roasted, baked or boiled." *(Looks up, furious.)* And that man was the Dean of the church![6]

SCHNUR: Maybe things in America are better today.

YABLONKA: In *wartime?* Who knows *what* they're eating over there.

(HAUPTMANN goes back into his cubicle, reading and muttering. SCHNUR resumes his silent instruction of the slaughter knife, demonstrating how it is to be painlessly drawn across esophagus and windpipe in two swift strokes. YABLONKA, bored, goes over to KRAUSE's cubicle and pushes aside the curtain.)

Maybe you could sell me some arsenic? Morphine? Codeine? Aspirin?

KRAUSE: Whatever drugs I carry with me are purely for my personal use.

YABLONKA: I could sell it for you at the hospital. Not just for money—for gold, or even cigarettes.

KRAUSE: Not interested *(he tries to turn his back).*

YABLONKA: Not interested in gold? You know the story of the man who tried to hide his gold from the police by shoving it into his . . . you'll-excuse-the-expression? *(But his gesture is graphic enough.)* But the military policeman, you see, he was a joker, too. He said, "Do you know that I'm greater than your Moses?" "How?" "Moses hit a stone, and water came out. I kick you in the ass, and gold comes out." *(He helpfully leads the laughter, but gets no response from KRAUSE, who regards him with righteous disapproval.)*

KRAUSE: They warned us about types like you. Layabouts. Parasites. War profiteers.

YABLONKA: Believe me, sir. I try my best to profit by the war. But it gets harder every day. How about you?

KRAUSE: Whatever I am now, at least I did my bit in the *last* war.

6. Hauptmann is taking seriously Jonathan Swift's satirical essay, "A Modest Proposal" (1729).

HAUPTMANN: Ah! *Those* were the days! Man against man. Hot lead and cold steel. Not all this *machinery* . . . Tanks! Bombers! *Submarines,* if you please. Everyone wants to fight sitting down.

KRAUSE: My feelings exactly. In former times, when your bayonet went into a man's belly, at least you looked him in the eye.

SCHNUR *(sympathetically):* And still they sent you here.

KRAUSE: It was my own fault. I was over the draft age. I could have sat out the war comfortably at home. But my wife . . . the embarrassment of an able-bodied man not doing his bit. So I volunteered for the Home Guard. Naturally they made the usual routine inquiries into my background . . . And that's when it all came out . . .

YABLONKA: One of your parents was not quite . . . pure?

KRAUSE: My grandfather. On my mother's side only.

SCHNUR *(sympathetically):* That's even worse.

(KRAUSE turns on him angrily.)

KRAUSE: Dammit to hell, I wasn't even *born* then! How can *I* be held responsible for the kind of a man my grandmother married when she was an empty-headed little slut of seventeen? . . . The dirty swine! Polluting an innocent Aryan girl with his bestial Asiatic lusts!

SCHNUR: It's extremely unfair, no question about it.

KRAUSE: And my daughter, Ursula, one of the most devoted members of the Youth Movement . . . It was all I could do to keep her from putting her head in the oven. *(Suppressing tears.)* Do you call that justice? . . . At least *you* people know why you're here . . . I mean, at least none of this comes as any *surprise* to you . . . But what about *me?* I never even knew I *had* a grandfather.

SCHNUR: And if you *had* known . . . ?

KRAUSE *(not listening):* Of course, my wife, the minute she found out, said if I didn't make a full confession, she'd leave me like . . .

YABLONKA *(helpfully):* . . . shit off a shovel? *(Under KRAUSE's glare.)* Excuse me. It's your story.

KRAUSE: Not that I blame her. After all, she had our daughter's future to think about.

YABLONKA: So if you hadn't been such a good citizen, you'd still be at home now . . . *(a dirty little gesture of illustration)* . . . making pitshy-potshy with your wife.

KRAUSE *(turns on him):* Well, let me tell you, I am not ashamed of what I have done for my country.

(YABLONKA *pins a yellow star to his breast as though it were a medal.* KRAUSE *stares at it, frightened, hesitates, then tears it off, stuffs it into an upper pocket.)*

SCHNUR: Why should you be ashamed? You'll see. It will turn out the whole thing was a mistake, a mix-up . . .

KRAUSE *(suddenly depressed):* I wonder. We do, after all, have a bureaucracy which is the envy of the civilized world. And if *they* have decided I am not fit to live among human beings, they probably know what they're talking about.

(BLAUSTAIN *comes in, awkwardly carrying, hidden under his jacket, a small, squirming bundle wrapped up in a dirty mattress ticking. He is trying his best, vainly of course, not to attract the attention of the others.* MME. HERSHKOVITCH *hovers nervously behind him.)*

BLAUSTAIN *(to the cat):* Patience, patience . . . tomorrow you're going to a place where you can lie on your back, and the food will come walking into your mouth. If the mice don't eat *you* first . . .

(YABLONKA, HAUPTMANN, KRAUSE, SCHNUR *and* BERYL *crowd around him, variously fascinated, envious, greedy, disapproving.* BLAUSTAIN, *prompted by* MME. HERSHKOVITCH, *draws back, shielding the cat with his arms. For a long moment they stare at one another, caught up in the sudden realization that the cat has turned all of them into potential antagonists.* BLAUSTAIN *now cautiously opens the sack, while* MME. HERSHKOVITCH *pushes to keep the others from getting too close.* YABLONKA *licks his lips.)*

YABLONKA: Ah, you little beauty. Look at him fight . . . Look, look. He's afraid. Don't worry, my good friend, you're much too

Yablonka tasting his bloody finger, from the 1969 production at the Royal Dramatic Theatre, Stockholm, Sweden. Photograph by Beata Bergström.

valuable to eat. *(He continues to tease it until he suddenly yanks back his bloody finger with a scream of outrage and shoves it into his mouth, dancing up and down with pain. The next moment, he looks rapt, regards his finger.)* Hey! *(Offers his finger to* BLAUSTAIN.*)* Here, taste it. Sweet as sugar.

KRAUSE: Naturally. Blood is a *protein.*

*(*YABLONKA *takes another suck at his finger.)*

YABLONKA: Why didn't I ever think of this before? Hey, Schnur. *(He offers his finger.* SCHNUR *politely shakes his head.)*

HAUPTMANN: What a lovely animal. I wonder who it belonged to. Perhaps one of their officers. Certainly not to an ordinary soldier. He would have eaten it already. In the last war, we found roast cat is a real delicacy. Why not? A cat is a clean animal. They say cat-meat is a bit on the greasy side, but with a glass of white wine to wash it down, and a good cigar afterwards . . .

MME. HERSHKOVITCH *(nervous):* I'd better get back to work . . . You'll come see me first thing in the morning, with my share of the bread? *(*BLAUSTAIN *nods.)* You won't forget?

BLAUSTAIN: Mme. Hershkovitch. I might be capable of *stealing* two pounds of bread. But not of *forgetting* about it.

*(*MME. HERSHKOVITCH *spits out fiercely.)*

MME. HERSHKOVITCH: Bite your tongue! Joking about a thing like that!

(She goes out. With her, some of the tension leaves the room. KRAUSE *stands in the entrance of his cubicle and watches disapprovingly as* BLAUSTAIN *inspects the cat once more, then takes the sack over to the cupboard, piles a camouflage of clothes on top of it, being careful it is left able to breathe. He locks the cupboard, puts the key in his pocket.* KRAUSE *shakes his head.)*

KRAUSE: You know what you're *doing* to that poor little creature, don't you?

BLAUSTAIN: What?

KRAUSE: Destroying its faith in man.

BLAUSTAIN *(thinks about it for a moment):* That makes two of us.

SCHNUR *(to* BERYL*)*: Don't listen to him. It is said, each time a human being suffers, the Almighty Himself feels the pain.

YABLONKA *(quietly)*: He must have nerves like iron!

(BLAUSTAIN *fetches one of his socks, ragged as a fishnet, and commences to darn it.* YABLONKA *sidles over to him.*)

Listen, Blaustain, if you need somebody with "elbows" to take that cat for you to the Ration Board . . . *I'll* take the risk of getting caught with it . . .

BLAUSTAIN: Why?

YABLONKA: She said four pounds of bread? I can get you twice that. Every one of those cheap bastards is afraid of me. If I told the world what I knew about them . . .

BLAUSTAIN: The world? Out there some place? You really think it's still there? *(He goes into the WC to urinate.* YABLONKA *follows him in, leaving the door open.*)

YABLONKA: Let me have fifty percent of the cat, and I'll throw in half a pound of chocolate cookies. Baked with coffee grounds from the *officers'* garbage cans only. Is your mouth watering?

(BLAUSTAIN *comes out, buttoning himself.*)

BLAUSTAIN: I don't *like* chocolate cookies.

YABLONKA: You want security? Here. Take any part of me. My teeth. My glass eye. One of my legs? First class mahogany. If I should cheat you, you'd have enough firewood for a week.

BLAUSTAIN: Listen to me. If I get that job at the Ration Board . . .

YABLONKA: Don't talk. You haven't got it yet.

BLAUSTAIN: . . . what will become of the rest of you? They *might* send another engineer. Or they might close down the factory.

YABLONKA: And if you stay, we will all live forever?

BLAUSTAIN: I had hoped to keep us going till the end of the war.

YABLONKA: And maybe tomorrow the sun will stand still? . . . You have a wife. You knocked her up. Take care of her. Don't bother *me* with your stinking conscience.

(He strides off toward his cubicle, seizes a broom, sweeps a cloud of dirt from under his bed into the common living area. BLAUSTAIN smiles, hunts for his pencil. YABLONKA stuffs another pile of straw and rumpled newspapers into his sleeves

*and trousers, curls up in his bed and, relaxed as an infant, tries
to suck a little more refreshment out of his scratched finger.*
BLAUSTAIN *is about to sit down and resume work.on his poem,
when* HUPERT *comes briskly into the room, briefcase under his
arm, cigar and homburg at a jaunty angle, a chairman hurry-
ing to a board meeting. As usual, no one pays any attention.
He fixes* BLAUSTAIN *with a penetrating stare. Then, in what
amounts to a parody of attempted casualness, he closes in on
him. He waits patiently until* BLAUSTAIN *is forced, wearily, to
look up and acknowledge him.* HUPERT *crooks his finger at
him.)*

HUPERT: You . . . come here. I've got something to discuss with you
in private.
  (A touch nervously, BLAUSTAIN *complies.* HUPERT *takes* BLAU-
  STAIN's *arm and leads him out to the balcony.)*

BLAUSTAIN: What do you want?

HUPERT: He's asking what I want. Listen, Mister. I'm a man of few
words. "Time is money," as we say in the States. Yes, yes, no,
no. You let me have that cat, and I'll make a fortune for both
of us.

BLAUSTAIN *(shakes his head):* Leave me alone!
  (He tries to go back inside. HUPERT *bars his way, continues
  mutely to harangue* BLAUSTAIN. *Inside,* ESTHER *sits up with a
  moan.)*

ESTHER: David . . . ? Is it time yet for the soup?
  *(*SCHNUR *hurries over to her.)*

SCHNUR: When they have cabbage, it takes a little longer to boil
the water.

ESTHER *(a frightened whisper):* Maybe there isn't any left? . . .
Where's David?

SCHNUR: Out on the balcony, negotiating.

ESTHER *(sharply):* For *what*?

SCHNUR: Who knows? Maybe an American passport. What is impossible to the One Above?

ESTHER *(firmly):* I wouldn't go *without* him. *(A sudden thought.)*
Would *he* go without *me*?

(SCHNUR, *after a moment's troubled hesitation, firmly shakes his head.*)

HUPERT: . . . You begin to understand? (BLAUSTAIN *tries to return to the room, but* HUPERT *clutches him fiercely by the lapel.*) Today, at Soup Kitchen Forty-Four, they're having potato soup. For this cat, I guarantee, I could get fifteen pounds of potato peelings . . . Do you know how much nutrition there is in potato peels? Enough iron to sink a battleship.

BLAUSTAIN: Idiot! What would I do with a sunken battleship? I want *bread*.

HUPERT (*a roar of impatience*): Shut up! I'm coming to that. I have a friend, a world-famous professor of chemistry, now polishing boots at Police Headquarters. He knows how to distill *vodka* from potato peels. You know what that means?

BLAUSTAIN: Mme. Hershkovitch is going to feed her children on vodka?

HUPERT: Let me *finish,* will you! From fifteen pounds of potato peels, he can make at least five gallons of vodka. And if you add a drop of water and stretch it to ten gallons, who'll know the difference? Of course, the professor will want fifty percent . . . (BLAUSTAIN *tries to cut him off.*) Then I sell the vodka to the Officers' Club, and with the money and some forged ration coupons, can you imagine what a reliable smuggler could buy on the other side? Meat, butter, eggs, fresh fruit . . . when is the last time you tasted an egg, eh? (*A wink, a nudge in the ribs.*) Tell me, what color is an egg, black or white? And does it have four corners or six? Ha-ha, he doesn't know any more . . . Of course, he'll also want fifty percent.

BLAUSTAIN: That's already a hundred-fifty percent. (*Another attempt to go back inside.*)

HUPERT: Ah, I understand. You don't trust me. Very well. All business must be founded on trust. What if I give you my short-wave radio for security? (*A lewd whisper.*) Wouldn't you like to know what *really* goes on in the world?

BLAUSTAIN: No! Why should I? Does the world want to know what's going on with *me*?

HUPERT: What are you being so arrogant about? Snotnose! An engineer you call yourself? Before the war, I used engineers like you to clean my toilets.

BLAUSTAIN: Hupert, I am not free to make any deals.

HUPERT: "Not free"! And where did your partner *keep* the cat? Right out there, under one of *our* garbage cans. And is it not a fact, that this plant is a cooperative? Eh? What's yours is mine, and all for one, and each according to the Capitalist System, my good friend, you'd better not cross swords with *me*. I know my rights. By Heaven, if I had my solicitors here, I'd instantly petition for an injunction, impound the cat, power of attorney, waiver of disqualifications, breach of promise, assignment of all rights, and objection overruled. You may not remember those days, old boy, but that's how we did things back in peace time . . . And as for your film career . . . Ha! You can go whistle for that.

BLAUSTAIN *(quietly ominous):* You're going to report me to the Blue Police?[7]

HUPERT: Heaven forbid! What do I look like? All I'm saying is . . . *(low, pitiful)* . . . give me ten percent, and I'll keep my mouth shut . . . ?
(BLAUSTAIN *brushes him aside and goes in.* HUPERT, *on the darkening balcony, looks down as though toying with the idea of hurling himself to the pavement. A freight train screams past.* HUPERT's *face follows it hypnotically. The sky turns livid. Inside,* BLAUSTAIN *checks the blackout curtain, then turns on the light, goes over to* ESTHER's *bed.)*

ESTHER: David . . .

BLAUSTAIN: Yes, my darling.

ESTHER: Does it hurt to die?

BLAUSTAIN: When I find out, you'll be the first to know.

ESTHER *(shyly):* I was wondering. What will he look like? Our son?

BLAUSTAIN: Probably a little disappointed.

---

7. Blue Police: the Jewish police (as opposed to the Polish police or the Nazis), who were responsible for keeping order in the ghetto.

ESTHER: Will you promise to name him after my father?

BLAUSTAIN: You plan to be out of town when he's born?

ESTHER: Don't laugh at me.

BLAUSTAIN: What else have I got to laugh at?

ESTHER: And you will teach him to say kaddish[8] for me? At least once a year. I know you don't believe in these things yourself, but . . .

BLAUSTAIN: You had a bad dream?

ESTHER *(shakes her head):* David, do *you* ever dream about . . . other women . . . ?

BLAUSTAIN: All the time.

ESTHER *(smiles at his "joke"):* I forgive you.

> *(He looks at her for a moment with utter detachment as she drifts back off to sleep.* HAUPTMANN *comes out of his cubicle and sits down opposite* BLAUSTAIN. *Very gently he shoves a much-folded newspaper clipping over to him.* BLAUSTAIN *glances at it politely.)*

HAUPTMANN: My son. When he graduated the Royal Military Academy. You will believe me if I tell you this photograph is the single most precious possession I have in all the world. Here! I want *you* to have it!

BLAUSTAIN: What are you doing? I don't want it.

HAUPTMANN: Of course. You are overwhelmed. But I insist. All I want in return is . . . *(excruciatingly humble and suspenseful)* . . . a twenty-five percent share of the cat. Not for myself. Oh, no. But there is a lawyer ready to take my case, to make inquiries of the American consulate in Stockholm, about the lapse of my visa. And once I am in America, my dear Herr Blaustain, you can be assured I will never forget what you have done for me today *(he tries to seize, even kiss,* BLAUSTAIN's *hand in abject gratitude).* I have this in the strictest confidence from Herr Hupert. The Alabama chapter of the American Red Cross is planning to send an impartial delegation to investigate alleged abuses in these Rehabilitation Zones . . .

---

8. *Kaddish:* the Jewish prayer for the dead.

BLAUSTAIN: Why? Have there been complaints?

HAUPTMANN *(shrugs helplessly):* You know our people. Notorious complainers. No wonder the world is bored with us. But you can depend on the Red Cross to be scrupulously impartial.

BLAUSTAIN: Next time they come around with a collection box, remind me to put in something extra.

HAUPTMANN *(indicates the clipping):* Look at his face. When they came to my villa to arrest me, he tried to explain to them, that I *was*, after all, a "Chevalier of the Iron Cross." But when the Lieutenant spat in my face, I think my son got a bit too excited and knocked him down. And for that, four soldiers held him pinned to the ground, while a fifth one, with the butt of his rifle . . . *(a silent scream).* And that, *that* is what has become of chivalry in this degenerate age of ours!

(He flings away his medal, hugs the clipping to his bosom for a moment, kisses it, moves back toward his cell, suddenly stops, turns and emits an animal sound of pain. ESTHER *awakens with a start.* BLAUSTAIN *runs to her, but* HUPERT *intercepts him.)*

HUPERT: Tomorrow morning, let me take the cat in for you as your broker . . . I'll take all the risks, and all I ask is . . . fifteen percent . . . ?

*(*BLAUSTAIN, *with a groan, turns away from him.)*

Twelve and a half, and I'll throw in my shortwave radio.

BLAUSTAIN: That's all I need. To be caught with a cat *and* a radio.

HUPERT: Why? They can only hang you once, ha-ha.

BLAUSTAIN: That's what you think.

HUPERT: Look at the money you could make, selling news bulletins, like I've been doing. Fresh merchandise every morning. Bad news, regular price. Good news, no limit. People *thrive* on good news. What else keeps them alive? Chopped liver?

BLAUSTAIN: Will you do me a favor and get lost?

HUPERT: Very well. You know where to find me. My offer remains in force until midnight. Not a moment later. This is no time for sentiment. You see this heart? A stone.

(And he's off. BLAUSTAIN *tries to get back to his poem.* BERYL,

like a mute, parodies HUPERT's *dignified departure.*

BLAUSTAIN *suddenly realizes there is someone standing quietly in the door. It is* ANYA, *his younger sister, a stocky, muscular ex-student with the red, coarse hands and arms of a laundress. Long, shapeless skirt, black stockings, wooden-soled shoes, a slight limp.)*

BLAUSTAIN: Anya . . . Did something go wrong?

ANYA *(shakes her head):* The price went up. Too much demand.

BLAUSTAIN: For what?

ANYA: Who would have thought one day a Certificate of Baptism would be worth more than a pair of gold earrings?

BLAUSTAIN: Your friend Karl Marx should have called it "the *caviar* of the people."

ANYA *(moves closer; confidentially):* Hey, listen . . . Is it true?

BLAUSTAIN *(guardedly):* What?

ANYA: The cat. I just heard about it.

BLAUSTAIN *(a groan):* Is there anyone in this town who *hasn't* heard the good news yet? I'm surprised the Blue Police isn't already surrounding the house.

ANYA: Listen, David, with that cat I can get papers, for you *and* for me. Passport, work permit, birth certificates . . .

BLAUSTAIN: Fine. And then what?

ANYA: There is a group of partisans hiding in the woods, not thirty kilometers from here . . .

BLAUSTAIN: Ours?

ANYA *(harshly):* They're workers like us.[9] They've learned by now we all have to be brothers.

BLAUSTAIN: Cain and Abel were brothers, too.

ANYA: And what have your fellow-intellectuals done to keep us out of this place?

BLAUSTAIN: Nothing. But at least they never *pretended* to be my brothers.

---

9. There were partisans (resistance fighters) of many national groups battling the Nazis throughout Europe; some were also hostile to Jews and fought them as well.

(ANYA *indicates* ESTHER *behind her curtain and lowers her voice.*)

ANYA: Listen . . . You wouldn't go without her, would you? (BLAU-STAIN *just looks at her.*) David, open your eyes. What good is she, even to herself? A living skeleton, with that obscene little vegetable growing in her belly . . . Lying there, half-dead, with nothing on her mind but the time for the next bowl of soup . . .

BLAUSTAIN: Half-dead is still better than half-alive. At least she has something to look forward to.

ANYA: You want to be buried next to her? Or maybe go up the chimney together, like Mama and Papa?

(BLAUSTAIN *hardens his face, turns away from her.*)

ANYA *(with bitter affection):* Ah, what a romantic you are. How did we two come to be in the same family? *(She reaches for his arm.)* All right, then, listen. How would you like to get her into the hospital by the back door?

BLAUSTAIN: How? They're stacked up to the ceiling right now.

ANYA: Give me the cat. One of the surgeons, he's been after me for months . . . a horrible little man, but he used to be an obstetrician . . . I've never let him touch me. But for Esther . . .

BLAUSTAIN: Anya, I can't. The cat isn't mine.

ANYA: An operation *with* anesthetics. And not with a kitchen knife, either. Two days in bed, and she'll walk out with blooming cheeks, all clean inside, as pure as the day she stood under the canopy with you,[10] all in white, like a little porcelain doll, flaming with innocence.

BLAUSTAIN: No.

ANYA: Idiot! Even if she *should* manage to squeeze out a live baby without croaking herself . . . Suppose you have to go into hiding, eh? Who would let you in with a crying brat? What's the use of growing to love the poor little thing, if in the end you'll only have to break its neck?

BLAUSTAIN: That cat belongs to Mme. Hershkovitch. Now will you shut up and leave me alone?

10. In a Jewish wedding ceremony, the bride and groom stand under a canopy.

ANYA: He worries about Mme. Hershkovitch! And what is she to you? Closer than your sister? Closer than your own wife? Are you responsible for every widow and orphan in the world?

BLAUSTAIN: And what makes *you* my business partner? Go out and find your own cat. Maybe *you* could cheat a helpless old woman. I can't.

ANYA: She wasn't too helpless to take advantage of your good nature. You do all the work, and risk your life on top of it, and she has the gall to demand fifty percent. What did she do, raise her skirt a little bit? *(Wearily shakes her head.)* Oh, David, you always were too good for this world.

BLAUSTAIN: Will you leave me alone?

ANYA: With that cat I could be *out* of here tomorrow. Alive. With papers in my pockets. And Esther . . . at least she'd have a chance.

BLAUSTAIN: And how will I face Mme. Hershkovitch?

ANYA: Pay her off with a pound of potato peels. If she makes a stink, smash her across the mouth . . . You want to live, don't you? Then forget you were born a human being. An animal has no shame . . .

BLAUSTAIN: This is how Mama raised you?

(Offstage, a train whistles. ANYA's *head follows it in rigid fascination.)*

ANYA: Ah . . . You want to talk about Mama? All right. Let us talk about Mama. Do you know why you're still here? Because you're making carpets for them? No. Because right now they need the rolling stock for their troops. That's all. And do you know whose clothing you are meanwhile turning into carpets for the parlors of their fat-assed housewives on the homefront?

BLAUSTAIN: Their own people's. Their air-raid victims. I can tell by the styles.

ANYA: You know perfectly well whose clothes these are.

BLAUSTAIN: No, I don't. There's no way of being sure.

ANYA: Isn't there?

BLAUSTAIN: No!

ANYA: Yesterday, one of the workers showed me a blue dress she
was about to put into the boiler . . . One of the pockets had a
little picture in it. *(She takes it out, forces him to look at it.*
BLAUSTAIN *averts his face.)* Remember when that was taken?
We were such a handsome family, weren't we? . . . You know,
I could almost face the thought of somebody *killing* Mama.
But taking her dress off . . . *(She crushes the picture so hard,
her fingernails cut right into her palms.)* And you're making
carpets out of it, for them! *(She flings the crumpled picture
into his face.)* All right, you dreamer, go ahead. Let her have
the little parasite. You know what they do with the mothers
afterwards, don't you?

(BLAUSTAIN *covers his ears. But she keeps right after him,
clawing at his shoulders to make him look at her.)*

Twenty officers a night. It's really not such a lot, when you
think about it. But Esther is a little out of practice, isn't she?

BLAUSTAIN: Will you shut up?

ANYA: Think she'll be able to handle it? If not, you know how they
get rid of them, don't you?

BLAUSTAIN: Shut up! Just shut up now.

ANYA: . . . Turn her over to the Ukrainian volunteers.[11] On a good
strong bed, it sometimes takes two, three hours before anyone
even notices she's dead.

BLAUSTAIN: Shut up, you whore! *(He flings off her hand so violently, she falls to the floor.)*

ANYA *(as she scrambles to her feet):* Murderer! You don't love your
wife. You *want* her to die!

(BLAUSTAIN *hits her with his open hand as hard as he can, but
ANYA doesn't even seem to notice.)*

You *want* to bring a child into this beautiful world? Ask Mme.

---

11. Ukrainian volunteers: After the German conquest of the Ukraine (a province
in southwestern Russia), Ukrainians fought alongside the Nazis; they had a long and
ugly history of anti-Semitism.

Hershkovitch what they do. She cleans up around the hospital. Ask *her* how it feels to throw away a smashed baby along with the rest of the garbage!

(KRAUSE *comes bursting out of his cubicle, holding his ears.*)

KRAUSE: Will you stop it with those stories! I can't stand it any more!

(BLAUSTAIN *and* ANYA *turn to him, surprised.*)

BLAUSTAIN *(mildly):* Don't you like to know what goes on in the world?

KRAUSE *(quietly hysterical):* This is not the world. Oh, no. This is no world *I* ever heard of. Even in Sunday school, when they taught us about the everlasting tortures of the Damned, it was nothing like this . . .

BLAUSTAIN *(to* ANYA, *casually):* He just arrived today. He hasn't gotten used to the routine yet.

KRAUSE: Used to it! Used to this? Not in a hundred years!

BLAUSTAIN *(reasonably):* That's true. A hundred years would probably not be enough. Two thousand years would be more like it.

KRAUSE: Don't you people have any human feelings, for Christ's sake?

ANYA *(reproachfully):* How can you ask? For nine years my brother has been dreaming of the day when he would bring a child into the world. Now like any normal father, all he wants is the best for the little bastard.

KRAUSE *(points an outraged finger):* I heard him! He wants an abortion. He wants to kill his own child.

ANYA: Of course. Like every good father, he wants it to have the best possible start in life.

KRAUSE *(almost spitting):* No wonder you are the most hated people in the world! *(He rushes back into his cubicle with every evidence of righteous disapproval.* ANYA *shrugs, withdraws toward the door.)*

ANYA *(affectionately):* All right, go on. Imbecile. Dreamer. Idealist. Let nature take its course *(shrugs).* Maybe you can get the convent to take it off your hands. They're already packed with babies, but I guess there's always room for another soul in need of salvation.

BLAUSTAIN: I imagine Esther would have something to say about that.

ANYA: And you haven't *asked* her yet?

BLAUSTAIN: How can I? You know how innocent she is. When we were married, that first night . . . she made me leave the room when she undressed.

ANYA *(drily):* Too bad you couldn't have kept her innocent a few years longer.

(ESTHER moans in her sleep.)

(ANYA offers her hand.) Goodbye, David. I'm going for a walk tonight. If I'm lucky, it'll be a long walk. If not . . . *(shrugs).* I'll also be lucky. *(She picks up the crumpled photo, smooths it out, hands it to him.)* We *were* a handsome family, weren't we?

(BLAUSTAIN looks at it once more, then puts it carefully into his pocket. He goes over to the baby carriage, digs out the automatic, offers it to her.)

BLAUSTAIN: It's full. Save one for yourself. Put the narrow end into your mouth. Who knows, it might turn out to be the shortcut to Socialism.

(ANYA smiles at him, touched, but doesn't take it.)

ANYA: You hold onto that. And when they finally have room for you in one of their box-cars, and even you can see the time for poetry is running thin . . . let the world find out our blood is not for nothing . . . Make a little commotion. Leave them something to remember you. A couple of widows. A handful of orphans. Believe me, they'll respect you for it . . . For Mama's sake. Because they took her dress off.

(She kisses his cheek, starts for the door, stops, waves to him. BLAUSTAIN wanly waves back. She leaves. For a long moment he stands motionless, drained. Then, stubbornly, he tries to return to his poem.)

SCHNUR: Still trying to write poetry about all this?

BLAUSTAIN: I know just what I want to say. Only, the minute I put it on paper, it becomes a lie.

SCHNUR *(shrugs):* Words have been used crookedly for so long, perhaps by now they have all gone and died of shame.

(BLAUSTAIN *glumly picks up the piece of brown wrapping paper he's been writing on.)*

BLAUSTAIN:

"The kettles vomit forth
Their poison clouds.
The walls pour out their tears.
And on the clay floor,
Squatting like frogs,
Our wives and mothers,
With cracked hands and frozen fingers,
Dismember the smeared garments of the slain . . .
We are the privileged, the fortunate, the living . . ."

(He shakes his head hopelessly, scratches out what he has just read.)

I never suspected I had such a talent for writing sentimental trash.

SCHNUR: I had a sister who liked to read poetry. I once looked into one of her books. What did it say? Nature is beautiful. Love is beautiful. Birds are singing. The weather is nice. It didn't seem to *me* the kind of information on which a person could get fat . . .

BLAUSTAIN: If I could leave behind me only one line that would live . . .

(YABLONKA yawns elaborately, cranks up the phonograph.)

YABLONKA: And what if you did? One day after you were gone, somebody would need a piece of paper to wipe himself, and . . .

BLAUSTAIN: Even if I *could* describe what went on here . . . would anyone really *believe* it? And if they did, what would they do about it—feel bad?

YABLONKA: Eh! A man's own toothache is more tragic to *him* than rivers of blood flowing in the next town. *(He puts on a record. Then sees* BERYL, *on the balcony, motioning him to come out and shut the door behind him.)*

BERYL *(to* YABLONKA*):* Didn't you hear him? We're going to study "The Book of Civil Damages."

YABLONKA: So what's your hurry? You have a case coming up in court?

BERYL: I'm tired of being treated like a kid. I know where he buried his books. Let him see I can do things on my own.

YABLONKA: You know what will happen if the soldiers catch you with a copy of the Talmud?[12]

BERYL: So I'll die ignorant.

(He starts to climb over the side. YABLONKA *watches him worriedly, until he is out of sight, then goes back into the room.* MME. HERSHKOVITCH *enters.)*

MME. HERSHKOVITCH: The soup wagon broke down in the mud, two blocks away. They won't get to us before curfew.

BLAUSTAIN: We'd better get over there, before they dump out what's left of the soup and poison every mouse in the neighborhood.

(Each man hurriedly collects a tin utensil of some sort. HAUPTMANN *comes out, carrying a military mess kit.)*

BLAUSTAIN *(to* ESTHER*):* Stay in bed. I'll try to get a little extra for you . . .

ESTHER *(clings to him):* I'm strong enough. I can go anywhere. With you.

BLAUSTAIN: I need you here to keep an eye on the cat. I'll play you some music to keep you awake *(he goes to wind up the gramophone).*

ESTHER: David . . . Come here a minute. *(He obeys.)* Did you *want* to go away with Anya . . . and leave me behind?

BLAUSTAIN *(after a moment; harshly):* Of course I wanted to. You think I'm made of wood?

ESTHER: David . . .

---

12. Talmud: Jewish law.

BLAUSTAIN: Yes?

ESTHER: Why didn't you?

BLAUSTAIN *(another long pause; then):* Because I'm not made of wood.

(ESTHER, *with a peaceful smile, goes back to sleep.* YABLONKA *goes up to* BLAUSTAIN, *indicates* KRAUSE's *cubicle.)*

YABLONKA: What about him?

BLAUSTAIN: Better wake him up.

YABLONKA: Don't they have a special soup kitchen for *them?*

BLAUSTAIN: Only for Catholics and converts.

YABLONKA: So what is he?

BLAUSTAIN: A Protestant.

YABLONKA: What's the difference? They all believe in the same Jesus, don't they?

BLAUSTAIN *(shrugs):* By *them* there's a difference. (YABLONKA *shakes his head, baffled.)*

YABLONKA: You mean they also fight among themselves?

BLAUSTAIN: Worse than we do.

YABLONKA: *Worse?* About *what?* What have *they* got to fight about?

BLAUSTAIN: Do me a favor, ask them.

YABLONKA *(loud):* Herr Krause!

(He *whistles the old Prussian military mess call, "Kartoffel-Supp."* KRAUSE *rises sleepily. The other men begin to straggle out.* BLAUSTAIN *cranks up the phonograph.)*

MME. HERSHKOVITCH: Herr Blaustain . . . please forgive me if I . . .

BLAUSTAIN: What?

MME. HERSHKOVITCH: . . . but I heard from someone, they said you had bargained away my cat . . . excuse me, *our* cat . . . to get your wife a place in the hospital.

BLAUSTAIN *(furious):* Mme. Hershkovitch, I haven't had a peaceful moment, ever since you brought me that damned cat. If you don't trust me, take it back right now. Right now! *(He moves to unlock the cupboard. She stops him.)*

MME. HERSHKOVITCH *(bursts into tears):* What did I say? Engineer Blaustain, I know you're not a murderer, a man who would take bread out of the mouths of innocent orphans. But . . .

BLAUSTAIN: But, but, but. The plain fact is, you don't trust me.

MME. HERSHKOVITCH: Can I help hearing things? Can I help worrying? A mother's heart isn't made of stone . . .

(She gives him a pleading look and shuffles out. BLAUSTAIN *puts a raucous Warsaw music hall record on the turntable, kisses* ESTHER *on the forehead, turns off all the lights, except for one small lamp on the floor next to the exit, and hurries out after the others. In the semidarkness, the phonograph blares its brash, derisive song, and* ESTHER *tries to remain awake and watchful.*

The door opens and a shadowy figure creeps over to the cupboard. He pries a tool into the fragile wood. The door flies open with a squeak. ESTHER *rises painfully from her bed.)*

ESTHER: Is somebody there? Hello? . . . Who's there?

(The intruder rummages for the cat. The cat howls.)

No! No! Not the cat! Please! Take anything. Not the cat. Please.

(Holding the squirming bundle pressed to his chest, the thief makes a dash for the door and disappears. ESTHER *weakly pursues him as far as the door.)*

Stop, thief. Stop, thief. *Stop, thief!*

(Her strength exhausted, she glides down the door frame and remains crumpled on the floor. A moment later, the phonograph comes whining to a halt. Blackout.)

ACT 3

Fade up. The moment before sunrise. The doors of the cupboard hang reproachfully open. The nightshift workers are sleeping, each one in his own way struggling with cold, hunger, and nightmares. Offstage, the fearsome howl of a passing freight train. YABLONKA *follows the sound with his eyes. Huddled inside his threadbare blanket, he tries clumsily, intently, to roll and light a cigarette from a piece of newspaper and some foul-smelling weeds.*

We now notice SCHNUR, *at the window after a sleepless night, as he moves from side to side to follow the path of a rare passing vehicle, foot patrol or worker.*

Dawn begins to seep into the room. The tempestuous sound of the toilet being flushed. BLAUSTAIN *carrying* ESTHER *to her bed. He darts* YABLONKA *a savage glare of suspicion.*

SCHNUR *(leans out, excited):* Beryl?

(No answer. SCHNUR *pulls back his head.)*

YABLONKA: Was it? *(*SCHNUR *shakes his head.)*

ESTHER *(almost flirting):* Do you think my breasts will have milk enough . . . for the baby?

BLAUSTAIN: Your breasts are . . . *(to* SCHNUR*)* How did King Solomon describe the breasts of his beloved?[13]

SCHNUR *(distracted):* Very poetically. But he was speaking of *our* relations with the Almighty—not of a woman's body.

BLAUSTAIN: He could have fooled me.

*(*HAUPTMANN *comes out and disapprovingly examines the broken lock of the cupboard, then casts an accusing look at* YA-BLONKA.*)*

YABLONKA: You want my fingerprints?

*(*SCHNUR, *at the window, anxiously watches a passing patrol.)*

---

13. Blaustain refers to a book of the Bible, The Song of Songs, which some attribute to King Solomon. It is often interpreted as an allegorical poem describing the love of Jews for their God.

BLAUSTAIN: Beryl's been gone the whole night? *(SCHNUR nods.)* Well, what's the good of standing there with full pants? Even if he ran into a patrol, what could they find on him—diamonds?

YABLONKA: Worse than that. *(To SCHNUR.)* He went to dig up one of the books you had hidden.

SCHNUR: I *told* him I would get it for him.

YABLONKA: He wanted to show you he can wipe his *own* nose.

(SCHNUR turns away, shaking his head. Clatter of ascending steps. SCHNUR turns hopefully. MME. HERSHKOVITCH bursts in, trembling with anticipation.)

MME. HERSHKOVITCH: Engineer Blaustain? *(BLAUSTAIN flinches with shock, and for a moment wishes he could hide. But he forces himself to face her.)*

MME. HERSHKOVITCH *(happily):* Well? . . . Don't keep me in suspense. All night long, my children were sitting up, blessing your name. They could hardly wait for it to be morning. I never saw them so happy. They spoke of *you* as if their own father had come back to life. Two pounds of bread! Quickly, where is it? I don't want to be away from them any longer.

(Each of her words goes through BLAUSTAIN like a knife.)

BLAUSTAIN: Madame Hershkovitch . . .

MME. HERSHKOVITCH: What? Is something wrong? Your wife, is she all right? *(He nods.)* They didn't give you a loaf that was underbaked, did they?

(All this time, her eyes have been roving the room, trying to discover where the bread has been hidden. Now she goes over to the cupboard, idly looks inside.)

You have a few minutes? I want you to come back with me, to see how their faces will light up.

BLAUSTAIN: Will you listen to me! *(She flinches back, as though slapped.)*

MME. HERSHKOVITCH: What's the matter? . . . Why do you look at me like that? *(Softly.)* What is it you want to tell me?

BLAUSTAIN: I didn't get any bread.

MME. HERSHKOVITCH: What? You didn't go yet? My children are
lying on the floor screaming, and he stands there with a finger
in his nose. Murderer, what are you waiting for?

BLAUSTAIN: Madame Hershkovitch, I don't have the cat . . . Somebody stole it during the night. *(*MME. HERSHKOVITCH *just looks
at him.)* Did you hear me?

MME. HERSHKOVITCH *(suddenly smiles):* All right now, you've had
your joke. For a minute, I . . . my heart almost fell out . . .
Come on, the children have been crying all morning.
(Tortured, BLAUSTAIN *shakes his head.* MME. HERSHKOVITCH
is suddenly very calm, ominously calm.)
You got the bread. But you don't want to share it with me. So
you made up this story . . . *(Shakes her head, still speaking
quietly.)* Never in my life would I have believed that my old
friend David Blaustain should have turned out to be a common thief, a swindler, an assassin of innocent children . . .
*(*BLAUSTAIN *continues, agonized, to shake his head.* MME.
HERSHKOVITCH, *in a burst of sudden hysteria, rushes at* BLAU-
STAIN *with her fists.)*
Criminal! Eating my orphans' bread!
*(*BLAUSTAIN *wards her off, grimly opens his suitcase, takes out
the shriveled remainder of his own bread ration and cuts it in
half.)*

BLAUSTAIN: Here. This is all the bread we have left for the rest of
the week. This is my wife's half. This is mine. Here. *(Hands
her his half.)* For your children. May they grow up to be
healthy and strong, and never go through a day like this one.
*(*MME. HERSHKOVITCH *stares at the bread, torn between taking
it and admitting that* BLAUSTAIN *may not have been lying after
all. At last, tortured, she takes the proffered piece, picks up the
knife and divides it once more and returns half to* BLAUSTAIN.
*She looks at the bread hungrily for a moment, but masters the
temptation and stuffs it carefully into the pocket of her overcoat.* YABLONKA *comes out, reproachfully shaking his head.)*

YABLONKA *(to* MME. HERSHKOVITCH*):* You see? Go into partnership with an idealist. He still believes in this world only thieves are allowed to steal.

BLAUSTAIN *(turns on him):* All I know is, it was stolen by one of *my* workers. One of the people *I* am keeping alive . . . Who *made* you an "essential industry"? Where do you think you would be without me? On your way to the "Rest Camp" at Treblinka.[14] "In through the gate, and out through the chimney." How would you like a taste of that, eh? . . . Pigs! Parasites! Thieves! Scum of the earth! . . .

(In the course of his harangue, HUPERT *has come in but remains standing in the shadowy doorway.)*

YABLONKA: Don't spit in the well. You may still have to drink from it.

*(*HAUPTMANN *humbly goes over to* BLAUSTAIN *with a rag, kneels down, and attempts to shine his shoes.* BLAUSTAIN *kicks him away.)*

BLAUSTAIN: All right . . . if that's the way you want to be . . . Why should I throw away my life, protecting scum like you? I'm young. I'm still young enough to start all over again . . .

ESTHER: David . . .?

BLAUSTAIN *(ignores her):* I should have gone away with my sister, and left you *all* to die like dogs. What *good* are you?

ESTHER *(frightened):* David . . . ?

BLAUSTAIN *(instinctively):* You, too!

*(*ESTHER *starts weeping quietly into her pillow.* BLAUSTAIN *pointedly turns his back on her. He addresses the men, but* ESTHER *keenly feels it is all meant for her alone.)*

Ten times I had a chance to get out of this place. To go join the partisans, or hide in the mountains. But no. Not David Blaustain. He felt *responsible* for his workers. And this is how you pay me back, hah?

*(*YABLONKA *tries, with gestures, to warn* BLAUSTAIN *of the effect his words are having on* ESTHER.*)*

14. Treblinka: One of the most notorious German concentration camps where Jews were exterminated. See the first part of the Editor's introduction.

She *told* me to go. She *told* me. Because she loves me. She wants me to live. Well, from now on, my good friends . . . *(indicates the open cupboard)* . . . I have learned my lesson. From now on, I look out for myself. You treat me like an animal? All right, I'll be an animal.

ESTHER: David . . . I'm thirsty.

BLAUSTAIN: Now I woke her up! Why did you let me go on talking? *(He runs over to her cubicle, kneels down by her bed, presses his face to her shoulder, weeping.)*

Yes, my darling, my treasure . . . I'm here . . . What is it?

ESTHER: I had a dream . . . that the war was over . . .

(BLAUSTAIN shuts his eyes, but can't shut out her voice.)

You were just running home to tell me, when I woke up. You believe in dreams, don't you?

BLAUSTAIN: What else have I got left to believe in?

(SCHNUR gives him a troubled look.)

ESTHER: David . . . when you get the bread . . . Remember . . . don't gulp. You'll make yourself sick if you don't chew every bite very slowly.

BLAUSTAIN: I think I still remember how to eat a piece of bread.

ESTHER: Ah, you're a good husband . . . How was I so lucky? You don't want the baby to be born, and still you feed it like a prince . . .

(BLAUSTAIN takes a rag, dips it in the firebucket, goes back and dabs it across his wife's feverish forehead. MME. HERSHKOVITCH is still sitting slumped at the table, without the strength to go home. Only SCHNUR has remained alert, posted at the window in desperate anxiety.

BLAUSTAIN goes over to MME. HERSHKOVITCH, gently helps her to her feet.)

BLAUSTAIN: Your children are waiting.

(She nods, shuffles toward the door. And stops, stares. HUPERT steps out of the shadows, concealing something behind his back.)

HUPERT: Heard the latest? America finally declared war!

YABLONKA: On who?

HUPERT *(irritably):* What's the difference? Either way, the war can't last another week. They've taken all the profit out of it now.

BLAUSTAIN: What's that you've got behind your back?

HUPERT: What? Oh, you mean this?

(He holds up the smeared mattress ticking with the cat squirming inside it. The others look at him in amazement. MME. HERSHKOVITCH *has begun to tremble as though she had suddenly aged another thirty years.)*

HUPERT *(listless):* Here.

(Looking at no one, he puts his bundle on the table. Inside, a plaintive meow. *All eyes are fastened breathlessly to the bag. All except* BLAUSTAIN'S *who moves slowly toward* HUPERT *as though ready to tear him in half. But* HUPERT, *instead of trying to escape, sinks into a chair and contemplates his swollen feet with a heartbreaking sigh.)*

Well, take it! I risked my life to bring it back, didn't I?

BLAUSTAIN *(softly):* Where did you get this?

HUPERT *(angry):* Where? Idiot, you think cats grow on trees? I'm a businessman. How do you *think* I got it? I stole it! *(And abruptly all the wind goes out of him; plaintive.)* I would have shared it with you . . . Whatever I got . . . I only wanted to be a partner.

BLAUSTAIN *(contemptuously):* Then why didn't you go through with it?

HUPERT I did. *(They look at him, astonished.)* I've just come from the Ration Board. They offered me ten marks for the cat.

MME. HERSHKOVITCH: He's lying! *(She's ready to claw out his eyes.* BLAUSTAIN *holds her back.)*

BLAUSTAIN: Ten marks wouldn't buy even one slice of bread.

HUPERT: Why should I lie? I brought you back the cat, didn't I? . . . *(viciously).* They don't *need* it.

MME. HERSHKOVITCH: Of *course* they need it! What about the rats eating up the grain in their cellars!

HUPERT: Exactly what I asked the "Emperor." He said, "A *job* you want? A loaf of bread? Ha! Give *me* a loaf of bread, and I'll give you *twenty* cats" *(re-creating the desperation of his at-tempt).* I said, "And who's going to catch the rats in your cel-lars?" So he laughs. He says, "I have a dozen two-legged cats down in the cellar right now. Know what I'm paying them? If they catch a rat, I allow them to keep it, to take home to their family. Why not? I hear that if you haven't eaten chicken for some time, you can hardly tell the difference."

(BLAUSTAIN *looks at* MME. HERSHKOVITCH.)

MME. HERSHKOVITCH: I'm sorry I . . .

BLAUSTAIN: It doesn't matter.

MME. HERSHKOVITCH: I cursed you. I distrusted you. I took your bread.

BLAUSTAIN: It doesn't matter.

MME. HERSHKOVITCH: And now what'll we do with the cat?

BLAUSTAIN *(shrugs):* It's your cat.

MME. HERSHKOVITCH: My cat? Heaven forbid! *(she backs away.)*

YABLONKA *(abruptly):* I'm going over to the Ration Board, to see if he's lying. *(He picks up the bag, to see if he can carry it inconspicuously under his jacket. Hesitates.)* Even a business-man *(refers to* HUPERT) has to tell the truth *sometimes.*

(BLAUSTAIN *puts the cat back down.* SCHNUR *is walking back and forth, trying to decide whether to go outside. The cat wails frightfully. At this moment,* KRAUSE *steps forward, with an odd mixture of shyness and arrogance.)*

KRAUSE: Herr Engineer . . . ?

(SCHNUR *goes downstairs.)*

BLAUSTAIN: Yes?

KRAUSE: If I might be permitted . . . to make a suggestion . . . I mean to say, look at your skin, your hair, your nails, the swell-ings in your legs . . . All that is due to nothing more than a lack of protein in your diet.

BLAUSTAIN: Thank you for the news.

KRAUSE: Now, speaking purely from a biochemical point of view . . . the flesh of a cat, you know, is edible.

HAUPTMANN: Exactly what *I've* been telling them.

KRAUSE: *(warming to his subject):* I mean, like any other meat, it contains all the essential amino acids necessary to regenerate muscle tissue, bone marrow, white blood cells . . .

MME. HERSHKOVITCH: How does *he* know all that?

KRAUSE: Madame, these things have been scientifically determined.

MME. HERSHKOVITCH: How?

BLAUSTAIN *(shrugs):* Experiments on animals, how else?

KRAUSE: Oh, no. That has been strictly forbidden by law in our country for almost ten years now.

BLAUSTAIN: What has?

KRAUSE: Vivisection. Any sort of experimentation that might inflict cruelty on a living animal . . . We may have our faults as a nation, but thank God, we *are* civilized.

YABLONKA *(fervently):* Ah. Where would we be without German science?

KRAUSE: Now, a cat, properly skinned, eviscerated and roasted, might yield as much as three, four pounds of meat . . .

HAUPTMANN: There is no animal cleaner than a cat! Ask any soldier.

(The others turn away, disgusted.)

KRAUSE: Dammit, I'm just trying to be helpful. Heavens knows, I want no part of it for myself.

(HUPERT suddenly buries his face in his hands, and his shoulders shake despairingly. BLAUSTAIN watches him without sympathy. HUPERT abruptly looks up, dry-eyed, cunning.)

HUPERT: Herr Engineer . . . Could you, I wonder, see your way clear to letting me have something to eat?

BLAUSTAIN: *What?*

HUPERT: Well, I missed dinner last night on your account, didn't I?

(YABLONKA laughs rudely.)

BLAUSTAIN: Stealing from a helpless widow! With all the money you've been making out of your radio . . .

(HUPERT cuts him off by dramatically opening the front of his shirt, pushing aside the insulation of old newspaper underneath, and displaying his bosom.)

HUPERT: Look at me! *(With horror and fascination.)* I'm developing breasts!

KRAUSE: A simple deficiency of vitamin B complex . . .

YABLONKA: Let me know when you're ready to give milk.

HUPERT: I'll be raped by every soldier in the street!

YABLONKA: Better you than my sister.

HUPERT: Listen, Blaustain, I'm in trouble. Somebody informed on me to the military police. Yesterday they came to look for the radio . . . If I'd had one, I'd be hanging like an apple right this minute.

BLAUSTAIN: You didn't *have* a shortwave radio? (HUPERT *guiltily both nods and shakes his head.*) And all the "news" you've been selling us all these months . . . You never had a radio?

HUPERT: I did. Until they put up the notices with all the death penalties for owning radios or babies or dogs . . . I dropped it into a cesspool, to be rid of it.

BLAUSTAIN: And since then, all that wonderful news, how the war might be over any month, any day . . .

HUPERT *(a touch of pride):* Made up. Every word. Out of my own head . . . After all, you can't be in the cinema without a gift for fantasy . . .

BLAUSTAIN: And now all your neighbors know that you're a liar and a cheat.

HUPERT: Two of them told me yesterday, if I don't pay back every penny, they'll find room for me, too, at the bottom of that cesspool.

YABLONKA: Never mind. You know what they say in Warsaw: "Shit always floats to the top."

(But HUPERT's *posture, as he makes for the door, is so overwhelmingly abject,* BLAUSTAIN *can't help a twinge of pity and amusement.)*

BLAUSTAIN: Tell them, if they lay a hand on you—you won't let them be in your film.

HUPERT: *That's* what I'll tell them!

(He exits almost jauntily, as SCHNUR *returns. Before the others again succumb to the ever-present drag of physical apathy,* MME. HERSHKOVITCH *rises with a pleading look at* BLAUSTAIN.)*

MME. HERSHKOVITCH: Herr Engineer . . . your piece of bread . . . I have to return it to you, don't I?

BLAUSTAIN *(shakes his head):* To realize large profits, one must be ready to take large risks. That is one of the cornerstones of capitalism, and I am a confirmed capitalist. *(She nods gratefully and, before he can change his mind, hurries out.)*

SCHNUR *(at the window):* There's a policeman on a bicycle ... *(They freeze.)* It's all right. He only seems to have left some kind of a letter downstairs.

(BLAUSTAIN hurries over to the window. HAUPTMANN has appeared in the door of the cubicle, his body clenched in a posture of unreasoning hope.)

YABLONKA: I'll get it. *(He starts for the door.)*

HAUPTMANN: My visa! *(With surprising energy, he sweeps YABLONKA aside and clatters down the stairs.)*

SCHNUR: Why not? For bad news, do they have to write letters? They come and take you by the beard ... Maybe *he* is the only one here who's *not* crazy.

(HAUPTMANN comes in with the letter, remains in the door.)

BLAUSTAIN: Well?

(Crushed with disappointment, HAUPTMANN holds out the letter, waits for BLAUSTAIN to come and take it. BLAUSTAIN looks uneasily at the return address.)

HAUPTMANN *(low):* It's for *him.*

(He nods toward KRAUSE's silent cubicle, then, shadow-like, withdraws, leaving only the amputated sight of his cavalry-booted feet and his three-legged stool. SCHNUR resumes his increasingly frantic vigil by the window. BLAUSTAIN takes the letter, knocks at the entrance of KRAUSE's "apartment.")

BLAUSTAIN: Herr Krause. A letter for you.

(KRAUSE appears instantly, his face moving rapidly between terror and hope. He is afraid to touch the envelope.)

KRAUSE: From who?

BLAUSTAIN: *(gently):* "Headquarters, Military Government, Relocation Zone B."

KRAUSE: Not from my ... wife? *(BLAUSTAIN sympathetically shakes his head.)* What ... what could they want from me? I just got here. *(BLAUSTAIN once more offers him the letter. KRAUSE withholds his hands.)*

YABLONKA *(under his breath):* Maybe it's a "Wedding Invitation."

KRAUSE: What?

BLAUSTAIN: Nothing. *(Gently.)* Why don't you open it? *(KRAUSE takes it with shaking fingers.)*

KRAUSE: What does he mean, a "Wedding Invitation"? My daughter isn't even menstruating yet.

BLAUSTAIN: Nothing. A joke. It's what we call a Deportation Order.

KRAUSE: Deportation! I've just *been* deported, to *this* place.

BLAUSTAIN *(quietly):* There are others . . . not quite as convenient. *(KRAUSE tears open the letter. He reads it and remains expressionless for a long moment. BLAUSTAIN and YABLONKA lean toward him with almost unbearable curiosity. KRAUSE abruptly looks up, holds out the letter to BLAUSTAIN, who reads it, hands it back. KRAUSE disappears abruptly back into his cubicle, throws himself down on his bed, and starts weeping unashamedly.)*

YABLONKA: Well?

BLAUSTAIN: Herr Krause's pastor, back home, arranged for "proof" that his mother was illegitimate. Which makes him a pure-blooded Aryan, after all. So now he can go back home to the arms of his loving wife and daughter, who rallied to his side so loyally in his hour of need. *(To KRAUSE.)* Better get ready. Now that you're a human being again, they'll probably send a car to pick you up. *(SCHNUR, fascinated by this turn of events, glances at KRAUSE with a pleased kind of amazement at the inscrutable workings of Providence. YABLONKA crowds forward and stares at KRAUSE who, blank-faced, has sunk fervently to his knees.)*

YABLONKA *(to BLAUSTAIN):* Ah, if my poor parents had known what a useful thing it would be one day to be baptized . . . they would have held me under till I drowned. *(KRAUSE gets up. YABLONKA beams at him benevolently.)* Hey, listen, now that you're one of *them* again, you're not going to squeal on us about the cat, are you? *(KRAUSE looks at him empty-eyed, abruptly draws the curtain of his cubicle between them.)*

Well . . . I wish him luck . . . Why not? He wasn't a bad fellow.
I've seen worse.

*(Uncertain footsteps on the stairs outside. The door opens
slowly and* BERYL *enters, hunched, white-faced, each hand
pressed into the opposite armpit, as though for warmth.*
SCHNUR *jumps to his feet with explosive relief.)*

SCHNUR: What took you so long? You got the book? *(*BERYL *shakes
his head)*: Ay, what a scatterbrain you are. No. You're fooling
me. You've got it under your coat. *(He reaches playfully into*
BERYL'S *tattered coat.* BERYL *fiercely pulls back. Only now
does* SCHNUR *become aware of the boy's chalk-white, pain-
twisted features.)*

BERYL: Get away from me!

SCHNUR: Beryl, what happened?

*(*BLAUSTAIN *and* YABLONKA, *too, gather around him.)*

BERYL *(quietly)*: Police patrol . . . they caught me digging up your
books. They wanted to know where is my school, who is my
teacher, who is teaching me this poison? They took me to the
station, down in the cellar and . . . I *told* them! Everything!
Your name, address, everything! They'll be coming for you any
minute.

SCHNUR *(overlapping)*; No. No. I don't believe you. Come. Sit
down. It's late. We've lost time. From the beginning. "All may
slaughter, and their slaughtering is acceptable . . ." *(He tries to
put his arm about the boy.* BERYL *averts his face.)* Don't you
know it is only the breath of children studying the Law that
keeps the world from falling apart?

BERYL: Let it fall apart!

SCHNUR: Beryl!

*(*BERYL *suddenly draws his hands out from under his armpits
and thrusts them at* SCHNUR, *just long enough to show several
fingertips streaked with blood.* YABLONKA *hurries to get a wet
rag.* SCHNUR *fiercely embraces* BERYL'S *head, trying to comfort
him.* BERYL *violently breaks away from him.)*

BERYL: Yes. I am finished with God! You have lied to me. He is not
our father. If *this* is how a father loves his children . . . then let
me be an orphan!

SCHNUR: *(gently shakes his head):* Remember what they said last year when they put up the barbed wire? They said, "Hunger will turn them into mad dogs. They will eat each other alive."

BERYL: I *want* to be a mad dog! I want to eat, I want to be warm, I want to kill, I want to be like *them!*

SCHNUR: Like them? Without the knowledge of having been made in His image? A beast of prey, without shame, without conscience, living for no higher pleasure than the smell of blood?

BERYL: Why not? What makes us better than they?

SCHNUR: Because you are a man! A man, and not an animal.

(KRAUSE has put his face through the curtain, impervious to BLAUSTAIN's look of open, jealous hatred. Now he withdraws again. But a moment later, he comes out with several pills. He puts them on the table, obliquely addresses BLAUSTAIN.)

KRAUSE: Pain-killers, for the boy. Take two every three hours, with water.

(He draws the curtain behind him. BLAUSTAIN picks up two pills, gets a tin cup of water and makes BERYL swallow them. SCHNUR faces the wall, glances slightly upward, speaking in a conversational tone of reproach and weariness and anger and pain.)

SCHNUR: Master of the Universe. You whom we call our Merciful Father. I, Alter ben Soroh,[15] I am calling You to judgment . . . Yes . . . We have trespassed, we have been faithless, we have robbed, we have been presumptuous, we have done violence, we have rebelled, we have been stubborn, we have corrupted ourselves, we have committed abominations . . . *(He continues the recital in an undertone for a moment, then:)* But how, how can You begin to weigh all our crimes in the last five thousand years against *what they do in one day?*

BLAUSTAIN *(indicating KRAUSE's cubicle):* Shall I ask him if he has any arsenic? Quick, before they knock on the door. *(SCHNUR*

---

15. Alter ben Soroh: Schnur's Hebrew name, literally, "Alter, son of Soroh."

shakes his head. He embraces BERYL, *strokes his hair.)* Goddamn it, Schnur, do you know what they can do to you?

SCHNUR: And if I cheat them of that pleasure? What is to stop them taking somebody else? *(Indicates* BERYL.) Maybe him.

(He shakes his head. BERYL *stares at him. Downstairs, the roar of approaching vehicles; a staff car and two motorcycles. They honk impatiently.*

BLAUSTAIN *looks down. Then abruptly goes over to the baby carriage, takes out the automatic.)*

BLAUSTAIN: Anya was right. You want the world to respect you, first become an animal! Let them say of us, "This beast is wicked! When attacked, it will defend itself."

SCHNUR *(seizes his arm, shakes his head):* Not yet. Not yet.

(BLAUSTAIN makes a convulsive effort to restrain himself. He jams the weapon into his belt, presses himself against a wall as though trying to merge with the plaster. SCHNUR *follows him.)* Life could be so simple, couldn't it? One grand gesture, and honor has been satisfied, and who cares if this afternoon they kill two thousand others to balance the books? You want to be Samson? Pull down the whole works on top of yourself? Fine, fine. No more complications, no more responsibilities. A holiday! Only afterwards, who will be lying under the rubble? *Their* women, *their* children? Or yours? . . . Oh, no, Blaustain. Even when the day comes to pay them back . . . remember, Samson was a bachelor. But you, you are a man with responsibilities.

BLAUSTAIN: I don't want responsibilities! I can't breathe!

SCHNUR: What makes you think you have a choice?

(BLAUSTAIN meets his eye and after a moment wryly nods his head in agreement. SCHNUR *starts for the door, turns again.)* Blaustain . . .

BLAUSTAIN: What?

SCHNUR: A favor?

BLAUSTAIN: What?

SCHNUR: Don't kill it.

BLAUSTAIN: Get away from me!

SCHNUR: Have your child. Let it be born. Who knows? One more act of mercy to the smallest of God's creatures could bring the Messiah like a whirlwind.

BLAUSTAIN: And where is He *now?*

YABLONKA: A blind shoemaker is sewing his boots.

SCHNUR *(seizes* BLAUSTAIN's *wrist):* Don't do their work for them. Let it be born.

BLAUSTAIN: What for? Another soul to rise to heaven and make its accusation? What about the millions already standing in line? You think one more would tip the scale? And what if there is no scale?

SCHNUR *(patiently):* He who saves one life is counted as though he had saved an entire world.[16]

BLAUSTAIN: I don't *want* to save any world. It's His. He made it. Let *Him* save it! I'm tired.

SCHNUR *(a sudden smile):* You mean you no longer believe *Darwin* created the world? *(Puts an arm around* BLAUSTAIN's *shoulder; downstairs, the piercing shrill of a whistle.)* Let it live. Give me your hand.

*(*BLAUSTAIN *refuses to meet his eye. But* SCHNUR *seizes his unresisting hand. Then moves decisively to the baby carriage, throws out its pitiful attempt at a garden and rolls the empty carriage at* BLAUSTAIN.*)*

Clean it up. Your child will need a place to sleep.

*(*BLAUSTAIN *mechanically obeys.* BERYL *suddenly rushes at* SCHNUR *and embraces him with all his strength.* SCHNUR *pats his head, smiling.)*

It's nothing. In our family, dying is an old tradition.

*(*BERYL *releases him, turns away. Downstairs, another whistle. Hobnailed footsteps clattering across the cobblestones.*

SCHNUR *pulls off his boots and hands them to* BERYL, *then fetches the book they've been studying from.* BERYL *only looks at it, clearly afraid to touch it.* SCHNUR *makes no effort to force*

---

16. Schnur cites a well-known statement on moral behavior from the Talmud.

it on him. For a moment, their eyes meet. BERYL *suddenly takes the book, dives into a hiding place, as the stairs begin to vibrate under the pounding of ascending boots.*

SCHNUR *and* BLAUSTAIN *exchange a farewell look of perfect understanding. A pair of fists begin to hammer on the door.* SCHNUR *places his fingers upon the doorpost to his left, kisses them,*[17] *glances once more behind him, then opens the door, behind which he is snatched up as abruptly as a jumper stepping out of a plane in flight. The sounds indicate that he is being dragged downstairs, feet first. At the bottom of the stairs, a bull-like roar, more rage than pain.* BLAUSTAIN *and* YABLONKA *listen, petrified.)*

BERYL *(mechanically):* "All may slaughter, and their slaughtering is acceptable . . . All except . . . *(fading)* . . . the deaf-mute, the imbecile, the child . . ."

(BLAUSTAIN *at the window stands arched in a state of excruciating tension, watching* SCHNUR's *removal. Downstairs, some hearty masculine shouts, as though some healthy young men were kicking around a football.* BLAUSTAIN *averts his face, slides to his knees, his hand clawed about the weapon in his belt, and pounds his head impotently against the window sill. The vehicles roar off. Awed silence. No one moves.* YABLONKA *is the first to break the silence.)*

YABLONKA: I tell you, it's a good thing God lives so far away, or they'd break His windows. *(He begins softly to hum a Yom Kippur*[18] *melody, his voice just bordering on the edge of parody.)*

BERYL *(no longer mechanically):* Why? Because we cannot trust them not to inflict pain . . .

BLAUSTAIN *(with savage self-disgust):* "Not to inflict pain"! No wonder we're so popular with the world.

YABLONKA: You would rather be unpopular?

---

17. A common gesture of faith is to kiss the *mezuzah*, a small container which encloses a Biblical passage which hangs on the doorpost of every Jewish home.

18. Yom Kippur: the Day of Atonement, the holiest day of the Jewish year.

BLAUSTAIN: All I "would rather" is to stop standing on air!

YABLONKA *(amused):* Ah, you want ground under your feet? Maybe a whole country of your own? With hot and cold running water? Where? In Argentina? Uganda? Jerusalem, maybe? Without having to fight the whole world? The Messiah will come and hand you the key? "Here, Blaustain. Time off for good behavior"? You also believe babies are brought by the stork?

BLAUSTAIN: *I'm tired of being "popular"! (He goes over to* ES-THER's *cubicle. They stare stubbornly at one another.)*

YABLONKA: Hey, Krause, you got anything you want to leave behind? *(No answer.* YABLONKA *rudely pulls aside the curtain. And reels back.* KRAUSE *lies spread across the bed, his head almost touching the floor, dead.)* Blaustain! *(*BLAUSTAIN *rushes over, checks his heart and eyes, tries to massage his wrists.)* So he *had* arsenic, after all . . . *(*BLAUSTAIN, *pained, tries to stop him rummaging through* KRAUSE's *bag.)* Two pounds of coffee . . . a bag of sugar . . . a bottle of cologne . . . a bathing suit!

BLAUSTAIN: Let's take him downstairs *(They pick up the body and stagger with it toward the door.)*

YABLONKA: I tell you, it's a bad world when you can no longer tell the difference between a funeral and a garbage collection.

(They go out with the body. BERYL *continues to sway over his studies.)*

BERYL: First we say, "All may slaughter," and in the same breath we go and raise a difficulty . . .

*(*HAUPTMANN, *from his cubicle, stares after them, open-mouthed. Then hurries over to* KRAUSE's *open bag, takes out the cologne, guiltily sniffs at it, splashes some under his arms and, just before the others return, takes a quick, cautious sip.*

Offstage, the train whistle, approaching. For a moment, the whole room trembles with the impact of the passing train. But this time no one pays attention. YABLONKA *and* BLAUSTAIN *come back in.* BLAUSTAIN *rinses off his hands, then goes into* KRAUSE's *cubicle, to hide the suitcase under* KRAUSE's *bed, while* YABLONKA *sniffs suspiciously at the mysterious cloud of cologne.* YABLONKA *opens the sack containing the all-but-forgotten cat.)*

YABLONKA *(to the cat):* You're hungry? Me, too.

(MME. HERSHKOVITCH *comes in furtively, with mop and pail.)*

MME. HERSHKOVITCH: Engineer Blaustain . . .

BLAUSTAIN: What?

MME. HERSHKOVITCH *(breathless):* I just spoke to the head nurse at the hospital. I told her you were willing to pay her with a cat for a quick little cutting job. She said to bring it right over.

BLAUSTAIN: What?

MME. HERSHKOVITCH: Both. The cat, and your wife.

BLAUSTAIN: Have you forgotten, the cat is worthless?

MME. HERSHKOVITCH: But *she* doesn't know it yet. By the time she finds out, the operation'll be over. What can she do to your wife? Stuff the kid back into her belly?

(BLAUSTAIN *stares at her a moment, goes over to* ESTHER. *Her eyes are open.)*

BLAUSTAIN: You heard what she said? *(No answer.)* Esther, it's up to you. You'll have to decide right now.

ESTHER: *I* will have to decide? Only I?

MME. HERSHKOVITCH: Quickly. She's waiting.

ESTHER: And you, David? What do *you* want, what do you *really* want?

(For a moment, he trembles at the outrageousness of the question.)

BLAUSTAIN: What do *I* want? I want the sun to be black. I want a crust of ice to cover the earth. I want my mother to wake me and say it was all a bad dream. What do *I* want? I want a baked chicken to fly into my mouth.

ESTHER: Do you *want* a child? *(She sees him avert his face.)* Animal! Do you want to be a father?

(BLAUSTAIN *remains silent, unable to meet her eye.* ESTHER *begins painfully to sit up.)*

ESTHER *(to* MME. HERSHKOVITCH): I'm ready to go.

BLAUSTAIN: Esther, do you know what a child can do to you?

ESTHER: I know what it can do. Do *you* want your child?
(He starts to walk in a circle, torn in all directions. Then suddenly stops, in tears.)
BLAUSTAIN *(quietly):* I want to be a father.
YABLONKA *(bouncing with enthusiasm):* Good, good. Let it be born. Why should it be better than the rest of us?
(ESTHER laughs, almost gaily, for the first time. BLAUSTAIN picks up the sack with the cat, brings it over to MME. HERSHKOVITCH.)
BLAUSTAIN: Here. Three pounds of meat. Want me to twist her neck for you?
(BERYL looks up, sharply. Even HAUPTMANN rises, takes a step into the room, looks at MME. HERSHKOVITCH suspensefully. MME. HERSHKOVITCH stares at the sack, terrified at the responsibility. The cat meows pathetically. BLAUSTAIN opens the sack, looks inside.)
MME. HERSHKOVITCH *(abruptly):* I'm late for work.
(She retreats toward the door, afraid to make such a decision. BLAUSTAIN looks at her, then opens the window, takes the cat, and places it where it can escape along the outside gallery. For a long moment, the cat remains on the window sill, purring happily in the golden morning sun. Its shadow looms immense on the opposite wall. BERYL has put aside his book, and is watching it with all the excitement of a little boy once more.
  The cat abruptly streaks away. ESTHER manages a smile at its happy cry of escape.)
YABLONKA: Go . . . go in peace . . . Enjoy the sunshine . . . and tell the other animals . . . tell them . . . tell them what it was like to be a Jew.
(BLAUSTAIN remains framed in the window, watching the cat disappear. The lights fade slowly.)

THE END

Harold and Edith Lieberman

THRONE OF STRAW

We should like to thank the following for helping the play along the way: Mel Helstein, Donald Freed, Dorothy Sinclair, Bob Skloot, Halina Charwat, Carl Lieberman, Lillian Hara. Special thanks to Abbey Fraser for writing the original music. Thanks to Ellen Schiff for her article about Holocaust playwrights in the *New York Times*, Dec. 2, 1979.

A Note on Historical Accuracy

Throne of Straw is a play, not a work of history. We have made every effort to remain true to the major events and characters of the Lodz ghetto during the years of the Holocaust. Rumkowski, Greiser, and Biebow actually lived. Rabinowitz, the police chief, is a distillation of the men who held that office at various times. Rumkowski's wife was named Dora, but her character is our own invention. The other characters in this drama are entirely our creation, based on the interviews we did with Lodz survivors. The choices of action, scene, and time frame were made to serve the stage and not historical scholarship, although there are several excellent books available on the subject of the Lodz ghetto. To cite only two obvious changes: Biebow did not assume his post until the creation of the ghetto; and the gypsies were moved into the *Balut* (the ghetto area of the city) at a later time. Therefore, we ask your indulgence in viewing this drama as both factual and an act of imagination. Our aim was not to judge—but to reveal—so that you might form your own judgments.

Production Notes

Throne of Straw is both Epic and folkloric in its form and substance. It is Epic in that the play is episodic with narrative bridges, which seems the best way to cover historical time as it moves through the action for a particular kind of audience catharsis. Epic should not be equated with cold. Sartre pointed the way when he wrote: "Anti-emotionalism is not what Brecht wanted. All he wanted was for the spectator's emotion not to be blind. The ideal would be to 'show' and 'move' at the same time. I don't think Brecht considered that contradiction as an insoluble absurdity." The director must try to fuse both aspects.

It is folkloric because Jewish folklore is a collective social and psychological outlook that accumulated through the many years of living in the Diaspora. The noted historian Solomon F. Bloom writing about the "ghetto dictator" described him in exactly the terms in which we see our protagonist, Rumkowski: "[He] may turn out to reflect one or another popular and conventional attitude. He may derive his ideas from folklore rather than the more self-conscious and sophisticated culture. His significance may thus be broadened. The notion that the Jews are a clever people; the circumstance that, being an unclerical people, every man is potentially a priest and a leader, and that Everyman may assume the mantle of social protector and even of a sort of prophet—the sense, in short, of mission; the hope or conviction that the Jews are an indestructible and eternal people, that 'The Lord will leave a remnant'—all of these, and other such, turn up in the thinking and self-justification of the dictator; and they are not individual discoveries or inventions."

Any work on the Holocaust is bound to produce emotion, but care must be taken to avoid any sentimentality. This is especially

117

true during those *moments of moral choice* in the play, of which each character has at least one.

The *mise-en-scene* is best done simply; this is a "poor" play. The poems of Yankele may be set to music, sung simply on their own, or done with his own accompaniment on a kind of crank-up hand organ he would carry on the street, or even a harmonica. However achieved, the music should avoid schmaltzy Jewish melodies. Kurt Weill will not help either, since he wrote for a different milieu. There is a complete musical score by Abbey Fraser, which may be used, subject to the composer's permission.

Slides may or may not be used depending on the aims of each particular production. A full set may be obtained from the author for a copying fee.

CAST OF CHARACTERS
In Order of Appearance

ARTUR GREISER, *Gauleiter*[1] of Warthegau *(an arbitrarily named region of German-occupied Poland),* he was an early supporter of the Nazis; he is arrogant and overweight, is fond of beer, and has developed a passion for art, fancying himself an expert.

HANS BIEBOW, the son of a Bremen coffee merchant, who joined the Nazi Party to help advance his commercial interests. His well-fitting black business suit and pants are neatly tucked and tell us much about his character. An undistinguished looking man who has just turned forty, he has one overwhelming passion: to turn Lodz into a great war production center. He and Greiser are different types of Nazis, and should be played differently.

MORDECHAI CHAIM RUMKOWSKI, known in prewar Lodz as "Father of the Orphans" for his work as director of its orphanage. Twice widowed and twice a millionaire (both times ending in bankruptcy), he was an active Zionist. He became the "Eldest" of the Lodz Jewish Council under conditions not historically verified. He was of average height and walked erectly despite his advanced age. His white hair, worn long, was his most distinguishing characteristic. His wardrobe grew apace with his power, and he took to having stamps and coins made bearing his portrait. He was obsessed by the idea of saving his people, and felt he was responsible only to God and history. His growing megalomania must always be linked to the possibility of achieving his goal.

AVRAM RABINOWITZ, a small-time gangster who has managed to

---

1. *Gauleiter:* district leader or commander.

become the chief of the Jewish police. He is completely unprincipled and is despised by the ghetto population.

YANKELE, an ageless Hassid (religious Jew) who scrounges a living singing topical songs and doing odd jobs. His clothes reflect his low economic status. His search for a master to follow has proved fruitless and has left him only partly of this world, thus appearing to the people as slightly "mad." He is the play's witness and narrator.

ISRAEL WOLF, the patriarch of the Wolf family. Despite his three score and ten years, his mind is fresh, active, and witty. A deeply religious man, he wears fringes;[2] he is also cranky and stubborn.

ADA WOLF, the widow of one of Lodz's most famous writers. A demanding woman of immense energy, she is determined to save her family. She has just passed fifty and still retains an attractive face and figure. Her wardrobe reflects her former position and her present distress.

GABRIEL WOLF, son of Ada Wolf. Full of fantasies at age twenty-two, he has always been protected by his mother. At her insistence he becomes a member of the Jewish police, one of the most hated roles in the ghetto.

ROSA WOLF, daughter of Ada Wolf. She is the embodiment of the enlightened socially conscious woman of the 1930s. A Bundist (Jewish Trade Union) organizer and active Zionist. Her face and body movement reflect the new exhilaration of the freer atmosphere of the times; she smokes and wears the proletarian-looking garments of the period.

ZOSIA WOLF, daughter of Ada Wolf. A sensitive girl undergoing the trauma of adolescence, her dress reflects her growing maturity throughout the four years of ghetto existence.

MOSHE LEWIN, an orphan boy living in the Wolf household. Small and extremely bright, he makes his living by begging in the streets.

---

2. Fringes: a short undershirt with knotted fringes at the corners worn by orthodox Jewish men. The fringes hang outside the trousers.

DAVID ABRAMOWITZ, also adopted by the Wolf family; in the
ghetto, he quickly learns how to smuggle and steal.

MIRIAM GOLDSTEIN RUMKOWSKI, executive secretary to Rumkowski
and later his third wife. Came from a wealthy family. Attractive and in her middle 30s, she had almost completed medical
school but was prevented from finishing by anti-Jewish decrees.

DOCTOR ARI COHEN, leader of Lodz Jewish Health Services, he is a
distinguished-looking man in his 40s.

HANNAH ADLER, Israel Wolf's niece. A Berlin lawyer of middle age
deported to Poland.

The play is set in Lodz, Poland, during the years 1939–44.

THRONE OF STRAW

Prologue

In the darkness a single spotlight finds YANKELE *in a crucifixion pose. He speaks to audience:*

Oberammergau:[3] home of the Passion Play.

(drops one arm; raises other in Nazi salute)
Litzmanstadt:[4] former home of the Jewish ghetto of Lodz.
What lies between performance
And puffs of common smoke?
Crucifixion gave birth to exile
And the wandering stopped in a zyklon cloud.[5]

(moves back and forth as if in prayer)
In me you see a prophet
That can only look backwards
From my mouth into your eye's mind
With some Talmudic injunctions
To worry your head about.
On the one hand we are told
"It is an honor for a man to keep aloof from strife"
And on the other
"If someone comes to kill you, kill him first."

3. Oberammergau: a town in Bavaria, southwest Germany, where once every ten years a play about Christ's passion is staged; the performances are internationally attended and the text, until recent changes, was generally acknowledged to be anti-Semitic.
4. Litzmanstadt: the German name for Lodz.
5. Zyklon (syklon): a poison gas developed by the Germans for the mass murder of concentration camp inmates.

So, if a Jewish community
Like the one you will see tonight
Is confronted with physical destruction
Should its leaders rescue what is possible
Or should all perish together as at Masada?[6]
No idle question, then or now.
And please before you sit in judgment
Sit *shiva*[7] first
A mourner needs only a hard box
An undraped soul
A stage bare of everything
But recognition
So the darkness can burst through.

(Lights down.)

6. Masada: the fortress near the Dead Sea in ancient Israel where, in the first century, A.D., 936 Jewish zealots committed suicide rather than be taken as prisoner and enslaved by the Roman armies.

7. *Shiva:* from the Hebrew word for seven, this is the name given to the solemn week-long mourning period which follows the burial of the deceased.

ACT 1

Scene 1

*The Nazi office. October, 1939. It gives evidence of its new instal-
lation. A desk, two chairs, some unpacked crates and a cart filled
with confiscated paintings.* GREISER *enters and looks around. He
grows annoyed at the absence of anyone to greet him. He goes to
the paintings and looks through them, showing his obvious disgust
at their quality. Enter* BIEBOW, *without his jacket. His sleeves are
rolled up and his tie is loose. He has a Nazi banner under one arm,
and a tray with a pot of coffee and two cups in the other. He tries
to click his heels in salute while holding the objects, and almost
upsets the tray.*

GREISER: Interesting uniform you have on. What were you doing,
    out looking for more masterpieces?

BIEBOW: Please forgive me, sir. But as you can see we just moved
    in . . .

GREISER: How long have you been in the Party?

BIEBOW: Six years, sir. *(Puts tray on desk.)*

GREISER: *After* we rose to the top. Are you always that cautious?

BIEBOW: I wanted to join earlier. But my father insisted on my stay-
    ing in the business.

GREISER: A proper bourgeois, huh? Your aide, what's he doing
    now? *Your* job?

BIEBOW *(hangs Nazi banner on wall):* I wanted this ready to greet
    you. *(Gives Nazi salute. Greiser ignores it.)*

GREISER: You should have hung a Deutschmark. That's your real
    banner, isn't it? *(Strained silence.)* What happened to the
    paintings that I asked for?

BIEBOW *(goes to cart with paintings):* These were all I managed to
    round up, thus far. Give me a few more days . . .

GREISER: Can't you tell the difference between a Dürer[8] and ma-
    nure?

8. Dürer: Albrecht Dürer (1471–1528), one of the most influential and popular
artists in the history of German art.

BIEBOW: I must confess my knowledge of the former is very limited.

GREISER: You don't have to step in it to know horseshit.

BIEBOW: Production and efficiency are my chief assets.

GREISER: What am I to do with you, Biebow? Are you one of those rare Germans with no taste?

BIEBOW: I do indeed have taste, but of a special kind. If you were to place a bag of coffee beans in front of me, I could not only tell you where it came from and what time of the year it was grown, but, and this is most important, when it finally appears in your cup *(while speaking he pours coffee into cup)*, whether it will have the aroma of a . . . Rembrandt. *(Offers him cup; GREISER does not take it.)*

GREISER: He painted old and ugly Jews, did you know that? *(BIE-BOW shakes head "no.")* How many do we have here in Litz-manstadt?

BIEBOW: Three hundred thousand, sir.

GREISER *(motions for coffee):* And what shall we do with them? *(BIEBOW starts to respond but GREISER continues.)* Sooner or later the solution will present itself in a productive and effi-cient manner. In Berlin there's talk of a mass exodus to Mada-gascar.[9] After the Louvre is ours, of course.

BIEBOW *(entering the spirit):* Where they will sit in the sun turning black.

GREISER *(laughs; bids him sit):* I like that. You haven't forgotten that they've learned to adapt to all kinds of conditions. We are at heart the real Zionists. One way or another we shall see to it that they remain together.

BIEBOW *(excitedly):* I have thought of nothing else since I was as-signed to this position. The factories will be their Palestine. *(GREISER is unmoved.)* Here's a complete survey of all the available plant facilities.

---

9. Madagascar: for a brief time in the years 1938–40, the Nazi high command considered a plan to deport all of the Jews of Europe to Madagascar, an island off the East coast of Africa. The "Madagascar Plan" was abandoned, and a more as-suredly "final" solution put in its place.

GREISER (*doesn't look at paper; throws it on table*): If we rush to put them to work, they'll become essential to our economy, and then what? The only thing they can do to help us is to disappear. Are we to let a few stinking smokestacks stand in the way?

BIEBOW: But sir, Marshal . . .

GREISER: I know that some want to increase war production so badly, they'd even use them. But it would be most unwise on your part to see this as anything but a short-term matter. We didn't create National Socialism to end unemployment for the Jews. It's *their* end we're after and we are going to let them help that process. How far along are you in the creation of the Jewish Council?

BIEBOW: It is done, sir.

GREISER: Excellent. That will be a spectacle worth watching. Put Jews in charge of Jews and they'll get what they deserve. Who have you chosen as chairman?

BIEBOW: He was not my choice, sir.

GREISER: I asked for a name, not a complaint.

BIEBOW: Rumkowski.

GREISER: A rabbi?

BIEBOW: No. Director of the orphanage.

GREISER: And before that?

BIEBOW: A businessman.

GREISER: Oh, one of your kind.

BIEBOW: He's hardly that, sir. He went bankrupt twice. And I intend to see that he stays that way. You must have seen him as you came in.

GREISER: That broken-down old man?

BIEBOW: That was my concern. But he's proven most energetic. He's very eager to make good on this job.

GREISER: Who's that hoodlum with him?

BIEBOW: The head of his Security. Some Poles have already threatened him.

GREISER: And what of his own flock? The measures you're going to insist on will make him very unpopular.

BIEBOW: Beginning with this *(takes out armband with Star of David).*[10]

GREISER: Ah, pure Chagall.[11]

BIEBOW: Since they're still free to roam the city, it will make surveillance a routine matter.

GREISER: Routine. I've no doubt you'll be very good at that. However, you'll have to keep them off-balance so that they're never quite sure of their bearings. Can you manage that or shall I bring in one of our Party members?

BIEBOW *(nervously):* No need for that, sir. I'll have him performing like a Viennese dancing horse.

GREISER *(with irony):* Horses are clean. Do they have a health service so that you can be kept plague-free?

BIEBOW: Why don't we ask him? *(GREISER nods. BIEBOW calls out.)* Rumkowski. *(RUMKOWSKI and RABINOWITZ enter.)*

GREISER *(looks RUMKOWSKI over):* Why have you come, old man?

RUMKOWSKI: We are starving, your honor.

GREISER: Who is we? You look well fed. *(RABINOWITZ smirks.)* What's so funny?

RABINOWITZ: It's just that he has a good appetite for a man his age.

GREISER: Your name?

RABINOWITZ: Radnitski, Gauleiter Greiser *(snaps heels together in imitation of German soldier).*

GREISER *(to RUMKOWSKI):* So your chief bodyguard is a Polish spy.

RUMKOWSKI: Rabinowitz! All I want to hear from you is silence.

RABINOWITZ *(to GREISER):* I'm not really Jewish, sir.

GREISER: I think you're really nothing.

RABINOWITZ: You've got it exactly. I tried to convert but no one would have me.

RUMKOWSKI: When we leave here, he'll hear lots of names, all unpleasant.

10. Star of David: one of the earliest Nazi proclamations was to order Jews in all the occupied countries of Europe to display conspicuously on their clothing the six-pointed Jewish star.

11. Chagall: Marc Chagall (b. 1887), one of the most famous Jewish artists of this century.

GREISER *(to* RUMKOWSKI*):* What is it you want from us? To help line your pockets a little?

RUMKOWSKI: I was twice a millionaire, and once you've had money it's not that important. Whatever years the Lord grants me, I want to use in the service of my people. They'll be here long after I'm gone.

GREISER: So you want us to underwrite your good name, is that it?

RUMKOWSKI: I ask nothing for myself. Go out into any street and you'll see hungry Jews. There's no food to be had anywhere, and there's nothing to work with. We can't go on much longer this way.

GREISER: Do I smell a Semitic proposition about to come my way?

RUMKOWSKI: I'm certain your nose and my mouth will get along.

GREISER *(throws coffee from cup into* RUMKOWSKI's *face):* No. Your nose and my behind. *(To* BIEBOW.*)* A funny old man isn't he? *(To* RUMKOWSKI.*)* You are proving to be more of a nuisance than you can imagine. Come back tomorrow.

RUMKOWSKI: By tomorrow fifty of us will fall dead in the street. I will not serve as their undertaker. I was assured that you wanted me to preside over a living community.

GREISER *(to* BIEBOW*):* Does he always exaggerate like this? *(To* RUMKOWSKI.*)* You have fasting days. Take them now.

RUMKOWSKI: We've had more than our share.

GREISER: Then you should be used to hunger by now. *(To* BIEBOW.*)* Tomorrow I'll be gone and you'll have to deal with him. *(Points to* BIEBOW.*)* He's not indifferent to you like I am. He detests Jews.

RUMKOWSKI: Gentlemen, what you have here are not ordinary laborers, but highly skilled workers. We want to put Lodz back on its feet again, to fill the air with smoke . . .

GREISER: Enough.

RUMKOWSKI *(continues):* I thought you might be busy, so I brought my proposals about the factories in writing.

(RUMKOWSKI *hands paper to* BIEBOW, *who starts to look at it.* GREISER *tears it from his hand, crumples it, and tosses it on table.)*

BIEBOW *(to* RUMKOWSKI*):* Tomorrow morning at eight o'clock.

RUMKOWSKI: I'll be here, Herr Commandant. *(Motions to* RA-BINOWITZ *and they start to leave.)*

BIEBOW: Our work is not yet finished and when it is I expect you to ask permission to leave.

*(*RUMKOWSKI *starts to apologize.)*

GREISER: The Jewish Hospital. Who's in charge?

RUMKOWSKI: Dr. Ari Cohen.

GREISER: Is he any good?

RUMKOWSKI: Good? He's a genius. Studied in Heidelberg. That's how well you taught him. May we leave now, please? *(*BIEBOW *nods.)*

GREISER: Just one last small matter. Are you fully acquainted with the duties of the Council?

RUMKOWSKI: I know what has to be done.

GREISER: Good, then read it again. *(Holds out paper for* RUMKOWSKI*.)*

RUMKOWSKI *(reads aloud):* "In each Jewish Community, a Council of Jewish Elders is to be set up. It should consist of influential persons and rabbis. It is to be made fully responsible, in the literal sense of the word, for the exact execution of all instructions released or to be released." *(*GREISER *speaks along with him.)* "In case of sabotage of such instructions, the Councils are to be warned that the severest measures will be taken."

GREISER *(confidentially to* RUMKOWSKI*):* Just between us, I can tell you, the Council is window dressing. The Führer rules us and *you* rule the Jews.

(Lights out; the next scene has begun.)

Scene 2

A street. ISRAEL WOLF *is writing in a notebook.* ROSA WOLF *carries leaflets.* YANKELE *is cranking out a Jewish tune.*[12]

ROSA *(calling out):* The Jewish Trade Unions of Lodz call upon all the workers of our great city to discuss our position on the Jewish Council. Tonight at eight o'clock.

YANKELE *(to* ROSA*):* Can you please be a little quieter? I've got a public too. (ROSA *gives him and* ISRAEL *a leaflet and starts to post one on the wall.* YANKELE *doffs his cap at her; sings:)*
I'm a Hassid by incantation.
A fool by inclination.
And I cash poems to keep from starvation.
I can make up words to fit any occasion.
And I'll keep you informed of the latest invasion.

(As he is singing ADA WOLF *enters carrying a box in her hands. She sees* ROSA*.)*

ADA: Put those away. Not here. *(To* ISRAEL*.)* I've been looking all over for you, Papa.

ISRAEL *(tapping his notebook):* That's where I've been, all over.
(GABRIEL WOLF enters with a box on his shoulders. He's struggling with it. ADA *calls out.)*

ADA: Yankele, quick! What kind of helper are you that disappears his first day on the job?

YANKELE *(helping* GABRIEL*):* First, I am a helper second. When there's a clientele I work for myself.

ADA: You know my Gabriel isn't very strong.

YANKELE *(sniffs at box):* I've changed my mind. It smells like bad advice.

ADA: When business is slow I wouldn't mind what you did. However, today, when word gets around that we're first on the street, we'll be overrun with customers. *(She gives him coin; he bites on it.)*

---

12. Jewish tune: see the authors' Production Note, pp. 117–18.

YANKELE: Thanks, but a stone should live alone.

ADA: Yankele, when will you learn to be responsible? You leave a dying father all alone to search for a holy man. Did you find him, our new Baal Shem Tov?[13]

YANKELE: I found only myself. And that wasn't easy.

(He exits. ZOSIA WOLF *has entered with a box.)*

ADA: What are you children waiting for? Unpack and please try to make our merchandise as attractive as possible.

ROSA: Mama, how can they be made attractive? I've told you a hundred times that in this matter I'm out. I'm so glad Papa's not here to see this. He would have been so ashamed.

ADA: That was your father all right. He never went near money so he could never feel ashamed. If I hadn't slaved in the textile shop, who knows where we'd be today?

ROSA: And just where are we? Peddling our own humiliation.

ADA: Rosa, please keep your politics away from this family.

ISRAEL *(writing in notebook; reads aloud):* October 25, 1939. Everywhere you go, it's always the same question. How did a nobody, a *knocker*[14] like Rumkowski, get the biggest job of all?

ADA: He's still our friend. Let's hope now he can help us.

ZOSIA: What are you writing, Grandpa?

ISRAEL: A diary. Whatever happens will have a home here.

GABRIEL: Give it up. At your age it's foolish to play the man of letters.

ISRAEL: And when will *you* stop playing?

GABRIEL: Taking a good photograph is an art.

ISRAEL *(suddenly getting idea):* Now you can put your camera to real use. Me with my words and you with pictures. How about starting with these? *(Takes armband from box.)*

---

13. Baal Shem Tov: the name given to Israel ben Eliezer (c. 1700–1760), the gentle visionary who founded the Chasidic movement of Judaism on the philosophy of simplicity, love, and joy.

14. Knocker: pronounced "k-nocker," a derisive Yiddish word for a braggart or someone pretending to be important.

GABRIEL: I don't want anyone telling me what to notice. To just record what ordinary people do would be so boring.

ISRAEL: Let's hope so. I'd like nothing better than for this to be a book of boring days. Tuesday, nothing happened. The same for Thursday. We should live so long.

ROSA: Grandpa, sometimes I think you and I are the only ones who know the kind of people we're dealing with.

ISRAEL: The others will learn. You must be patient.

(Sound of trucks in distance.)

ADA *(looking around apprehensively)*: Where's Moshe?

ZOSIA: I sent him to get David from the orphanage to help us.

ADA: A seven-year-old you allow to go by himself in the street? I've a revolution on my hands.

GABRIEL: Not from me, Mama.

ADA: From you I'd welcome it. Now go, both of you, and don't come back until you've found him. (GABRIEL *and* ZOSIA *run off.)*

ROSA *(to* ADA *in last appeal)*: Mama, how can I make you understand this is all wrong. We must not allow ourselves to be singled out this way.

ADA: We have to eat.

ROSA: This is just the beginning. First they start by separating us. *(*RUMKOWSKI *and* RABINOWITZ *enter.* ADA *quiets* ROSA. ROSA *gives* RUMKOWSKI *a leaflet and exits. He hands it to* RABINOWITZ. YANKELE *enters.)*

ADA *(boldly)*: Mr. Chairman, to put it plainly, my family could use some help.

RUMKOWSKI: That's just what I'm in a position to do.

YANKELE: Yes. We've seen the position. *(Laughs.* RABINOWITZ *starts for him.)*

RUMKOWSKI: Rabinowitz, let me handle this.

YANKELE: Please let him, for he can handle anything. *(Dances around* RUMKOWSKI.*)* Court Jew,[15] Council Jew. Do you think

---

15. Court Jew: it was not unusual in the centuries following the Renaissance in Europe for petty rulers to include among their retinue of advisers (often financial

you can pull us through, this time? Oh yes, Commandant Bie-bow. I can do this. I can do that. I can do everything. And Rabinowitz will oblige.

RUMKOWSKI: Why must you make a fool of yourself in public?

YANKELE: So you don't fool the public and yourself? You know, I wanted to be Chairman myself, but I didn't know what to promise.

ADA *(to* YANKELE*):* You'll never work for me again. *(*YANKELE *squeezes own lips tight; joins* ISRAEL. *To* RUMKOWSKI.*)* Between you and me, there's nothing wrong when a man wants a job badly enough.

RUMKOWSKI: Mrs. Wolf, what man in his right mind would apply for this job? But when a German officer grabs you by the hair and says "You are the oldest," take my word for it, you are the oldest *(takes off his cap revealing his white hair)*. Still, it doesn't matter how the job comes, what counts is if you feel ready.

ISRAEL: A leader is not a mailman for barbarians.

RUMKOWSKI: Letters can be interpreted in many ways, our rabbis have shown that. I will turn and twist them until it suits only our purpose. This is not the first place nor the first time someone has tried to do us harm. We managed before and we'll manage now.

ISRAEL *(writing in diary):* We are *all* orphans now. *(*RUMKOWSKI *glares at him.)*

ADA: Papa, not here. And to a man who wants to do only good.

YANKELE *(to* ISRAEL*):* I know exactly what you had in mind.

RABINOWITZ *(to* YANKELE*):* We all know what's in your mind: nothing.

YANKELE: Nothing? Nothing is more corrupting than the illusion of power. *(To* RUMKOWSKI.*)* Your plumage casts no shadow and your throne is made of straw. *(He exits.)*

ADA: Don't bother with him. He's not worth the trouble.

RUMKOWSKI: Who knows what's worth nowadays, Mrs. Wolf.

---

advisers) selected members of their Jewish communities. Their position might be a delicate one, and Yankele here (and later in his song in act 1, scene 4) means the term as an insult, implying that Rumkowski has "sold out" to the Germans.

ADA: What's with Mrs. Wolf all of a sudden? When I was young and unmarried you used to call me Ada. You even looked at me on a first name basis.

RUMKOWSKI: You were very beautiful. It was only natural.

ADA: For a widow only one thing is natural.

RUMKOWSKI: How long have you been alone?

ADA: Almost a year. It's time.

RUMKOWSKI: Wait a little longer and you'll get proposals by the dozen.

(ROSA *enters with more leaflets. She watches* RABINOWITZ *pull the one she has posted off the wall. She goes to him and argues. He tries to tear leaflets from her.* RUMKOWSKI *motions for him to desist and he does.)*

ADA: My family can't eat proposals.

RUMKOWSKI: Then let them begin to provide for themselves. *(Thinks for a moment.)* How about your Gabriel for my security force? It's a very privileged position.

ADA: I can tell you right now he'll be very pleased.

RUMKOWSKI: Good. I promise your family need never worry. *(Points at* ROSA.) Provided you keep them in hand. Your Rosa, she worries me. A real firebrand she's turned out to be. I want you to calm her down. *(To* ROSA.) That leaflet your group put out about me wasn't very nice.

ROSA: Starvation isn't nice either, Chairman Rumkowski.

RUMKOWSKI: I've been on this job only ten days and already there's a Social Welfare Department that's working. The schools will begin next week. And soup kitchens opened this morning. So?

ROSA *(somewhat meekly):* It's a start, but it's not enough.

RUMKOWSKI: So why don't you give me a chance before you begin to bark? *(Enter* MOSHE *and* DAVID *followed by* GABRIEL *and* ZOSIA.)

MOSHE: There he is!

DAVID *(to* RUMKOWSKI): We were looking for you.

RUMKOWSKI: Have they changed the rules in the orphanage? Are you allowed to come and go as you please?

DAVID: Everyone misses you a lot, me most of all. Do you still care about us?

RUMKOWSKI: What a question. I love you all more than ever.

DAVID: Then why have you left us?

RUMKOWSKI: Leave? I'd never do that. Right now I'm helping every boy and girl there.

MOSHE: Can David help us here? Can he live with us? He's the best friend I've ever had, even though he is an orphan.

RUMKOWSKI: But Moshe, only a month ago, when I arranged for you to live with Mrs. Wolf, you were an orphan, too.

MOSHE: I forget things like that very quickly.

RUMKOWSKI: Is that what you'd like to do, David?

DAVID: Yes, sir.

RUMKOWSKI: Then I'll try to make it possible (*he nods to* ADA *and she nods back*).

MOSHE (*to* RUMKOWSKI): Can the Germans make us do anything they want?

RUMKOWSKI: Nobody can make you do what you don't think is right.

DAVID: And if they tried, we'd fight them (*makes staccato noise of gun*).

RUMKOWSKI: We are not fighters. Let others use bullets. We are still a people of the word. We persuade. We argue. We petition. Never forget, we live in a sea with sharks all around us. If we fought them all, could we have lasted these thousands of years? (ADA *and* RABINOWITZ *applaud.*)

ROSA: We can't bargain for our lives. Not with those who've sworn to have done with us once and for all. Not this time. (RABINOWITZ *moves to her.* RUMKOWSKI *calls him off. He points his finger at her angrily and they exit.*)

ADA: Don't you dare ever to speak to him like that again.

ROSA: I'm sorry you feel that way.

GABRIEL (*to* ADA): Did you ask him whether he could hire me to take pictures?

ADA: Your mother didn't forget her only son. He went so far as to make you an offer.

GABRIEL: He wants me to do his portrait?

ADA: He has something better in mind. He's making a place for you on his police force. You can set an example. All he's getting now are crooks and God knows what.

ROSA: That's because every decent organization has refused to let any of its people join.

GABRIEL *(to* ADA*):* But that would mean I'd have to arrest Jews!

ADA: You'd just be making sure people behave themselves.

ROSA: If there's any dirty work to be done, let the Nazis do their own.

ADA: The Germans are not as bad as the Poles.

ISRAEL: A very fine distinction.

ADA: Everywhere you hear it's going to be like 1914 all over again. They marched into Lodz and all that happened was a lot of people got rich. You should remember that, Papa.

ISRAEL: What I remember is that when I rub elbows with a rich man, I get a hole in my sleeve.

GABRIEL *(to* ADA*):* You know I don't mix into politics. I'm not cut out to be a policeman.

ISRAEL *(to* ADA*):* Why do we need police at all? We have our rabbis. All they would have to do is say one word and it would be followed.

ADA: None of you seems to understand: a war has been lost!

ROSA: Only temporarily.

ADA: And until our time comes, would you rather have German police over us? Isn't it better that we do it ourselves? *(to* GA-BRIEL*.)* I won't let you turn it down.

GABRIEL: Mama, you can't do this to me.

ADA: We'll talk about it later. A decision like this shouldn't be made in the street. David, the Chairman gave permission for you to live with us. *(*MOSHE *and* DAVID *are joyous.)* And what's more, you'll be working and earning money as our new salesman. So pay close attention, for I'm about to give you a lesson in how to sell armbands *(takes one out)*. This is a guaranteed product. Unfortunately, we are in a seller's market, fortunately; every-one over the age of twelve must wear one. You call out: "Arm-bands! Get your armbands here!" Now let's say a prospective customer comes over to you and inquires about the price. You answer: "I've one to fit every pocketbook. You want it plain, so it's plain *(takes out linen armband)*. You want it from the best linen? I have it. It costs a little more but it's beautiful. We even have some in the finest velvet, very becoming. I even have a few in celluloid, in case you want to see through it." *(Hands one each to* GABRIEL, ZOSIA, *and* DAVID. *Tries to give some to* ISRAEL *and* ROSA; *they refuse.)* Now you demonstrate the right way to wear it. Not too high and not too low. And never dirty or torn. Here you make a suggestion that they buy two; this way one will always be clean and ready to wear. Remember, the more you sell, the more you make.

ISRAEL: So now we sell our Jewishness on a commission basis. *(Exits.)*

ROSA *(starts to leave):* I've a meeting.

ADA *(to* ROSA*):* You forgot this.

(Hands her an armband. ROSA *hesitates a moment, then takes it and exits.)*
Well what are we waiting for? Let's start selling!
(They start to hawk armbands. Lights down. The next scene has already begun.)

Scene 3

BIEBOW'*s office the next morning.* RUMKOWSKI *is standing alone.* BIEBOW *enters drinking coffee. He finally turns to* RUMKOWSKI.

BIEBOW: Waiting will be part of your duties, too.

RUMKOWSKI: It's an old story. I'm used to it.

BIEBOW *(in a confidential tone):* What is your age, really?

RUMKOWSKI: A never-felt-better sixty-three.

BIEBOW: Going on seventy? My choice would have been a lot younger. This job is going to require a great deal of energy.

RUMKOWSKI: I'm prepared to see that no one, myself in the first instance, works by the clock.

BIEBOW: Do that and there might be a bonus for you. Under the table, of course.

RUMKOWSKI: Thanks. But I've no wish to start a private bank account. May I speak plainly? (BIEBOW *waves him to go on.*) You and I, we need each other.

BIEBOW: Need? I need you?

RUMKOWSKI: Yes. We're bound together, we're partners. (BIEBOW *laughs derisively.*) We both want the same thing. The machines moving. The chimneys belching black smoke. Am I right so far? (BIEBOW *is silent.*) I will guarantee you a large supply of very good workers, in return for food and materials for the shops. However you add it up, it won't come to charity.

BIEBOW: My superiors insist that losers in war be taken from, not given to.

RUMKOWSKI: And just how many Jewish divisions did you defeat? Our biggest loss was to be born in Poland. And yours will be not to use our manpower. Remind your superiors that unfed horses don't run.

BIEBOW: They have no need for hay, either.

RUMKOWSKI: But what employer in his right mind would starve his own workers?

BIEBOW: When it comes to Jews, there are quite a few that I know. You can't look for any help from me.

RUMKOWSKI: Lodz can be your Manchester. You won't be just another commandant, but the boss over the largest work center in the East.

BIEBOW: Are you asking me to collaborate?

RUMKOWSKI: I never forget that butter sits on top of bread. And I'm sure you've friends in Berlin to help smooth our way.

BIEBOW: I like your nerve, but I've no friends in Berlin.

RUMKOWSKI: Give me three months and the factories will hum like before the war. And the money, it will come. The rich will pay their way this time.

BIEBOW *(change of tone):* You realize that even if I could arrange these matters, it would require a great deal of cash.

RUMKOWSKI: How much is a great deal?

BIEBOW: Everything. A good Jewish Council should be able to accomplish that.

RUMKOWSKI: If we give you everything, what will we have for the next time?

BIEBOW: What next time?

RUMKOWSKI: There always is for us. Give me three months. I'll stake my life on it.

BIEBOW *(ironically):* That could be arranged. *(Sudden change to conciliatory tone.)* Not everyone in Berlin thinks like Greiser. And I do have contacts there who are well placed. But to consummate these matters will require a substantial return. A commission if you like.

RUMKOWSKI *(feeling he has turned him around):* It will be my pleasure to deliver it to you personally.

BIEBOW *(with a sigh):* Oh you Jews. Three months, eh? Tell your people food and supplies will start arriving tomorrow.

RUMKOWSKI: Thank you, Herr Commandant.

BIEBOW: And it would be appreciated if you spread the word that you're dealing with an honorable man. *(Hands paper to* RUMKOWSKI.*)* I've a gift for you. A few gypsies will arrive next week, and you shall be their master.

RUMKOWSKI: But why me?

BIEBOW: Mordechai, everyone needs someone he can look down on. Oh, those gypsy women. They'll set you on fire. No matter how old you are. Have you ever had one?

RUMKOWSKI: No. It is forbidden.

BIEBOW: I'd like to see what makes you Jews so special *(gestures for him to open his fly).*

RUMKOWSKI: It's not special.

BIEBOW: I could stop the rations from coming in and tell your people why.

(RUMKOWSKI *decides to call* BIEBOW's *bluff.*)
It's your decision, not mine. Your pride or your people. Which will it be?

RUMKOWSKI: I can't believe what gives some people pleasure.

BIEBOW: I'm merely curious. After all, you are the ones that make a big fuss about it.

RUMKOWSKI: Take my word for it. Yours and mine do exactly the same thing.

BIEBOW: Really. Would you care to see the difference?

RUMKOWSKI: Not especially.

BIEBOW *(putting his hand on his fly):* You'd finally get to see what a real man looks like.

RUMKOWSKI: I don't doubt that you're real or a man. I doubt that you're human.

(BIEBOW *gets up from chair and in angry mood pulls* RUMKOWSKI *by the coat lapels towards him.*)
You can threaten me as much as you like. I can't get much older than old. (BIEBOW *pushes him away.*)

BIEBOW: I'm waiting.

RUMKOWSKI: For your enjoyment, no.

BIEBOW: For what, then?

RUMKOWSKI: For my children at the orphanage. A little something extra for them and you can look to your heart's delight.

BIEBOW *(sits, takes paper and speaks each word as he writes):* "Lunch . . . for . . . Chaim's . . . children" *(pushes paper towards him).*

RUMKOWSKI *(pushes paper back):* You didn't sign it.

BIEBOW *(signs it;* RUMKOWSKI *takes it):* Well?

(RUMKOWSKI *unbuttons his trousers and reveals himself.*)

RUMKOWSKI *(after a long moment):* Are you finished?

BIEBOW *(nods):* I had to see what kind of man you were. And I'm very pleased. Isn't it lucky for us both that textile spindles are not circumcised?

(He laughs. Lights out. The next scene has begun.)

Scene 4

YANKELE, *accompanied by music, sings directly to audience:*

"Courting the Jews"

In Polish history we often read
About pogroms to make Jews bleed
The King would sometimes stop the deed, if
For a Court Jew he had a need.

Court Jew, Council Jew
Do you think we'll make it through
This time?

When the Queen ordered all Jews from Prague
And set that community agog
Only the gift of hard cash down
Got the Jews back into town.

Court Jew, Council Jew
Do you think we'll make it through
This time?

Now a blitzkrieg sits on our shoulders
And a Judenrat squats on our heads
Rumkowski won't ever grow older
And we'll never die in our beds.

Court Jew, Council Jew
You think that you can get us through
This time?

(Lights down. The next scene has begun.)

Scene 5

RUMKOWSKI's *office. January, 1940.* MIRIAM *is seated at a desk working on papers. There is another chair. A coat hanger and a few graphs of factory production on a board or wall.* RUMKOWSKI *comes bursting into office shaking the snow off his overcoat. He removes his coat, hat, and gloves, and hangs them up.*

RUMKOWSKI: Today the frost didn't bother me at all. *(He jumps in air.)*

MIRIAM: Be careful.

RUMKOWSKI: See, I'm still in one piece. Hot-blooded men, like myself, are strangers to, you'll pardon me, hernias. That's for the old ones past their prime. Mine is still ahead of me. Look at me: young and successful. After four months of eating my heart out, we now have a real health system! *(waves paper).* You said we needed it and here it is *(hands it to her).* Now am I entitled to ask you something?

MIRIAM: As long as it's not about me.

RUMKOWSKI: Was it really this hair? Suppose I didn't have any?

MIRIAM: They'd be looking for somebody who was bald.

RUMKOWSKI: Suppose I had a cold and missed that meeting?

MIRIAM: Suppose doesn't add up to why. Accept it.

RUMKOWSKI: As what? God's will? Is such a thing possible?

MIRIAM: He works in mysterious ways and He doesn't always choose rabbis.

RUMKOWSKI *(long moment at acceptance of his mission):* There's a time for a Moses and a moment for Mordechai. *(Looks upwards and speaks to God.)* Whatever it is You have in mind for me, I accept. I make You this promise: You won't be sorry you chose me. *(Looks at* MIRIAM.*)* Now only one thing's missing. An intelligent and attractive wife at my side *(takes ring out and slips it on her finger).* I've been assured that I'm not unattractive. Imagine me with thick black hair, wouldn't I look at least twenty years younger?

MIRIAM: Your hair goes very well with the rest of you.

RUMKOWSKI: Miriam, it's only an engagement ring. In these modern times it doesn't bind anyone, especially someone like you. Please, keep the ring on your finger. As long as it's there it gives me hope.

MIRIAM: And it gives me problems.

RUMKOWSKI: Is that what I am to you, a problem?

MIRIAM: The ring is, not you. So much has happened. My parents get stranded in America. My school decides it doesn't want to teach Jews anymore. And now suddenly a proposal.

RUMKOWSKI: It wasn't so sudden. I've had my eye on you ever since you came to work here.

MIRIAM: Is it just what you see?

RUMKOWSKI: There's a lot more, believe me.

MIRIAM: You said you wanted an intelligent wife, why?

RUMKOWSKI: To share this great burden.

MIRIAM: And give you advice?

RUMKOWSKI: Why not?

MIRIAM: Would you take what I had to say seriously?

RUMKOWSKI: Would you take love from a man like me?

MIRIAM: You're very appealing, but that's not the only reason for marriage. There must be other things too.

RUMKOWSKI: You're negotiating. I'm still not out of the picture.

MIRIAM: I've given no thought to my personal life. All my energy and thought have gone into this work: to serve our people against a very dangerous enemy.

RUMKOWSKI: That's why I need you.

MIRIAM: It could happen, sometime in the future, under certain conditions.

RUMKOWSKI (*laughingly*): It's like doing business with Biebow.

MIRIAM (*trying to control anger*): No. You and I are equals. None of us could ever be with him. (*He's taken aback by tone. She adopts a friendlier voice.*) I know someone had to take this thankless job. And even though I don't always agree with you, I feel in these times, you're right for the part. You can be flexible, sometimes too much for my taste, but you can also be decisive and stand your ground. And your patience seems inexhaustible.

RUMKOWSKI: Not when it comes to you. I'm ready to deal right now.

MIRIAM: If, at some future time, it came to pass, as a wife I'd see to it you got your full share. But here and now, in this work, a colleague, that's what I'd like to be.

RUMKOWSKI: You'll be my Mrs. Roosevelt.

(*Enter* DR. COHEN.)

MIRIAM: Ari, what are you doing here?

RUMKOWSKI: You two know each other?

MIRIAM: Of course. We're old friends.

RUMKOWSKI: What kind of friends?

COHEN: Very good ones.

MIRIAM (*reacting to* RUMKOWSKI's *jealousy*): I introduced him to his beautiful wife.

RUMKOWSKI: What can I do for you, Doctor?

COHEN: We're out of everything at the hospital. This morning I had to cancel all surgery for lack of anesthetics.

RUMKOWSKI: You'll be receiving a full truckload of supplies tomorrow. I was well aware of your problems (*hands paper to* COHEN).

COHEN (*reading aloud*): Two clinics. An invalid and convalescent home.

RUMKOWSKI: Serving only kosher food.

COHEN: A facility for the aged and the mentally ill.

RUMKOWSKI: All to be in operation in the next six months.

COHEN: Is this some sort of joke?

RUMKOWSKI: I don't deal in that kind of merchandise.

COHEN: Since when have the Nazis taken an interest in our welfare?

RUMKOWSKI: Since it was called to their attention by me that we can match England when it comes to production. They were very impressed. But I can see you're not (*looks disdainfully at him*). I realize I don't have your big reputation or fancy wife, not yet anyway. But then I'm in a job that nobody's ever had before, so anything might happen.

COHEN: I've nothing but respect for the way you've managed our affairs thus far. But it troubles me that Jewish skills are producing goods on their behalf.

RUMKOWSKI: So maybe we should tell our people to go without hospitals and medical care because it might help the Germans. *(Growing more sarcastic.)* I've even got a better idea. Why don't you stop saving Jews, because if they're dead, they can't be useful to anybody.

COHEN: I help men and women get well again. I don't point them in any direction.

RUMKOWSKI: Stop kidding yourself. You point them right to the factory gate.

COHEN: There are no other gates possible.

RUMKOWSKI: Now you're catching on. We work or we starve. There's nothing in between.

COHEN: There's the Council. It must act on our behalf and not theirs.

RUMKOWSKI: So what would you have us do?

COHEN: How far are you willing to go to meet their demands?

RUMKOWSKI: How far is far when it comes to the life of one of your patients?

COHEN: I'm bound by my oath.

RUMKOWSKI: And we by our faith. So for us, enough is never enough. And why? Because the price of survival is always right.

COHEN: Always?

(RABINOWITZ enters running.)

RUMKOWSKI: What girl friend are you running away from now?

RABINOWITZ: A big roundup . . . The Gestapo . . .

RUMKOWSKI: Slow down and tell me what happened.

RABINOWITZ: They started by picking up some political people and then they went for all the Council members.

RUMKOWSKI: Where did they take them?

RABINOWITZ: To the jail.

RUMKOWSKI *(looking up):* Why have You spared me?

RABINOWITZ: He hasn't. This whole building is surrounded. *(Self-pitying.)* I think we're all going to get it.

RUMKOWSKI *(nastily):* Rabinowitz, if anyone manages to come through this, it'll be you. *(Starts to put on coat.)* They won't keep me here. Not when they're up to no good. I'll find out what this is all about.

COHEN: I insist on accompanying you.

RUMKOWSKI: I don't need any more loud mouths. Mine will do.

RABINOWITZ: They've announced that some will be shot.

COHEN: They must not be allowed to butcher our Council.

RUMKOWSKI: I'll keep that in mind. That is if they don't butcher me *(stares into space)*. Please God, help me now. So I can help You. *(Turns to them.)* I want the three of you to stay here. I'll need you if I get back. *(Looks at* MIRIAM.*)* A tear? For the groom? *(He exits quickly.)*

COHEN *(to* MIRIAM*):* Mazel Tov.[16]

(Lights out.)

Scene 6

Lights up on YANKELE. *He sings:*

"Maimonides"[17]

A group of men, like you and me
Had a big problem and rushed to see
Maimonides, who else?

16. Mazel Tov: literally "good luck," Cohen means this derisively, indicating his disapproval of Miriam's relationship with Rumkowski.

17. Maimonides: (1135–1204), one of the greatest and most influential philosophers in the history of Judaism. The applicability of the "Code of Maimonides" to

They told him of the enemy plan
To pick from their own a simple man
To be killed, what else?

(change of voice)
But should we fail, then we'll be flailed
We'll be punished like that blameless Jew
Oh mamanu, mamanu, give us some clue

(imitating Maimonides)
"Since you judged him innocent
In no way must he die for you.
What to do? What to do?
Join him. Nothing less will do!"

(speaks)
Rabbi Maimonides, if we do as you suggest
How will a remnant be saved?
But on the other hand
If we don't do as you say
What kind of remnant will it be?

(Lights out. Lights up in RUMKOWSKI's *office.)*

Scene 7

RUMKOWSKI's *office.* RUMKOWSKI's *face has been beaten and* DR. COHEN *has just finished tending the wound.*

RUMKOWSKI: One by one he informs me of who's been killed. I managed to save some. Just a few. Too few. But if I didn't stand up to them, they would *all* be out there, buried in some ditch

---

conditions the Jews suffered under the Nazis is one of the central philosophical concerns of the play.

where only God could find them. (*Talks to God.*) You're not making it very easy for me, are You? And we both know what lies ahead now. (*Lost in his reverie.* COHEN *breaks silence.*)

COHEN: Who did this to you? Biebow?

RUMKOWSKI: At first he only used words. I did too. Only louder. That got him very upset. He doesn't like me to raise my voice in his presence. So he took off his belt and started to beat me. I stood there and didn't make a sound. He didn't like that either, so he stopped. Then he suddenly remembered that he had two Council members left, Berger and Levine, so he gave them to me for 2,000 marks each.

RABINOWITZ: We've always been very good at fund raising.

COHEN: There's not enough money to ransom us all. (*To* RUMKOWSKI.) Are you prepared to say who will live or die?

RUMKOWSKI: (*with anger*): Are you telling me it was wrong for Rumkowski to save some?

COHEN: No. I'm saying it's right to save all.

RUMKOWSKI: Even God doesn't save all.

MIRIAM (*to* COHEN): If you were in his place, would you have behaved differently?

COHEN: I'd never be in his position.

MIRIAM: You and I, Ari, we're never in charge, are we? We make sure to leave that to the Chaims of this world.

COHEN: You will discover, to your regret, there's a very thin line between benevolence and betrayal.

RUMKOWSKI: Enough! Both of you. There's important business to settle. We must inform all the families of what's happened. They've taken over a hundred people to the jail.

COHEN (*apprehensively*): Are any of them Zionists?

RUMKOWSKI: Some. I tried to warn them against carrying on like they did, but they wouldn't listen.
(COHEN *starts to exit.*)
Where are you going? I didn't give you permission to leave.

COHEN: Where is my wife?

RUMKOWSKI: Home. And only because of me will she still warm your bed. They need you, so I told them you needed her.

COHEN: I'm very grateful for what you've done.

RUMKOWSKI: Let's see how grateful. For instance, what would you say, Doctor, if I told you that your hospital must be completely evacuated by next week.

COHEN: Have you any idea what it takes to evacuate an entire hospital?

RUMKOWSKI: No. But obviously you do. That's why you're in charge.

COHEN: What else do they want moved?

RUMKOWSKI: Everything. Everything Jewish moves to the *Balut*.

COHEN: But why?

RUMKOWSKI: We'll be much safer.

COHEN: That never concerned them before.

RUMKOWSKI: It will be completely under our jurisdiction. Free from the possibility of any pogrom. They're putting a ring of *Volks Deutsch*[18] around us to protect us from any Polish hooligans. It will be our area, under our authority.

COHEN: What kind of authority are you talking about, when they alone give the orders? Can't you see that they're pushing us straight into a ghetto? Back to the Middle Ages. You're mad. It's a ghetto.

RABINOWITZ: Think of it as a small piece of Palestine.

RUMKOWSKI: Of course I could propose another option: mass suicide. We've already proven in our history that we can do that quite well.[19] Are you ready to kill yourself?

COHEN: I'm not ready to let them kill me.

RUMKOWSKI: So let's resist. Take a stand. Plant our feet. Such fine phrases. Such bad advice. To go on breathing, *that* is the rebellion of this time.

COHEN: There is a step which once taken, locks in all the other steps to come. We must not do that voluntarily.

18. Volks Deutsch: ethnic Germans who forcibly displaced the Poles who lived in the area surrounding the ghetto.

19. "Quite well": Rumkowski is referring to the mass suicide of Jews at Masada. See Yankele's prologue, p. 124.

RUMKOWSKI: If we don't organize the move with decency and humanity, they'll do it by terror.

COHEN: Not me. *(To* MIRIAM.*)* And you?

MIRIAM: Ari, we need you. This is no time to refuse.

COHEN: There will never be a better time. After the gates are locked and barred, it will be impossible to say no.

MIRIAM: Please, don't turn away from us now. I need . . . *(stops and looks at* RUMKOWSKI*).* We all need you.

COHEN *(savagely):* For what? To become like you?

RUMKOWSKI: She at least will stay on the job. Not like you, a lousy quitter.

COHEN *(to* MIRIAM*):* You thought you could influence this man. But he's turned your head around, so you can't see what's right any more. Stay with him and your life will be one compromise after another. *(To* RUMKOWSKI.*)* You make decisions for those who will not make their own. I will not move into that ghetto. *(He exits.)*

RUMKOWSKI *(yelling after him):* You're finished as a doctor. *(Turns to* RABINOWITZ.*)* You'll need to recruit at least a hundred new men. *(To* MIRIAM.*)* You are to draw up a list, street by street, so we can have an orderly evacuation. Everything must be done properly. Everyone must be ready to leave by Thursday. *(Lights out.)*

Scene 8

YANKELE *sings to audience:*

"The Ballad of Bloody Thursday"

The unloved dawn so slow to rise
Let out a mournful yawn
And tried to close its tear-stained eye
So light would not be born

And on the ground, on every street
The frozen stalks pushed through

They marched in silence 'neath the sleet
That danced to wind the winter blew

Some stayed behind, the S.S.[20] came
And beat and kicked and shot
Without the slightest trace of shame
Those rooted to their spot

The blood meandered through the snow
The bodies flaked with white
The brutes had staged a bloody show
To make us run in harried flight

Bloody Thursday
Muddy curse day
While the world stood mute
And did its best to turn away
While ghetto walls rose round *Balut*
Round *Balut*, round and round
The barbed wire dropped
And we were bound.

(Some scenic effect should be used to indicate the total isolation of the ghetto, perhaps a simple barbed wire fence downstage to separate audience from actors.)

Scene 9

The barbed wire is up. YANKELE *speaks to audience:*
That first winter in the *Balut*
The frost slept on our empty stomachs
Only the fire was sometimes fed

---

20. *S.S.:* the Nazi elite troops who were usually in charge of the organized deportation and murder of the Jews of Europe.

With our tables and chairs.
Soon bad tempers gave way to resistance
And strikes started to melt the snow.
In the beginning were the furniture workers
Then out came the others
The ghetto was as silent as a mirror
And we liked our own reflections
Until Rumkowski began his own winter offensive.

(Single spot picks up RUMKOWSKI.*)*

RUMKOWSKI: A general strike has to be handled by a real general. So we'll start by cutting the furniture workers' rations in half. Then we'll see to it that the extra share is given to those in the textile mills, provided of course they go back to work.

(Lights out on him and up on YANKELE.*)*

YANKELE:
They went back
The strike collapsed
The unions were made illegal
And solidarity sat in the corner like an orphan
As each acted according to his need.
Only the few, always the few
Refused the bribe of silence.

(Lights out. Single spot on ROSA *with leaflet.)*

ROSA *(reads aloud):* "Starving Jewish masses. In order not to fall from hunger and cold, you were forced to give in to Rumkowski. What had we demanded? Nothing that was not possible. More rations for those who did the hardest work. A piece of bread with the watery soup. That's all we asked for. But he threw our demands away. We understand that you couldn't look at your starving children any longer. We sorrow with you that there was no other recourse. To hell with our Jewish betrayers. They will not avoid revenge."

(Lights out; lights up in RUMKOWSKI'S *office.* RUMKOWSKI *is*

handed a copy of the leaflet by MIRIAM. *He crumples it up and throws it away.)*

MIRIAM: Are you afraid to read it?

RUMKOWSKI: I know what they have to say.

MIRIAM: That you are evil.

RUMKOWSKI: Who cares? When it's all over, then I'll be very popular. You see, it's a lot easier to keep my people from falling than it will be to have them picked up.

MIRIAM: I don't like what you're becoming, Chaim.

RUMKOWSKI: So divorce me. That might give me real pleasure *(laughs loudly)*. You don't anymore. Even the devil will take anything but a cold wife.

MIRIAM: I'd thaw out very quickly if you started to hear what I have to say.

RUMKOWSKI: I listen. I just think your advice is foolish. *(Changes his tone.)* Now, take a letter for my darlings *(paces)*. "Dear children. I want you to know how much I love you. So stay in school and learn. Don't hang around in the streets. And never go near the barbed wire. Remember, whatever happens, you can always look to me as your Father."

(Lights out. Lights up on YANKELE. *He speaks to audience.)*

YANKELE:

Now another spring
Hangs on this line[21]
Like dirty underwear.
The new Exodus is two years old
But it's the old one
That's still being celebrated.

(As he speaks we hear the last lines of the song "Dayenu"[22]

---

21. "This line": Yankele refers to the barbed wire that first appeared at the end of act 1, scene 8.

22. "Dayenu": a Hebrew song often sung at the end of the Passover *seder* (festival meal). It is a song of many verses in which Jews thank God for His many blessings, each one of which would have been "dayenu"—"enough for us."

being sung softly in the background. It grows louder in inten-
sity as lights come up on the Wolf household. Everyone has
joined in that final song of the Passover service.)

Scene 10

Passover, 1942.

ADA: It was such a lovely seder.[23]

ISRAEL: I've seen better.

ADA: Tell Grandpa the truth, children. Did you ever hear a seder conducted with such feeling?

ISRAEL: I wanted to remind, blessed be His name, that in 1942 we are in bondage again.

ADA: This year, unlike the last, thanks to the generosity of our Chairman, we were able to serve matzos.[24]

ISRAEL: I've tasted better.

ROSA: What shady deal did he make this time so we could have this unbleached cardboard?

ISRAEL *(to* ROSA, *with his diary):* There's nothing like a bad taste to stimulate a good question. Listen to this, Rosa. "If tragedy is the tale of an unsuccessful ruler, what shall we call the story of his people?"

ROSA: Not bad, Grandpa. Will you enter one for me? *(He nods.)* "Is a successful leader one who makes an offer five minutes before he's asked?"

ISRAEL: I've heard—worse.

ADA: A fine bunch of comedians. One writes funny things in a book that no one will read and the other does all kinds of funny

23. Seder: the festive, ritual meal which begins the week-long celebration of Passover (*Pessach* in Yiddish and Hebrew), a holiday commemorating the Jews' escape from the ancient Egyptians as told in Exodus. It is known as the Festival of Freedom.

24. Matzos: the unleavened bread which is eaten during the Passover holiday.

things out there in the streets. Rabinowitz made it a point to tell me that they're keeping a close eye on you and your group.

ROSA: And we're doing the same thing to them. Tell me, Gabriel, when your club hits a body, does it make you feel like the man you always wanted to be?

GABRIEL: Don't push me, Rosa. I keep order and safety in this ghetto. I wouldn't want my own sister getting in the way.

ZOSIA: You'd never arrest her, would you?

ADA: What kind of stupid question is that, Zosia?

GABRIEL: I refuse to talk about such a remote possibility.

ZOSIA: I want an answer. Would you ever touch her?

GABRIEL: I might if you two don't shut up.

ADA: Stop this nonsense right now. The truth of the matter is that your brother cares more for the future of this family than anyone else, even me. Which of you has made a sacrifice as big as his? (*Turns to* ROSA.) Please don't give him or the others the slightest cause to do anything to you. On this, our happy holiday, promise me you won't do anything foolish.

ROSA: My answer is still the same. A new regime and I turn over a new leaf.

ADA: We're still here, aren't we? Doesn't that say something for his leadership?

ISRAEL: Only that our turn hasn't come yet. When we got to the place to say, "Next year in Jerusalem," [25] all I could think of was "Fool, pray for a next year here in Lodz. The year after that can be in the Holy Land."

ROSA (*to* ISRAEL): How did you like my wine?

ISRAEL: I've drunk better.

ROSA: From beets?

ISRAEL: As soup, it's first rate.

GABRIEL (*scornfully*): Just like your Polish comrades, Rosa, who haven't managed to get you a single gun—not one.

ROSA: We'll get some.

---

25. Jerusalem: at the end of the seder, the participants express the traditional wish to be able to enjoy the next Passover in Jerusalem.

GABRIEL: You should ask David to help. He's very good at taking other people's things.

DAVID: I don't know what you're talking about.

GABRIEL: I hear you're one of the best bread grabbers there is.

MOSHE: He's learned a very good trade for these times.

DAVID: Can I close the door now? I'm freezing.

ISRAEL: Give him a few more minutes.

GABRIEL: Let him close it. If he wants to see us badly enough, he'll knock.

ISRAEL: It stays open. You don't wait two thousand years for Elijah and when he finally decides to come, he finds the door closed.[26]

(MOSHE and DAVID play. GABRIEL, ZOSIA and ADA are seated at table.)

GABRIEL *(to ADA)*: You said it was all set up. Where is he?

ADA: He's coming. He's very pleased with your work. So I can tell you, only act surprised when he tells you, you are going to be promoted. He's decided to make you one of Rabinowitz's assistants.

ZOSIA: But he's the worst crook and bully of them all!

GABRIEL: Zosia, I'm warning you. *(Turns to DAVID.)* David, shut that damn door.

(DAVID hesitates and GABRIEL gets up to close the door. We now see YANKELE in the doorway, carrying a once-elegant suitcase.)

ADA: For this we had to keep the door open?

(Into the room comes HANNAH ADLER, middle-aged, German. She is wearing a fashionable coat and hat with Star of David prominently displayed. The others all stare at each other in disbelief. YANKELE follows her in. No one speaks. ISRAEL rises and crosses to HANNAH.)

ISRAEL: You're my sister Sarah's daughter. *(She nods. He embraces her.)* I recognize you from the picture she sent me. Welcome. How is Sarah?

---

26. "Door closed": at the seder, a door is opened in anticipation of the arrival of the prophet Elijah, whose task is to announce the coming of the Messiah.

HANNAH: It was all too much for her. She passed away last month.

ISRAEL: May she rest in peace.

ZOSIA: Are you the lady lawyer Grandpa keeps bragging about to all his friends?

HANNAH: I haven't practiced in seven years. Jewish women lawyers are not exactly in great demand in the Third Reich.

ADA: Do you plan on staying in this city?

HANNAH: I've no say in the matter.

ADA: Have you been to the Council?

HANNAH: There are no rooms to be had anywhere.

ADA: Just look at how we live. Two grown-ups and five children, two of whom are young girls, in one room. It's not healthy.

ZOSIA: It's not that bad, Mama. A lot of families live ten to a room.

ROSA: Privacy is a bourgeois affectation.

HANNAH *(laughing at* ROSA's *ironic remark)*: This star is my guarantee of privacy, and of public attention. *(She pauses, lost in her thoughts.)* Have you ever had your food spat upon while shopping? *(Looks around room for answer.)* The vegetables, I can tell you, don't take very kindly to it. So I tried to eat nothing but eggs. Can you guess why? Because eggs have a natural cover against spit. I ate them so often that I imagined myself an egg. Oh, to be inside that shell, hidden, protected. Even to be bitten with affection. I'd settle for that. I had to sell my law books for cabbage, and Goethe bought me first place at the garbage heap. *(To* ADA.) I don't need very much at all. Really, just a . . .

ADA *(interrupts)*: We've got nothing to give. So many of us living on top of each other. *(Goes to* HANNAH *and examines her coat.)* Now, if you had come in the old days, I would have worn my black satin dress with real pearls. And my daughters, how lovely they looked in their new spring ensembles. You would have had a place of honor at our seder. And over a glass of tea, what conversations you would have heard. But then, you never came. And now you've made a terrible mistake in coming here. Why didn't you run to America like the others?

HANNAH: Because I thought I was a German. Until the Nazi travel agent tied me to this suitcase and sent me on a journey of humiliation and *(to* ADA*)* self-abasement *(she begins to cry).*

ADA: Tears don't buy anything here. We have more than we can use.

ISRAEL: My daughter has become a regular businesswoman. But she hasn't come to selling her own family. Not yet, anyway. So you'll stay here with us.

ADA: Just like that? One more mouth to feed.

HANNAH: Did you think I was asking for charity? No. I can pay my way.

ADA: What with?

HANNAH: I had a friend. A former friend. He made it possible to take some money with me *(takes out roll of marks, holds it out to* ADA *who takes it).* There's more.

ROSA: Mama, what kind of family are we . . . ?

*(*ZOSIA *in shame turns away from* ADA*.)*

ADA: Gabriel, what are you waiting for? Take her coat *(*GABRIEL *takes coat; offers* HANNAH *his chair).* Please sit down *(*HANNAH *sits).* My two daughters don't approve of their mother's behavior these days. They'd like to turn their backs on me, but they can't. Because I see to it that their backs are up instead of flat. I've managed to keep us all together and I'll do anything to keep it that way.

ROSA *(to* ADA *and* GABRIEL*):* Whatever it is you're doing, don't pretend it's for me. I don't want it. Not your way.

ADA: But not everyone acts that way anymore. Last week there was a mother who, when it was her turn to go, offered her own child in her place. That's what some of us have become.

*(*YANKELE *fills the silence.)*

YANKELE: Some of us have even become Pharaoh,[27] in honor of the season.

ADA *(to* HANNAH*):* You're in very good hands now. A part of our

---

27. Pharaoh: Yankele's joke is to associate Rumkowski with Pharaoh, the Egyptian ruler who enslaved the Hebrews and from whom they escaped; the story is recounted and celebrated during Passover: "Slaves were we unto Pharaoh of Egypt . . ."

family. And I've got connections where it counts the most. Understand? Now which corner would you like?

HANNAH: Any one will do.

ADA: It won't be so bad. Tomorrow Yankele will buy you a mattress on the black market and you'll be our regular boarder.

YANKELE: I went yesterday for a client to buy some cyanide. It was so expensive that I advised him it was cheaper to live.

(RUMKOWSKI *and* MIRIAM *enter. Both are dressed well.* ADA *and* GABRIEL *applaud him. The children crowd around him and he gives each boy a crisp new bill.*)

MOSHE: Look, it's got his picture on it.

YANKELE: That's to make it easier to part with (*waves bill around*). He puts his face on money so everyone knows he can be bought.

ROSA: And we get sold out in the bargain.

ADA (*seeing* RUMKOWSKI'S *irritation*): Chairman Rumkowski, we have a guest from Germany, Miss Adler.

RUMKOWSKI: And I'd like you to meet my wife, Miriam. She's my third, that's how I believe in marriage. In my ghetto, I give an extra ration to every new bride and groom. So now the engagements are very short (*he laughs and* GABRIEL *follows along*). I once asked a young man if he would love, honor and obey, and he said: "After I've eaten."

(*They all laugh.* MIRIAM *greets* HANNAH *in German and they exchange a few words when* RUMKOWSKI *interrupts and points directly at* HANNAH, *angrily.*)

A word of advice for you. Don't speak German around here, unless you want to get a reputation as an informer.

HANNAH: I shall do whatever you think best.

RUMKOWSKI: Good. Don't be like the others who don't want to understand what this ghetto is. They think they can live their old ways, but I assure you that's finished. You German Jews used to look down your noses at us. We were never important like you. We break our backs here but all I get from your kind is a negative attitude towards work. And do you know where it leads them? To the top of my Work Relocation List.

HANNAH: I need to get back to work. Do you have a legal system here?

RUMKOWSKI: You're looking at it.

HANNAH: I was a lawyer for over fifteen years.

RUMKOWSKI: The time would have been better spent if you were a seamstress. *(To MIRIAM, derisively.)* Of brains there is no shortage here. Can you sew a dress? A brassiere? Stitch lingerie? Make parachutes and camouflage? That's what my women do here, and that's what you'll have to do *(points to ADA, ROSA and ZOSIA)*. Be like them. They're fast and good. You work as hard as they do and you'll be here a long time. *(To MIRIAM.)* Come on *(he starts to go, looks at ROSA, goes to her)*. Some friendly advice for you, Rosa. I know what you and your hotheads have in mind. So remember this: I'd rather not use force, but I won't hesitate if you force me. *(With all his authority.)* There will be no strikes in my ghetto. And you Ada, I'm glad you've decided not to be a stranger. My door is open to you any time. *(Starts to exit. GABRIEL fidgets. To GABRIEL.)* Be at my office tomorrow. I've got some good news for you.

ADA and GABRIEL *(bow to him and repeat a few times)*: Thank you, Mr. Chairman. Thank you.

(RUMKOWSKI and MIRIAM start for door.)

ISRAEL *(raising his voice)*: He deserves no thanks.

(Everyone reacts to his boldness. RUMKOWSKI stares menacingly at him.)

Dictators are now the latest fashion everywhere. So we had to get one of our very own.

ADA *(to RUMKOWSKI)*: My father is never happy unless he's had the last word. Please forgive the outburst. Half the time he doesn't know what he's saying.

RUMKOWSKI *(to ISRAEL)*: When I want your opinion, I'll ask. Until then keep this shut tight.

(He squeezes ISRAEL's lips hard. All are shocked by the violence of the gesture except ROSA.)

It's lucky for you Ada's a very old and good friend of mine, so
I didn't hear a thing. *(His face beaming.)* Happy Pessach,
everybody. *(To* HANNAH.*)* Happy Passover.
*(*RUMKOWSKI *and* MIRIAM *exit. Lights down. Everyone exits
except* YANKELE.*)*

Scene 11

YANKELE *looks at table, moves to Elijah's cup*[28] *and picks it up:*
Elijah told me
He tried to come that night
But lost his way
On those terrible Polish roads.
The Angel of Death
Who makes his own road maps
And is never too shy or embarrassed
To put in an appearance
Passed over that night
But not before he had gently nudged
The eldest son.
Meanwhile, we scan the skies
For a new David
A likely Solomon
A rabbi, anybody
To fortify our shadows.
As for me
I bandage my heart
With foolish words.
Can a song cry out

---

28. Elijah's cup: a cup of wine is poured for the prophet Elijah and remains on
the seder table during the festival meal.

Like my people are crying?
Can it be eaten?
Can it kill?

(Pause. Stares out into the darkness.)
Like good guests
You came uninvited
So this is your night too.
The roasted egg
The blasted bone
The bitter herb[29]

(Pours wine on white tablecloth.)
How do you like the taste?

INTERMISSION

29. The roasted egg, the blasted (roasted) bone, the bitter herb: these items are on the Passover table and are a central symbolic part of the seder meal. The egg and bone remind the celebrants of the burnt offering brought to the Temple, and the bitter herb recalls the bitterness of slavery. In the ghetto context, these objects assume special significance.

ACT 2

Scene 1

YANKELE *speaks to audience:*

Since we last met
This earth has made many turns on its axis
While the Axis[30] has turned on us.
It's all upside down
The sun is setting in the East
While the West explores deserts in Africa.
Here our ghetto is an *ersatz* Tel Aviv
We get pushed by our own policeman
Trade with our own currency
And deliver our own mail.
Already there are 10,000 "Addresses Unknown"
If we keep that up
The letters will have to answer themselves.
And through it all
Our Kaiser rides in his broken-down coach
Pulled by his nearly blind horse
Listening to verses fashioned in his honor
By his own poet laureate
Who exchanges praise for parsnips.

(Claps hands.)

"A Homage to Rumkowski"

When the Chairman grows weary
Of the struggle to keep us fed
It's no picnic, my friends
You just try it, my friends
To have such a ghetto on your head

---

30. Axis: the name given to Germany and its allies in World War II.

Then he goes to the children
And they speak of many things
Just to see them and hear them
Makes him grow a pair of wings
So Rumkowski goes smiling
As the children begin to sing

Then he goes from the children
He protects with his strong arm
Feeling good that on this Pessach
He has kept them all from harm
Then our Chairman is happy
For in his ghetto all is calm.

(Lights out. In the darkness we hear MIRIAM *reciting the litany of names.)*

Scene 2

RUMKOWSKI's *office.* MIRIAM's *appearance has changed for the worse.* RUMKOWSKI *enters wearing a well-tailored suit. He ignores her.*

MIRIAM: "Szymon and Leah Berger. Tadeusz Rubinsztein. Ester and Ida Goldberger. Mendel and Minna Brodsky. Hannah Kantrovitz."

RUMKOWSKI: You got it wrong. The production of textiles is up forty percent not twenty. An experienced secretary like you shouldn't make such mistakes.

MIRIAM: "Janusz and Elke Levine."

RUMKOWSKI: My factories are doing a remarkable job.

MIRIAM: "Jacob, Anya and Hannele Sztern."

RUMKOWSKI: Berlin couldn't believe it.

MIRIAM: "Isak Shulman."

RUMKOWSKI: So all morning they had their cameras in my shops.

Then they asked to film the hospital. "Why do you want to go there?" I asked them, "That's the only place production has gone down" *(laughs at joke).* Guess what they wanted to shoot? *(She is silent.)* Circumcisions. Nothing but circumcisions from every possible angle.

MIRIAM: And what did you do, join the spectacle?

RUMKOWSKI: A man's penis is not his soul. It's even possible to live without one.

MIRIAM: What would he be then, like you?

RUMKOWSKI: Shut that filthy mouth of yours. A good queen shouldn't have too much to say. You eat well, you are protected. What more do you want?

MIRIAM: I will not work on the lists any more.

RUMKOWSKI: You will stay here and do your work and I don't ever want to hear that kind of talk again.

MIRIAM: Then you'd better prepare to put me on your next list.

RUMKOWSKI: How would it look for me to deport my own wife?

MIRIAM: It would prove to all you rule with an equal hand. Privilege is dead. Long live the King! . . . and his mistresses.

RUMKOWSKI: You try my patience.

MIRIAM: And you my shame. The people you send out of here, have you any idea of what happens to them?

RUMKOWSKI: They're put to work.

MIRIAM: Since when is dying work?

RUMKOWSKI: Stop already with the dying.

MIRIAM: Only you can do that. *(Takes handful of bloody fringes from bag and holds them in front of him.)* This is from that new shipment of materials you asked me to look at. The clothes and undergarments of murdered Jews.

RUMKOWSKI: Who told you that, that crazy Yankele?

MIRIAM: No one has to tell me that. Who else wears fringes besides our men? *(She waves them at him.)*

RUMKOWSKI: They look to me like they came from some sick people. *(Looks at her disdainfully.)* Or who knows? You're acting so strange these days, maybe you used them to wipe away your unclean blood?

MIRIAM: You'd like that, wouldn't you? To turn your mania into my madness. (*Holds up fringes.*) We both know where they came from, don't we? This could be your chance not to be a camp follower. Take it. Refuse to participate in any new deportations.

RUMKOWSKI: All this on your say so, huh?

MIRIAM: No, not only mine. This morning a woman approached me in the street. At first I thought she was crazy and then she showed it to me. A letter from her husband. He was there, in the camp, and he managed to escape.

RUMKOWSKI: I'll listen to your street gossip some other time.

MIRIAM: Where do you think your Jews go when they leave here?

RUMKOWSKI: A lot of places.

MIRIAM: No. Only one.

RUMKOWSKI: They go wherever the Germans need workers.

MIRIAM: The Jews you send out of Lodz, like the Jews of Kalisz and Kutno,[31] I've found out where they go. They're assembled at a large mill near Zawadki and everything is taken from them. Then they are put on trucks for Chelmno.[32] There everyone is forced to undress. A soldier tells them to hang their clothing on a hook and to remember the number. He gives them breathing exercises. "Inhale 1—2—3—4. Exhale 1—2—3—4." It makes the gas line move more quickly. When it is over, they remove the bodies and place them in rows, one atop the other. In between kindling wood is scattered. Then one who was spared is sent to the top to start the fire. He can't get down in time and goes ablaze, his cries mingling with the crackle of the wood. (*Her voice rises.*) You are that Jew up there. And you will not escape the burning!

RUMKOWSKI (*who has listened impassively*): You think I'm an insensitive man, don't you? Well, for a change you're right. I've had to teach my heart to be like a rock. For if I grow soft or

---

31. Kalisz and Kutno: Polish towns north of Warsaw.

32. Chelmno: one of the most notorious concentration camps established by the Nazis, where thousands of Jews were murdered.

sentimental, all will be lost. I'm not responsible to you or any rabbi now, but to God alone! Save the crying for later when there'll be eyes to shed tears and ears that can listen.

MIRIAM: There is no later for us. Our people must be told now, and that is what I intend to do. And you can tell your Commandant, and he can tell his Commandant, that the secret he, they, *you*, worked so hard to keep is now out.

RUMKOWSKI: No one will believe you. Not when they find out I had to commit you because of your strange behavior.

MIRIAM: How will it look to send your own wife to the mad house?

RUMKOWSKI: Everybody knows that when it comes to wives, I've been very unlucky. Two went and died on me and the third has become muddleheaded.

MIRIAM: I don't know which is worse: the curses of Haman or the blessings of Mordechai.[33]

(Lights down; the next scene has begun.)

Scene 3

The street. Night. ISRAEL *enters and looks around. Hides.* ROSA *enters. He calls out.*

ISRAEL: Rosa! . . . over here. *(She approaches him.)*

ROSA: Grandpa, what are you doing out so late? It's not safe.

ISRAEL: I've been looking for you since this afternoon. And I wouldn't be a bit surprised if you were looking for this *(takes out large radio tube)*. You're getting very careless, especially with a policeman in the house.

---

33. Mordechai: Miriam refers to the Jewish festival of Purim which commemorates another Jewish escape from certain destruction in ancient Persia. Mordechai, the leader of the Jews, together with his niece Esther was able to defeat the evil plot of Haman, the Persian king's chief minister. Miriam's mordant joke is the more pointed because Mordechai Rumkowski and Haman had the same birthdate.

ROSA (*almost in tears*): I've been ashamed to face my comrades. (*He gives her tube.*) I may not get old, but this must (*puts tube in pocket*).

ISRAEL: I'm not prying, mind you, but that looks like something from a wireless set.

ROSA: As an old revolutionary, would you want me to violate security?

ISRAEL: Certainly not. Just give me a hint now and then, whose army is where.

ROSA: Sometime next week, regular bulletins will be issued throughout the ghetto. The only thing we've got left to fight with are our ears.

ISRAEL: A radio is like an angel who sings. I just hope his news is as good as his voice.

(*As they embrace,* GABRIEL *in his policeman's uniform enters.*)

GABRIEL: What are you two doing out here this time of night? (*They are startled.*) You could be arrested. It's long past curfew.

ISRAEL: Your sister took me to the theatre. A new play. What was it called, Rosa?

ROSA: "Eden Schmeden." Very avant-garde.

GABRIEL: For a lousy show, you went and jeopardized our family?

ISRAEL: It wasn't lousy. It was speculation. Which after all is a lower form of prophecy.

GABRIEL (*looks at watch*): Since when do shows last after midnight?

ROSA: Grandpa became a little faint.

ISRAEL: All that commotion made my head a little weak.

ROSA: So we thought it best to rest a while before going home.

GABRIEL: You expect me to swallow that? (*Laughs menacingly.*) I know you two were up to something.

ISRAEL: I was more down than up, believe me.

GABRIEL (*to* ROSA): And if you keep it up, Rabinowitz will start showing how tired he is of the work stoppages your group keeps organizing.

ROSA: I'm available any time he wants to jail me.

GABRIEL: He doesn't dare. Not yet. Not while Mama's got the

Chairman on her side. Did I say side? I meant her back. They make such a lovely couple.

ROSA: Can I please take Grandpa home now?

GABRIEL: Not so fast *(gestures with hands)*. Hand it over. He gave you something. I was watching.

ISRAEL: I gave her nothing.

GABRIEL *(to* ROSA*):* Hold out your hands. I'm going to search you.

ISRAEL: You'll do nothing of the kind *(steps in front of* ROSA*)*.

GABRIEL: Get out of the way, Grandpa.

(She starts to run. GABRIEL *grabs her and holds her hands behind her back.* ISRAEL *takes club from* GABRIEL'*s belt and starts to swing it at him.* GABRIEL *is forced to let her go.)*

ISRAEL: Run, Rosa!

(She runs off quickly. ISRAEL *hands him the club back. The two men stare at each other. Lights out; the next scene has begun.)*

Scene 4

The street. Bright daylight. YANKELE *is putting up poster. He points at it and speaks.*

YANKELE: Our Leader has ordered us to be happy. So ha-ha, ha-ha, ha. That's how you'll laugh and forget your troubles at the Old Yiddish Art Theatre production of "Life Will Be Better." Starting tonight.

(As he is speaking MOSHE *enters, carrying a stick. He looks at sign, turns to* YANKELE.*)*

MOSHE: Better than what?

YANKELE: Than . . . better.

MOSHE: You're right. What could be better? Do you mind if I set up shop here?

YANKELE: Go right ahead.

*(*MOSHE *sits down against wall, puts on dark glasses, throws*

his cap to floor and holds out his arms in beggar posture.
DAVID *comes running on stage with a loaf of bread. As he goes
past,* MOSHE *puts out his stick and trips* DAVID. *He falls to
floor and the bread goes flying through the air.* MOSHE *pounces
on it.)*

MOSHE: Finders keepers.

DAVID: Give it back to me or I'll blacken both your eyes.

MOSHE *(warily staying away):* Who'd you steal it from?

DAVID: That's none of your business. *(Turning friendly as he approaches* MOSHE.*)* I can teach you my best tricks. *(He slaps
bread from* MOSHE'S *hand and it falls to the floor. They dive
for it and begin to wrestle and roll over the ground.* YANKELE
picks up the bread and starts to exit. DAVID *yells out.)* Stop!
Thief!

YANKELE *(very seriously to* DAVID*):* You've got to stop talking fool-
ishness or people will think you're a bit looney.

MOSHE: You're the real lunatic around here.

YANKELE *(to* MOSHE*):* I hope you understand that this bread is now
mine, all mine.

*(*DAVID *grabs the stick and is about to swing it at* YANKELE'S
head. YANKELE *ducks and grabs it from his hand.)*
What? You'd kill me for this?

DAVID: Give me my bread back.

YANKELE *(starts to shake* DAVID *but suddenly stops):* Why is it
someone is always sent to test me? Our Lord, blessed be His
name, doesn't look on the evil side. Why can't I?

DAVID *(angrily):* Why did He let all this happen?

MOSHE: Maybe it's as hard for Him as it is for us?

YANKELE: He's not accountable to us. But we are . . . to each other.
Even here . . . where it's impossible.
*(Breaks bread into three pieces, gives one to each boy, keeping
a tiny crust for himself. Lights down and up; the next scene
has begun.)*

Scene 5

RUMKOWSKI's *office, September, 1942.* RUMKOWSKI *is at his desk when* BIEBOW *enters unannounced.*

RUMKOWSKI: Commandant Biebow! What a surprise to have you in my office.
(Offers him seat. BIEBOW *stands.)*
BIEBOW: The pleasure is mine *(puts hand on* RUMKOWSKI's *shoulder).* I'm fond of you, Chaim. I really am. You and I understand each other. Aren't we two doing a splendid job?
RUMKOWSKI: Couldn't be better.
BIEBOW: Some of my superiors haven't the faintest notion of what it takes to run this operation and how valuable this ghetto has turned out to be. *(Confidentially.)* They've proposed that we close this place down and ship everybody out, God knows where.
RUMKOWSKI: Who would turn out the uniforms, the boots, the parachutes? Who? Tell me?
BIEBOW: I've made this place do what those fanatics said could not be done. You and I will drink champagne together when Germany is victorious. In a few weeks we'll be bedded down in Stalingrad. It's almost in our hands now. Sometime next year the war will end and if I am to continue to guarantee your safety, you're going to have to be far more efficient and productive than you've been.
RUMKOWSKI: What do you have in mind?
BIEBOW: We must dispose of all the excess baggage.
RUMKOWSKI: What?
BIEBOW: Who are the least productive in your community?
RUMKOWSKI *(apprehensive and slightly angry):* Don't give me riddles. I prefer plain talk.
BIEBOW: Why keep the crippled, the sick and the insane on your payroll?
RUMKOWSKI: To turn our back on the sick is a terrible sin.
BIEBOW: Where do you enter sin in the ledger? As of tomorrow your rations will be cut. They plan to starve you out.

RUMKOWSKI: You want work but you don't want workers. We've over 7,000 machines going and they're better fed than those who run them. The more goods we turn out the less we eat. Two ounces of rotten bread a day. Could you live on that? One hundred people a week die from hunger now.

BIEBOW: They don't think it's fast enough. Those who've already had a full life can help the rest.

RUMKOWSKI: I will not trade my old people like broken-down furniture. We are a people of strong family ties.

BIEBOW: So are we Germans.

RUMKOWSKI: So when does the auction of your people start?

BIEBOW *(takes out piece of paper):* A report on you from one of your own.

RUMKOWSKI: Your favors sometimes tempt a few.

BIEBOW: And you? What tempts you? Your own carriage? Your special food rations? Your exalted position?

RUMKOWSKI: I will not let you or anyone else judge me. That's reserved only for the Lord Almighty.

BIEBOW: I wonder how He'll feel about this?

RUMKOWSKI: Since He won't talk to you, you'll never know.
(Long pause.)

BIEBOW: Himmler called me this morning.

RUMKOWSKI *(after a silence):* How many this time?

BIEBOW: Three thousand a day, but just for eight days.

RUMKOWSKI: What makes you think I'll do what you want?

BIEBOW: You always do, but I can't force you. I can only urge common sense. Some or all.

RUMKOWSKI: You feed me my own vomit. *(Pauses, then impulsively:)* The sick and the old. I'll settle for that. No more.

BIEBOW: How many are there in that category?

RUMKOWSKI: About 11,000.

BIEBOW: I appreciate your trying to meet me half way but I'm afraid it won't do. There is one place left to fill out that shipment.

RUMKOWSKI: *Them!* You'll never get them from me.

BIEBOW: I'm not asking for all of them. Just those under ten.

RUMKOWSKI: I forbid you from ever talking about my children.

BIEBOW: They are mine now.

RUMKOWSKI: Haven't I given you whatever you've asked for?

BIEBOW: So why stop now?

RUMKOWSKI: Because they are my life. And our future. If I do that, my name would breed maggots. There wouldn't be a single soul who'd say kaddish[34] for me.

(BIEBOW *is silent.* RUMKOWSKI *takes a new tack.*)

Have you ever watched them work? Efficient. Obedient. They're no trouble. They do as they're told.

BIEBOW: It's Himmler, not me.

RUMKOWSKI *(in pleading tone):* Can't you come down a little? To seven, maybe?

BIEBOW: I'm sorry, I can't bargain this time. But I can assure you this will be the last deportation.

RUMKOWSKI: No. I gave and gave, but it stops with them.

BIEBOW: Why are you carrying on so? They'll receive excellent care.

RUMKOWSKI: You'll give them dancing lessons?

BIEBOW: I'm a father too, you know. Two lovely daughters. I do understand. And that counted for a great deal, believe me. Their original demand was for all those through age fifteen. That I flatly refused. They threatened me and I still said "no," and that's a word they don't like to hear. But knowing that what's needed now—above all—is rationality, I stood my ground until they finally gave in and set the mark at ten. Much more sensible, ten. We both know how unproductive those little ones are. What do they produce? Baby shit. *(Raises his voice as* RUMKOWSKI *tries to interrupt.)* I had to draw the line somewhere and ten was it. Only when I convinced them that it would be stupid to send away those who produce a high work yield, did they agree. So you see, I did make them back down on your behalf. I know it's hard but weigh it carefully.

RUMKOWSKI: Will you please leave now?

34. *Kaddish:* the Jewish prayer for the dead, said first at the graveside of the deceased, then for eleven months after death by the deceased's family, and afterward on each anniversary of the death.

BIEBOW: You'll do it. There's no turning back now.

RUMKOWSKI: Don't be so sure. Even a worm turns.

BIEBOW: The worm, maybe. But not you. You're too much like me. We make duty a disease.

RUMKOWSKI *(angrily):* Get out of my office.

BIEBOW *(with irony):* Now that you've given me permission. Tomorrow, it will all look different. After you've had time to think it over.

(BIEBOW *has gone.* RUMKOWSKI *slumps into chair and cries.)*

RUMKOWSKI: No. No.

(He looks up, rises and paces back and forth in the following dialogue with God. This is not a form of madness—but is part of a long tradition of Jews talking and arguing with Jehovah.) So what do I do now? *(Pauses.)* I can still remember what You said when You got in touch with me. "Stay on the job. Forget the questions. Step confidently into the dark. Be like Noah. Don't worry too much about numbers. Rescue two Jews and this world can be put together again" *(stops).* Now it's growing very dark and there's no ark to carry us to safety. There's only me. And if that's Your idea of a joke, forgive me if I can't laugh. *(Angrily.)* Tell me, why the children? And why with *my* hands? Did You make me "Father of the Orphans" to mock me now? When this is over, I will be one of Your most detested creatures. Do You really want a wretched me serving an indifferent You? *(Calmer.)* One thing I promise You. I won't kill myself like Czerniakow[35] in Warsaw. Very cheap. And easy. To wash his hands of the problem with some poison. Only the problem didn't remove itself. I never ran away or cared about my life or reputation. I wanted only to serve You. So I feel I must tell You this. Nobody will understand about the children. Nobody. And You'll be treated as harshly as myself in allowing

---

35. Czerniakow: Adam Czerniakow (b. 1880) was the head of the Warsaw *Judenrat* (Jewish Council) who served in circumstances nearly identical to those of Rumkowski in Lodz. He took poison on July 23, 1942, no longer able to endure the horrible condition of the Warsaw Jews and the moral dilemmas of his position.

this to happen. You must have had something in mind. But it's much too deep for me. *(Long pause.)* Now if You'll excuse me, I've got some big decisions to make. Who knows better than me that to be both God and Jewish is not easy.
(Lights down; the next scene has begun.)

Scene 6

The WOLF *home, September, 1942.* DAVID *and* MOSHE *read.* ADA *and* ROSA *and* ZOSIA *do household chores.* ISRAEL *is writing in his diary.* HANNAH *is sewing. Her hands tremble. The sewing falls to the floor.*

ADA: Pick it up.
   *(*HANNAH *does not move.* ZOSIA *picks it up from the floor and puts it in* HANNAH's *lap.)*
   I've never seen anything like her. A lawyer who won't speak.
ISRAEL: I wish she could give Rumkowski lessons.
ADA: The only thing she could teach him is how to act crazy.
ISRAEL: How about us who've adjusted to all this? She's just re-placed this world with another.
ADA *(ignores him):* Where's Gabriel? He didn't come home last night. I hope nothing happened.
ISRAEL: He makes bad things happen to others—not himself.
   *(*GABRIEL *enters. He sees his mother and waves a paper at her.)*
ADA: Where have you been? I was worried sick all night.
GABRIEL: A special assignment. A new deportation. *(They all stare at him.)* Grandpa is saved. He won't go. We made an agree-ment among ourselves. Rabinowitz has the amnesty for him. There's only one to a family. But that's all we need. *(Nods towards* HANNAH.*)* She brought it on herself. Her work is bad and she dealt with the black market.
ISRAEL: I never saw you refuse to eat the food her money bought.

GABRIEL: Do you think I enjoy doing this? My life has been a nightmare since I put on this uniform. But without it, you'd be deported.

ISRAEL: Dying is natural. Complicity is not.

ADA: Did you ever save anybody with all your fancy talk?

ISRAEL *(waving his diary)*: Let's hope this hangs some.

GABRIEL: Diaries are illegal. Strictly illegal.

ISRAEL: So arrest me.

GABRIEL *(embarrassed)*: I have to report in now.

(He exits. The following three speeches of RUMKOWSKI *take place as background to the action of the scene. When he talks, a single light is on him and the Wolf family is only partly seen.)*

RUMKOWSKI: Brothers and sisters! A terrible fate is about to befall us. Yesterday they gave me an order, an evil, despicable order. And today, the most terrible day of my life, I have come here to fill it. I must cut off some limbs in order to save the body. Is what I'm asking of you cruel and inhuman? Yes. Is it worthwhile? I can't be certain. All I can do is plead with you: give me your sick people. In their place will remain healthy ones. We don't have enough for all so I had to rule in favor of those who still have some strength. I beg you to help me, for now comes the worst of all. They demand from us the best that we have: the old people and the children.

(Lights down on him and up on the WOLF *family.)*

ROSA *(to* DAVID*)*: Show me your papers *(he hands them to her)*.

ZOSIA: There's nothing to worry about. He's twelve.

*(*MOSHE *fumbles in his pockets and hands his papers to* ROSA.*)*

ISRAEL: Rosa, what is it?

ROSA: He won't be ten until next month.

ISRAEL: We must not let them take him.

ADA: Shall we all be taken then?

ROSA: Gabriel will be back any minute now. Moshe, you'll go with me. David, you stay here.

ZOSIA *(to* DAVID*)*: You'll be all right.

ADA: You'll be arrested.

ROSA: Only if you tell them.

ADA: What shall I do if they ask me?

ROSA: Lie a little. It won't be that hard for you.

(ROSA and MOSHE exit.)

ADA: Rosa, come back! Come back! *(She runs out; DAVID hides.)*

ISRAEL: I was asked the other day by one of our few remaining scholars what was to be learnt from all of this. Nothing, I replied, but the obvious. *(Reads from diary.)* "Man must never allow himself to be put in such a situation." *(To ZOSIA.)* If for any reason, I'm unable to finish this, will you do it for me? *(Before she has a chance to reply, enter GABRIEL and RABINOWITZ with a list, followed by ADA.)*

RABINOWITZ: Two here, is that correct?

GABRIEL: Yes, sir.

RABINOWITZ: "Hannah Adler." Let's go. "Moshe Lewin." *(No one moves.)* Where is he?

(Lights down on WOLF family, up on RUMKOWSKI.)

RUMKOWSKI: I never had the good fortune to have children of my own. Perhaps that is why I have given the best years of my life to them. I never dreamed that my hands would have to give them up as victims. Now in my old age, I reach out to you and beg. Give me your children. I must have your children. If not, God save us, they'll take everybody.

(Lights up on WOLF family.)

ADA: Haven't they informed you that he's no longer part of this household? Yesterday . . .

RABINOWITZ: For this evacuation, he's listed with you. Isn't that so, Gabriel?

GABRIEL: He's right, Mama.

ADA: But you weren't home yesterday, how can you say he's right?

RABINOWITZ: I could take the old man in his place.

ISRAEL: I'll go gladly so I don't have to see abominations like you any longer. He's a reproach to creation. *(Looks up.)* I want You to understand I'm not criticizing, just reporting.

GABRIEL: He's been out of his mind for months.

RABINOWITZ: Since he's such a nuisance, it might be best for everyone if . . .

ADA: My father wants and needs to be with me and his family.

RABINOWITZ: They recognize no such need.

ADA: Rabinowitz, I'm talking to you, not them. You lay one finger
on him and I'll go right to the top. The Chairman and I are
more than just good friends, understand?

RABINOWITZ: Oh, I know the kind of pull you have with our
"Chaim Try-'Em." Tell me, can the old bastard still make it
stand? Haven't you learned yet his position is a joke? He can't
even wipe his ass without their permission. He couldn't save
his own life if it came to that. (ADA *goes to* RABINOWITZ *and
kisses him.*) I appreciate your offer. But that wouldn't provide
the kind of body I'm looking for. (*Laughs. Fondles* ZOSIA's
hair.) I want to convince you I'm reasonable, so here's the amnesty for the old man. But I must have the boy. It's not like I'm
asking for your son. Blood should always come first (*gives* ADA
amnesty).

ZOSIA: He begs in the street all day and brings home whatever
people give him for all of us to share. If that isn't family, what
is?

RABINOWITZ: Call him cousin if you like, but he's no flesh of your
flesh.

ISRAEL: My daughter does not betray children.

ADA: It's for you, Papa.

ISRAEL: Such favors I don't accept.

RABINOWITZ (*sees* DAVID): Ah, I've been looking all over for the
boy and he's right under my nose.

DAVID (*fearfully*): I'm not Moshe. My name is David Abramovitz.
I'm twelve years old and I've got a job (*takes papers from
pocket and hands them to* RABINOWITZ). Here are my papers.

RABINOWITZ (*scans papers*): It says here you're nine.

ZOSIA: What?

DAVID: Look how tall I am. I couldn't be nine.

RABINOWITZ (*to* GABRIEL): He'll do.

DAVID (*yelling*): My name is David. David. You can't take my name away from me. I was one of Mr. Rumkowski's favorite orphans. Ask him, please!

ZOSIA: He works in our shop and never misses a day. Biebow himself commended him while going through the factory.

RABINOWITZ: It's not personal. It's bookkeeping. *(To* GABRIEL.*)* Hold him so he can't get away.

DAVID *(stuttering his words):* Moshe just left here a few minutes before you came.

RABINOWITZ: You're not so dumb. Save your own skin. Where is he?

ADA *(to* RABINOWITZ*):* Don't listen to him. He never tells the truth.

DAVID: Don't I have as much right to live as Moshe? I watch you people make deals every day. What's wrong with me doing it?

ISRAEL: Because in doing it this way, we become animals like them.

DAVID: So why don't *you* die?

(Silence.)

ISRAEL *(to* ADA*):* The amnesty, give it to David. I'm going in his place.

RABINOWITZ: It's for you alone. You can't give it away.

DAVID: Mr. Rabinowitz, give me my papers back and my own amnesty. Otherwise why should I tell you anything?

RABINOWITZ *(grabbing* DAVID *by the throat):* Are you trying to make a deal with me, Jew? *(*DAVID *nods.)* You're a smart boy. I'll have use for someone like you. *(*RABINOWITZ *scribbles a note on a paper and gives it to* DAVID.*)* Now, where is he?

DAVID: I can't tell the spot exactly, they never mentioned it to me.

RABINOWITZ: That tells me nothing. I could spend days tracking him down.

DAVID: You'll have no trouble finding him. *(Pauses.)* He went with . . . Rosa.

ADA *(slaps him across face):* Fine thanks I get from you. I take you off the streets, feed you, give you a home, and you dare to tell lies about my daughter. Get out of this house right now. And I never want to see your rotten face ever again.

RABINOWITZ: All right, you two. Let's go.

DAVID: But you just gave me my amnesty.

RABINOWITZ: Did I? Read it!

DAVID *(reads):* "This boy goes with us." You tricked me you bastard. *(Screams:)* Moshe! Moshe!

(He pushes GABRIEL *and they fall to the floor. He pounds on* GABRIEL *hysterically.* RABINOWITZ *kicks him.* ISRAEL *pushes* RABINOWITZ *away as* HANNAH *screams.)*

HANNAH: Stop!

(Lights down on WOLF *family, up on* RUMKOWSKI.)*

RUMKOWSKI: I know what it feels like to see your child dragged away. But what is better? To permit 80,000 Jews to remain or for all of us to be destroyed? I did everything and will continue to do all in my power to never let them bloody our streets. I know that one must have the heart of a bandit to demand what I ask of you, but put yourself in my position. Put yourself in my position. Put yourself in my position.

(Lights down on RUMKOWSKI; *up on* WOLF *family.)*

DAVID: I don't want to go. Help me someone, please.

ISRAEL *(to* DAVID*):* You and I will make fine traveling companions. When I ache you'll rub my back and tickle my bones. And when you're sad I'll tell you jokes that would make a stone laugh. And stories to stuff your head. I've enough to last us through all of Europe. A fine bargain is it not?

(All through ISRAEL's *speech we hear* ADA.*)*

ADA: Papa . . . Don't go . . . Papa . . . Papa . . .

*(*RABINOWITZ *motions to* GABRIEL *to take* DAVID. *He takes* HANNAH *and exits.* ISRAEL *stares* GABRIEL *down as he approaches, puts his arm around the boy and begins to tell story.)*

ISRAEL: Once upon a time there was a . . .

*(*GABRIEL *follows them out.* ADA *stands motionless. We hear trucks drive away.* ZOSIA *picks up the diary and begins to write in it. Lights out.)*

Scene 7

Lights up on YANKELE. *He speaks to the audience:*

It is July, 1944
And even our flies
Aren't around any longer
They're afraid they might be mistaken
For chickens and get eaten.
Ninety-five percent of our people are working
And one hundred percent are weakening
The Russians are seventy miles away and holding fast
The Allies are crossing the Channel at last
They bomb everything but the tracks to our doom
While we try to forget how to hope in our tomb.

     "The Riddle Song"

A riddle without a middle
Is a question that's lost its mind
Here's one with which you can fiddle
A knot at the edge of the wind.

I ask you: why are a blind man
And our Allies alike as two peas?
The man without eyes sees no one
And their armies none of us sees . . .

Maybe they think we're like the sun
That will set without any assistance
We're the one thing about which the world agrees:
To look on our fate with indifference.

(Lights down; the next scene has begun.)

Scene 8

RUMKOWSKI's *office, July, 1944.* RUMKOWSKI *with a full-length white cape and a cane is seated. In the distance we hear the steady sounds of artillery.* GABRIEL *is setting up his camera. He hands* RUMKOWSKI *a photograph.*

GABRIEL: Here's the one I took yesterday.

RUMKOWSKI *(looks at it):* My hair, it isn't white enough. And it isn't flowing. How many times already have I told you? *(Makes waves with hands.)* And what kind of background is that? It's too dark. It has no refinement. This is for my special postage stamp, not my funeral. It should be light and airy to inspire confidence. If you got a letter with that on it would it make you feel happy?

*(*RABINOWITZ *enters pushing* MIRIAM *before him. She's disheveled and her face is streaked with dirt.* RUMKOWSKI *turns to* GABRIEL.*)*

Come back tomorrow and make sure to bring your talent with you. *(*GABRIEL *takes stand and camera and exits. To* RABINOWITZ:*)* Where did you find her?

RABINOWITZ: Don't you recognize the uniform? You ordered them. Or have you forgotten that, too?

RUMKOWSKI: Who gave you the right to talk to me like this? You think I'm finished, on the way out, bankrupt, don't you? Who told you that nonsense? Biebow? While you were licking his boots? All your scheming for my job will come to nothing, because you are a nothing, interested only in graft, women and saving your own neck.

RABINOWITZ: Oh, I know I'm not blessed with your ideals or your righteous mission. That used to go over big before. Now, everybody's tired of your endless talking to God.

RUMKOWSKI: Who I do business with is nobody's concern but mine.

RABINOWITZ: Stop acting like the Messiah.

RUMKOWSKI: So let me return the advice. Since Biebow didn't do the hiring, he hasn't the authority to dismiss me. If I go, you

A photograph of an actual postage stamp from the Lodz ghetto showing Rumkowski's likeness provides the background for this scene from the 1978 production of *Throne of Straw* at the University of Wisconsin-Madison. Reproduction of the postage stamp in the photograph courtesy of B. M. Ansbacher Collection, Jerusalem, Israel.

go too. I've been told that by one of *his* bosses. Would you like to put it to a test? *(RABINOWITZ is silent.)* Good, now we can get back to her. Where was she?

RABINOWITZ: With the women who haul the crap from the ghetto. She seems to like the work.

RUMKOWSKI: I wonder why?

MIRIAM: The smell reminds me of you.

RABINOWITZ: She still has her wits about her. I'll say that.

RUMKOWSKI *(to RABINOWITZ):* I didn't ask about wit from a shit like you.

RABINOWITZ: Those women are the only ones permitted past the wire. If you wanted to send a message out, say to your Polish comrades, wouldn't they be ideal for the purpose?

RUMKOWSKI: What kind of message?

RABINOWITZ: They keep begging for guns and knives. Isn't that so, my *meshugene*[36] Miriam?

RUMKOWSKI: Rabinowitz, she's still my wife, so only I can talk to her that way.

MIRIAM: We'll settle for hammers or crowbars.

RABINOWITZ: She and that Rosa Wolf and her group were planning a strike.

RUMKOWSKI *(to RABINOWITZ):* What did you do—sit there and listen?

RABINOWITZ: We got her, didn't we?

RUMKOWSKI: And the rest?

RABINOWITZ: They managed to slip away *(laughs).* But they won't get very far.

RUMKOWSKI *(to MIRIAM):* This time I think you're really crazy. Don't you hear what I hear? We've come through. Can't you get that into your head?

MIRIAM: The Russians seem content to wait, God knows what for, even though they could march into this city with practically no opposition. And yet they wait. A strike will encourage them to attack.

---

36. *Meshugene:* Yiddish word for "crazy."

RUMKOWSKI: I know already what you want. To make this another total wreck like Warsaw.[37]

RABINOWITZ: They were big heroes and even managed to kill a few Germans. So how many are left?

MIRIAM: None. They died fighting or were deported.

RABINOWITZ *(laughs):* And that's your idea of a victory?

MIRIAM: The Nazis are afraid we might do the same thing here. They must not count on our servility any longer.

RUMKOWSKI: All the more reason we don't throw ourselves away now. If they're as hard pressed as you say, will they waste their time on us?

MIRIAM: They care only about our extermination now that they know they've lost this war. The Polish underground has informed us that Eichmann has prepared a hundred trains to deport us all in the next two weeks.

RABINOWITZ: Who takes anything Poles have to say seriously?

MIRIAM: I saw them myself at the railroad yard.

RUMKOWSKI: The Russians will be here long before your imaginary trains.

MIRIAM: Your factories supplied the Nazis. The Bolsheviks hang collaborators on the spot.

RUMKOWSKI *(stung by the accusation):* Are you telling me that for saving 70,000 Jews I'm to be judged guilty? I'll go willingly, with pleasure, before any court of Jews here or in the next world and state my case. And if they dare to put me on trial, they'll have to try God too. *(Looks up.)* If you ask Him, He'll tell you that we had an agreement and that I kept my part of the bargain.

MIRIAM *(solicitously):* You and I know that He would not want us to go voluntarily. Honor Him by ordering our people not to appear at the railway station, no matter what promises are made.

RUMKOWSKI: And to appear instead before their firing squads?

---

37. Warsaw: Rumkowski refers to the brutal suppression of the Jewish uprising in the Warsaw ghetto in April 19–May 16, 1943.

MIRIAM: Even they dare not do it now for all the world to see.

RUMKOWSKI: If the world hasn't choked on our blood up to now, it never will. *(Turns to* RABINOWITZ.*)* I want this provocation stopped. Can you do it or shall I call in someone tougher?

RABINOWITZ: I do my job now, in spite of you. *(Exits.)*

MIRIAM: Chaim, there are no guns, so we can't fight that way. All that's left is our refusal. Whatever they ask for we can stall, we can hide, we can strike, we can say no.

RUMKOWSKI: First ask yourself where are the other ghettos? Why is it that only mine survives? Because I understood that when the end is good, everything is good. I won't deny that I had to do terrible things. To give away my poor pigeons. But for every hundred I saved a hundred. I stood as a watchman before the door of death and snatched them from the furnace one by one. *And I am not ashamed.*

MIRIAM *(pause):* I wonder what I ever saw in you.

RUMKOWSKI: You wanted to be the shadow behind my throne. *(Mocks her.)* "A colleague, that's what I want to be." *(Forcefully.)* Leaders take shit, slaves carry it.

(She takes dab of excrement from her boot and smears it over his face.)

You bitch *(starts to wipe it from his face).*

MIRIAM: Now, will you send me . . .

(Lights down; the next scene has begun.)

Scene 9

The Street. RABINOWITZ *is saluting* BIEBOW. *Artillery continues under the scene.*

BIEBOW: Have my orders been carried out?

RABINOWITZ: I was unable . . .

BIEBOW *(nastily):* Are we about to lose to you Jews, too?

RABINOWITZ: I told Rumkowski they were going to strike but he did nothing to stop them.

BIEBOW: But that's *your* job, isn't it?

RABINOWITZ: I tried to get them to listen, but they booed and jeered me.

BIEBOW: In some matters they still show good taste. You fool. They smell the vodka on the other side of the river.

RABINOWITZ: There are all kinds of rumors about where you plan to send them.

BIEBOW: You must have started them.

RABINOWITZ: Not me. But I wouldn't put it past the old man. I hope you realize he's not reliable any more.

BIEBOW: What would a swine like you know about reliability? He's impatiently waiting for salvation. That's something that would never trouble your soul, Mr. Radnitski.

RABINOWITZ: He wants to die, is that it? Now that he's failed.

BIEBOW: The strikers seem anxious to make him a success. What a triumph would be his if the Bolsheviks showed up here tomorrow.

RABINOWITZ: Is there any chance of that?

BIEBOW: I haven't asked them. But I don't think they're in a great hurry to save your skins. *(In official tone.)* You are to arrange a meeting at which I and the Eldest will speak. And see to it that there's lots of bread on hand. Now go. I still need you, and the longer I see your ugly face the less convinced I become about your usefulness.

(RABINOWITZ *exits. Lights down quickly; lights up on* ZOSIA.)

Scene 10

ZOSIA *(reading from diary):* "July 15, 1944. Many of the workers, tired of the twelve-hour day and the constant lowering of rations, are not only going on strike and staying in their

shops, but are trying to stop all production. A few are even
setting fire to the factories. Rumkowski has issued a decree
that these 'elements' are creating havoc in the ghetto. Long live
havoc!"
(Lights down on ZOSIA.*)*

Scene 11

Lights up on BIEBOW *and* RUMKOWSKI. *They are preparing to
speak to a crowd which can be heard during this scene.*

BIEBOW: Your people are growing very naughty.

RUMKOWSKI: Before there was no Red Army pounding on your
head.

BIEBOW: Lovers of Jews they're not.

RUMKOWSKI: But haters of Nazis they are.

BIEBOW: So you think they'll come to your rescue?

RUMKOWSKI: Your generals must think so. Otherwise why have
they pulled out most of your soldiers. We're both finished, you
know.

(Crowd noise grows in volume.)

BIEBOW: They're growing restless. Speak to them now.

RUMKOWSKI *(begins, nervously)*: This ghetto like your Chairman is
now finished. You may well ask, was it worth the sacrifice? Let
others more distant answer that. For us who lived through it
know an extra hour was also life. It was only with the Almighty's assistance that I was able to bring you this far. So
don't blame Him, or yourselves. If it makes you feel better,
curse me. Only remember: nothing is over until it's over. The
sun does not shine on us yet . . . but it will! A bright *red* sun!

BIEBOW *(interrupting)*: My Jews. Give up this foolish strike.

(Voices are heard: "No," "We'd rather starve here," "You'll

have to give up when the Russians arrive." BIEBOW *ignores the heckling.)*
Germany is now struggling for her life. Therefore it is necessary that you replace the workers in our German factories so
that they can go off to fight. I know what good workers you've
been for us. But so do the Russians *(some cheering in the crowd)*. But do not worry. I will protect you from them *(voice:* "Who'll protect you from them?"*).*

ROSA *(comes forward and speaks):* Let the trains remain empty.
Stay in your shops. We'll see to it that you have food. The
Nazis are afraid of *us* now! And if they dare shoot us down,
let it be here and not at the end of a railroad trip to one of
their camps. What matters is that we do not go willingly. It
will matter to every Jewish boy and girl . . . (RABINOWITZ
drags her away).

BIEBOW *(as if nothing has taken place):* So my Jews, report to the
station tomorrow. Food is already on the trains. And I ordered
what I know you like. Herring, both kinds. Boiled potatoes.
Even chicken. Your future is now my main responsibility. I
promise not a single hair on your head will be harmed. And
please bring along your pots and pans. Now to show my gratitude in advance, a loaf of bread will be given to each of you.
*(Lights go down quickly. Long moment of silence. We hear
noises of trains backing and filling. Lights up, very bright. The
next scene has begun.)*

Scene 12

August, 1944. The Lodz railroad station. ADA *and* ZOSIA *enter each
carrying a heavy suitcase. An open boxcar awaits.* ZOSIA *looks
around and speaks to* ADA.

ZOSIA: Look, up there. The air, it's so clear. All I ever remember is a sky filled with soot and smoke. Now the chimneys are all at rest. They received a most proper burial. *(Pauses.)* Will we, Mama?

ADA *(ignoring her question):* When did you get home last night?

ZOSIA: Late. Almost not at all.

ADA: That's not an answer, Zosia.

ZOSIA: How did *you* sleep the last night, last night?

ADA: How could I sleep not knowing where you were?

ZOSIA: Or what I might be doing?

ADA: What kind of talk is that?

ZOSIA: I stayed up all night, and not by myself either.

ADA: Were you with a boy?

ZOSIA: You could call him that.

ADA: What were you doing?

ZOSIA: What you do with the Chairman.

ADA: That was different. It was for all of you.

ZOSIA: I made a wish, to have this one time, your experience.

(ADA *raises hand, stops and lowers it.*)

I was trying to catch up with life. To make up in a few hours for all the empty nights before, and to come. And of all the boys, guess whom I had to choose? A beginner, just like me. We didn't even know how to start. He didn't want to. It was I who insisted. *(Singing the following line like a nursery rhyme:)* "Eden, Schmeden, Zosia had no feeling." None. The more we tried, the worse it got. He wanted to give up, but I wouldn't let him. I finally made it happen and when it was all over we looked at each other and cried. There was nothing. It was like exercise. Is that all there is to it?

ADA: Maybe nothing now. But it wasn't always so.

ZOSIA: Where did it all go?

ADA: Sometimes you hide something and you forget where or what it was. You forget. You make yourself forget. Sometimes when you remember too much, you want to give up living. It wasn't you. I know the sickness. But it will pass. We've been through the hardest part already.

ZOSIA: Do you really believe that? These trains, they go one way.

Do you want to know where?
(In the distance we hear artillery.)
ADA: Rosa's cossacks will be here soon.
ZOSIA: There is nothing that can save us now.
ADA: It's only a train, my darling. It will take us there, and before we know it, turn around and take us back. The Germans are finished, kaput. Soon Lodz will be ours again. Gabriel is already hard at work for our homecoming. He promised me that he'll put together a nice place for us. And mark my words, it will be just like before.
ZOSIA: Nothing will ever be like before.
(BIEBOW *enters followed by* RUMKOWSKI. RABINOWITZ *enters pushing* YANKELE *ahead of him.* YANKELE *sees* RUMKOWSKI *and goes to him.)*
YANKELE: Court Jew, Council Jew, shall I tell why you didn't pull us through this time? Your hand was always open, so how could you make a fist? *(Shrugging his shoulders.)* But, even if you had, could a fist have saved us from them? *(Points to* BIEBOW.*)* Tell me Mr. Nazi, which is worse, hell or the trains that take you there?
(RABINOWITZ *punches* YANKELE *in the back.* YANKELE *curses at him.)*
May all the evil dreams that live in his head *(points to* BIEBOW*)* stay with you forever.
BIEBOW *(to* YANKELE*):* My bad dreams deserve someone better than him. *(Derisively.)* How about the Chairman?
YANKELE: No. You can't have him. He is still ours and always will be. The only thing of his you can have is the throne. And may you crash on it soon, in good health.
RABINOWITZ *(to* BIEBOW*):* May I put him on the train now, sir?
BIEBOW *(looking first at* YANKELE *then at* RABINOWITZ*):* No. I've decided to spare him.
RABINOWITZ: Why him?
BIEBOW: For the same reason I'm saving you. For a while at least, you two will represent the remnant. *(To* RUMKOWSKI.*)* That

was your aim Chaim, wasn't it? *(RUMKOWSKI is silent.)* The finest examples of natural selection. *My* selection. *(To YANKELE.)* Now you, get out of here. *(YANKELE exits. To RABINOWITZ.)* And you. Come with me.

(RABINOWITZ and BIEBOW exit. We hear the sound of railroad cars. Enter ROSA and MOSHE who carries a rolled-up blanket, followed by GABRIEL.)

ADA: Thank God you're here. *(Tries to embrace ROSA, who turns away.)*

ROSA: God had nothing to do with it. Gabriel deserves the credit. And what's left over I leave to you and Rumkowski. *(ADA goes to MOSHE. ROSA drags him away.)* Don't touch him.

MOSHE: Please Rosa, you promised. She did take me from the orphanage. *(ROSA releases him. He goes to ADA and kisses her.)* Where's David? Nobody seems to know.

ADA *(hesitates):* He was at our house yesterday and he talked of nothing but you.

MOSHE: I miss him a lot. But I don't think we'll ever see each other again. *(He stares at ADA. She goes to GABRIEL and they whisper together.)*

ZOSIA: I hoped they wouldn't find you.

ROSA: Did you hide the diary?

ZOSIA: Yes. But it will be harder to understand than to find. My final entry was a page of questions.

ROSA *(a trace of bitterness):* I also have so many . . . The workers go on strike and then for some lousy bread . . . *(her voice trails off)*.

ZOSIA *(plaintively):* Why did we all show up here like this?

ROSA *(gently):* Don't be too harsh on yourself, or us.

ZOSIA: Why not?

ROSA *(kissing her forehead):* Because everyone else will be.

ZOSIA: I'm not like you, Rosa. I'm afraid. Make me a promise. Don't let them strip me. I couldn't stand . . . *(ROSA puts arms around her)*.

ROSA: My dear, sweet sister. You and I are beyond shame. So we will dance there. *(Takes* ZOSIA's *hand and as they approach* RUMKOWSKI *she starts to dance around him.* ZOSIA *follows her.)* Mr. Chairman, am I dressed properly for the trip?

ZOSIA: Did you choose the trains personally?

ROSA: Will we drink as much beer as we want?

ZOSIA: And dance the waltz all night long?

RUMKOWSKI: Perhaps.

ROSA: Liar!

ZOSIA: Liar!

(BIEBOW *enters with* RABINOWITZ *who is prodding a reluctant* MIRIAM. BIEBOW *motions for* RABINOWITZ *to begin calling the names.)*

RABINOWITZ: "Ada Wolf." "Rosa Wolf." "Zosia Wolf."

ADA *(to* GABRIEL*)*: Goodbye, Gabriel. Take good care of yourself and be sure to write. *(She enters train.)*

ZOSIA: Come, sister. *(She and* ROSA *enter train.)*

RABINOWITZ: "Gabriel Wolf."

GABRIEL *(to* BIEBOW*)*: There must be some mistake. I was given a promise *(points to* RUMKOWSKI*)*. He gave me his word that I'd be one of the kosher ones assigned to clean up the ghetto.

BIEBOW: Don't you enjoy the company of your family?

GABRIEL: I just arrested my own sister.

BIEBOW *(removing club from* GABRIEL's *side and throwing it towards* RABINOWITZ*)*: A good policeman does his duty, nevertheless.

GABRIEL *(throws his cap at* RUMKOWSKI's *feet)*: But I don't think a good Jew would. *(He exits into train.)*

BIEBOW *(to* RUMKOWSKI*)*: You have all been good Jews, Chaim. Good Jews.

RABINOWITZ *(calls out)*: "Miriam Rumkowski."

MIRIAM: And the *former* Chairman, will he wait here like some homeless dog?

RUMKOWSKI: I made a sacred promise that as long as one Jew needed my guidance, I'd be here. Just one, any one *(he motions* MOSHE *to stand beside him)*. One. *(MIRIAM *exits into train.)*

RABINOWITZ *(calls out)*: "Moshe Lewin."

(When his name is called MOSHE *puts arms around* RUMKOWSKI. *As* RABINOWITZ *goes to get him,* RUMKOWSKI *is moved to violence to save* MOSHE. *He tries to beat* RABINOWITZ *with his cane.* BIEBOW *takes it from him and* RABINOWITZ *grabs* MOSHE.)*

MOSHE: Save me, Mr. Rumkowski! Save me!

RUMKOWSKI *(to* BIEBOW)*: I promised Him one Jew to carry on. Let it be the boy, please.

BIEBOW: It's out of the question.

RUMKOWSKI: But why, Biebow, why?

BIEBOW: Germany has no future. Why should you Jews? *(Hands cane back to* RUMKOWSKI.)* You can go with him if you want.

*(*RUMKOWSKI *holds out his hand for* MOSHE *to accompany him.* MOSHE *starts to take it, then enters boxcar by himself.* RUMKOWSKI *gathers himself together and follows him.* RABINOWITZ *slams the boxcar door shut.* BIEBOW *and* RABINOWITZ *are left alone on stage.* RABINOWITZ *picks up the blanket* MOSHE *has dropped, searches in it and finds the bread it conceals. He pockets it.* BIEBOW *notices but does nothing. They exit. We hear the sound of the train beginning its journey, first the mournful bell and sharp whistle and then the sound of the train pulling away.)*

(The stage is dark for a brief moment as YANKELE *enters. A spotlight picks him up. He peers out into the audience and speaks.)*

YANKELE:

You're curious
I see it in your faces
You want to know what happened to him?
Well, as always with us, there are two possibilities.
A certain Mr. Levy swears he saw Rumkowski
Alongside the Commandant at Auschwitz
Reviewing the long lines of new arrivals and then taking his place at the end of the line.
However a kapo who worked the gas chambers

And wants his name withheld
Says that he was pushed in first
And that the reason he's so certain
Is that Miriam was smiling, and that was highly unusual.
When the Russians finally arrived in Lodz
There were 801 Jews left. I am the one.
And why am I still here?
Because you are all still here.

(House lights come up.)
I've given up being whatever I was
Because I'm an impresario now
I take this passion play from place to place
And please while it's with you
Don't feed me your dinner table morals about how
They should have behaved;
Only say what you would have done.

(Turns to leave.)
A final question until I return:
Since shrouds have no pockets
And ashes no permanent home
Where will you keep them?

(He exits.)

THE END

George Tabori

THE CANNIBALS

Being the extraordinary tale of a dinner party as told by the sons
of those who attended the feast and the two survivors by whose
courtesy the facts are known.

In memory of Cornelius Tabori,
perished in Auschwitz,
a small eater.

CAST OF CHARACTERS
In Order of Appearance

THE LOUDSPEAKERS.

HEALTAI, a survivor.

HIRSCHLER, a survivor.

PUFFI, a fat man.

KLAUB, a medical student.

GHOULOS.

THE GYPSY.

UNCLE.

THE RAMASEDER KID.

WEISS, the cook.

LITTLE LANG.

PROFESSOR GLATZ.

THE SILENT HAAS.

S.S. SCHREKINGER, The Angel of Death.

KAPO.

Setting

A white room. A long table with benches. A three-tiered bunk.
An old-fashioned stove. A pisspot. A door. Against the back wall,
a mountain of clothes, shoes, hair, teeth.

THE CANNIBALS

SCENE 1

The Survivors

The room is empty. Over THE LOUDSPEAKERS *dying voices call for their favorite dishes. The guests enter and climb up the mountain to pick out pieces of clothing that might have belonged to their fathers or uncles. Soon they look like inmates of a death camp, except for* HELTAI *and* HIRSCHLER *who wear identical business suits. They all put on a little gray make-up and practice the "Auschwitz Trot." A ram's horn is heard.[1] They freeze and look out front, dribbling.*
   A silence.

HELTAI: I was at Howard Johnson's today.
HIRSCHLER: Which one?
HELTAI: On the Turnpike.
HIRSCHLER *(eagerly):* Yeh, but which one?
HELTAI: Near Exit 8-A.
HIRSCHLER: Oh yeh?
HELTAI: I love Howard Johnson's. Don't laugh, but I love Howard
   Johnson's.
HIRSCHLER *(laughing):* I wasn't laughing.
HELTAI: It's so cheerful, so simple.
HIRSCHLER: What did you have?
HELTAI: I always have a banana split at Howard Johnson's.

1. Ram's horn: in Jewish history, the ram's horn or *shofar* was blown as a warning, a call to battle, and, as today, on Yom Kippur to announce the ending of the old year and the beginning of the new.

HIRSCHLER: Anything to start with? A club sandwich? A cheese-
burger? *(Screams:)* Breaded veal cutlet?

HELTAI: Gotta watch my weight.

(They laugh, patting their stomachs.)

HIRSCHLER: So why did you have a banana split?

HELTAI: I can't help myself. Whenever I pass Howard Johnson's,
I've got to stop in for a banana split. I slide up to the counter,
I loosen my tie, I put the knife aside.

HIRSCHLER: Naturally you put the knife aside.

HELTAI: What's so natural about it?

HIRSCHLER: Did you ever try to eat a banana split with a knife?

HELTAI: That's not why I put the knife aside.

(A pause.)

HIRSCHLER: Personally, when I drop in at Howard Johnson's, I take
a strawberry shortcake.

HELTAI: There's no arguing about taste.

HIRSCHLER: After my first stroke I couldn't speak for awhile.
(Rises, bows to the audience; his mouth paralyzed.) There
were twelve of us left in Block Six after Christmas. Two of us
survived. Heltai makes toys. I'm a gynecologist in Yonkers.
Doing well, two cars, a fancy barbecue in the backyard.

SCENE 2

Puffi's Death

A camp bell is heard. They all trot to the bunk, jogging like stiff-limbed puppets, and go to sleep. A cock crows.

PUFFI *sits up, climbs off the bunk, and tiptoes to a corner. He sits down. He looks around. He takes a piece of bread from under his armpit. He feels it, he smells it, he kisses it. The cock crows again. He breaks off a piece and starts chewing. The bread is hard. He can't help making a sound.*

PUFFI: Crunch. *(The others sit up one by one.)* Crunch. *(The others listen incredulously.)*

KLAUB: Somebody is eating!

(KLAUB, GHOULOS, and THE GYPSY begin to hunt for the one who eats. They stop, they look, they listen. They force HAAS' mouth open to see if there are crumbs inside.)

PUFFI: C-r-r-runch. *(They turn. They watch him. They dribble like dogs.* LANG *faints.)* Crunch. *(He becomes aware of them. He tries to get out of the room.)*

KLAUB: Get him!

(They pounce on PUFFI. Only UNCLE stays out of the fight. PUFFI lets out a squeak.)

UNCLE: Children, this is no way to behave.

(The fighting stops. They flop down, exhausted. PUFFI *lies still, his clothes torn. His flesh looks pink.)*

Surely, these exertions are futile. What have you gained? Let me see!

(KLAUB shows him a morsel of bread. The others eat, grunting and giggling.)

Was that worth it? Aren't you ashamed? May I have a small piece?

(The others look up, surprised.)

It's just that I'm curious what bread tastes like.

(KLAUB *gives him a tiny piece.*)

(*Eating.*) What kind of bread d'you think it is, corn or rye?

KLAUB: Rye.

UNCLE: I think I'm tasting a caraway seed.

KLAUB: You think right.

UNCLE: Let's face it, it's magnificent. Give some to Puffi, too.

THE KID: He's dead.

(GHOULOS *pushes* PUFFI. *He rolls downstage.*)

UNCLE: See what you've done? You animals! (*To the audience.*) He was shaking with indignation. (*To the others.*) Pigs don't endure, dogs don't endure, and the flies are dropping in their tracks.

THE OTHERS (*looking for a fly*): Bzzzzz. Bzzzzz.

UNCLE: Only man endures. Excuse me while I relieve myself.

THE OTHERS: Bzzzz.

UNCLE (*at the pisspot*): There is no way of enduring except through courtesy, by saying even to the guards, "After you, sir." But if, God forbid, you ever become like them, that is the time to hang yourselves. There isn't by any chance another small piece left?

KLAUB: No.

UNCLE: Slow start this morning. (*To God.*) Not yet?—If ever.— Ramaseder, when was the last time I pissed?

THE KID: Monday.

UNCLE: How time flies!—Will someone please whistle?

(*They whistle.*)

Better luck tomorrow.

THE GYPSY (*pisses loud and strong*): Hope springs eternal.

(*He is applauded.*)

THE OTHERS: Bzzzz.

(UNCLE *catches the fly.*)

THE KID: May I have it, Uncle?

UNCLE: Go catch your own goddam fly!

THE OTHERS (*shocked*): Bzzz?

UNCLE: Wait, sorry, come back, boy. Ramaseder, I'm disappointed in you. I know you're only twelve, but that's no excuse. You keep breaking the rules. The other night I watched you at suppertime—when was the last official supper, a month ago?—and when you saw the food-fetchers cross the compound with the great pot, you wormed your way to the head of the chow-line. You know damn well it's better to lag behind, the best of the soup is on the bottom of the pot. Will you never learn? Open your mouth.

(THE KID *swallows the fly.*)

THE OTHERS: Bzzzzzz!

SCENE 3

The Funeral

UNCLE (*over* PUFFI's *body, a blanket around his shoulders, chanting a kaddish[2]*): Here cracks a noble heart, with some assistance from his friends. Puffi Pinkus, rest in peace. He was the second fattest man in Europe, a glandular freak, no mean achievement. The guards liked to take pictures of him, to prove to posterity how well they fed us Jewdogs. He loved his children and prospered by raising geese, and exporting their liver all over the civilized world, *sic transit gloria mundi.*

THE GYPSY: Never mind, speak to me about goose liver.

WEISS: Did he export it as such, as liver I mean, or in the form of paté?

(A silence.)

PUFFI (*coming back to life for a moment*): As liver.

THE GYPSY: Some rich bastard is eating it now with hot buttered toast.

LANG: Oh God!

UNCLE: Let his epitaph read: "He fed his fellowmen."

THE OTHERS: Amen.

UNCLE (*covers* PUFFI *with the blanket*): Take him outside and bury him among the dandelions.

KLAUB: Just a minute. (*He pulls the blanket off.* WEISS *feels* PUFFI's *belly expertly.* HAAS *makes a croaking sound.* LANG *collapses.* GLATZ *starts out.*) Sit down.

GLATZ: Yes, sir.

(They all look at PUFFI. WEISS *starts undressing him.*)

KLAUB (*steps forward, bows to the audience*): As a medical student he told them they needn't worry about any untoward effects— gastritis—constipation—toxic indigestion—and provided he was properly broiled or boiled or even fried—and properly

2. *Kaddish:* the Jewish prayer for the dead.

masticated—that goes without saying—each bite should be chewed—ideally speaking—six or seven times—the effect ought to be both pleasant and nourishing. After all, the difference is—negligible.

SCENE 4

The Knife

UNCLE: What are you doing, may I ask?

KLAUB: Making a fire.

GHOULOS: It's cold in here.

KLAUB: The stove's gone out.

UNCLE: The stove's been out for weeks.

THE GYPSY: Yes, but it started to snow last night.

UNCLE: Where did you get that firewood?

THE GYPSY: Found it.

LANG: Broke it off Bunk 21.

    (THE GYPSY hits LANG.)

UNCLE: Have you gone mad? Where will the kid sleep?

GHOULOS: There are plenty of unoccupied bunks.

UNCLE: That was his bunk, that was the only thing that was his!

KLAUB: He can have Altschul's bunk, which is out of the draft.

UNCLE: Altschul will be back from the hospital any day.

KLAUB: No, he won't be back.

    (GHOULOS crosses himself.)

THE GYPSY *(pointing at God):* He thinks of everything.

GHOULOS: Uncle, look, the fire is going.

LANG: A little turnip, with my compliments.

WEISS *(an apron round his waist):* I have the salt.

UNCLE: Where did you get that ridiculous costume?

WEISS: Puffi's shirt, d'you mind?

UNCLE: Couldn't you wait till his grave was dug?

KLAUB: He won't need a grave.

    (A silence. HAAS returns from outside with the pot.)

GHOULOS: The pot has been washed and filled with snow.

UNCLE *(knocks the pot off the stove):* I forbid you to proceed. May
    I rot in hell if you proceed!

KLAUB *(to HAAS):* Put it back on the stove.

UNCLE *(steps into the pot):* You shall be cursed in the city, and cursed in the field, cursed in your basket and cursed in the fruit of your body, cursed when you come in and cursed when you go out!

WEISS *(interrupting):* Excuse me, where is the knife?

UNCLE: What knife?

KLAUB: We entrusted you with the knife as a sign of our confidence the day the Gypsy tried to kill the Greek.

THE GYPSY: It's the only knife in the hut.

UNCLE *(sits on the edge of the pot):* Never heard of it.

KLAUB: I gave it to you.

HIRSCHLER: Search his bunk.

HELTAI: It's strapped to his leg!

UNCLE *(jumps out of the pot, brandishing a very long red kitchen knife):* Tell me what you need it for!

KLAUB: Send the kid out.

UNCLE: Send the kid out? Oh, very funny. Is there anything he doesn't know? What's in the rain when it rains?

THE KID: People.

UNCLE: Where were you when Altschul was eating his own shit?

THE KID: I was there.

UNCLE: I don't think this kid has to be sent out.

KLAUB: May I have the knife, Uncle?

UNCLE: Certainly not.

KLAUB: Then I'm going to take it away from you.

(They move toward UNCLE. HIRSCHLER *stops them.)*

HIRSCHLER: Listen, Uncle, let's have some perspective. The cake is too small. Whenever you eat, you take a crumb out of someone else's mouth. At this very moment, while you're making such a fuss, millions are starving to death in India; but today we may have stumbled on the most elegant solution. The graveyards are full of goodies; the chimneys are going full blast, and nice fat suicides come floating down every river and stream. All that perfectly good stuff going to waste. Aren't you bored with the same old menu? You know you'd make a lovely roast pig, with an apple in your mouth!

HELTAI: Uncle, be sensible!

HIRSCHLER: Listen to Mr. Weiss! Mr. Weiss, give us one of your succulent poetical examples.

WEISS: Sautéed kidneys!

(Applause. Cheers. Groans. Salivation.)

(Tempting UNCLE.*)* Prepare eight lamb kidneys. Quarter them. Sprinkle them with lemon juice. Heat three tablespoons butter and dripping. Sauté lightly in one cup chopped celery. Quarter cup chopped onions. Add the kidneys. Simmer them covered. Add salt if needed. Two tablespoons sherry. One tablespoon parsley, chopped.

(Applause. Cheers. Salivation.)

THE GYPSY: I'm so happy I could die.

UNCLE: You shall eat; you shall eat not one day nor two days nor twenty days but a whole month until it comes out of your nostrils and be loathsome to you, because you rejected the Lord who is among you.

THE GYPSY: You shut up. I want him to shut up. I tell you to shut up. One . . . two . . . three . . . SHUT UP!

(The others chant and squeak and cry "Shut up!")

UNCLE: Their lips against me! Their muttering against me! Their sitting down and their rising up! *(Steps forward, takes his beard off, bows to the audience.)* Raising maledictions! Cursing their heathen heads! Like a prophet whirling out of the wilderness! Waving his arms like so! His eyes starting out of his head! His throat bursting AOOOOOAI! Or words to that effect.

(The others keep chanting "Shut up!" UNCLE *turns back, puts on his beard; to the others.)*

Let vultures sit on your roof, a weasel under your blanket!

(Over PUFFI's *body.)*

The moonface loony haunt your dreams,

His great bloody fingers poking at your eyes!

You have sodden your father, and he is your food

I will oppose this abomination till my dying breath!

GHOULOS *(cupping his ears):* Breath? What breath? Dying breath?

Oh very well-spoken. Excuse me, we respect your beard, we are impressed by your white gloves, but I'm hungry. D'you understand what I'm saying? I . . . am . . . hungry. You are beautiful, but if you open your stinking mouth once more, I'll spill your brains! *(He picks up a stool, tries to throw it at* UNCLE, *staggers about, drops it, exhausted; to the audience.)* He was never a strong man.

HELTAI: Uncle, I sympathize but only for reasons of health. Puffi is too fat for my ulcers.

WEISS: Nothing that's boiled can hurt you.

HIRSCHLER *(astonished):* Oh? I never thought of it that way.

KLAUB: That's enough now. Give me the knife, Uncle.

UNCLE: I'm going to bury it in the snow where you can't find it. *(He starts out. Some give way; some jump him.)* Cannibals! I denounce this meal!
(A fight.)

SCENE 5

Fight

HIRSCHLER *and* HELTAI *step forward and light up cigarettes, talking to the audience.*

HIRSCHLER: The point about the fighting—
HELTAI: I wouldn't call it fighting.
HIRSCHLER: As I was saying—
HELTAI: Excuse me, I didn't mean to interrupt.
HIRSCHLER: It certainly wasn't fighting in any athletic or Anglo-Saxon sense. There was something profoundly Jewish—
HELTAI: You mean amateurish?
HIRSCHLER: D'you mind?
HELTAI: After you.
HIRSCHLER: It was a tussle—careful, nightmarish, green.
HELTAI: Like fighting under water?
HIRSCHLER: Yes, punches were thrown but didn't connect.
HELTAI: Little Lang's nose was bleeding.
HIRSCHLER: Oh for God's sake! Little Lang's nose! Little Lang's nose was a notorious bleeder. You said, "How are you?" and it started to bleed.
HELTAI: Uncle fell down.
HIRSCHLER: Uncle fell down because he was old.
HELTAI: Not at all. He'd been hit in the face, that's why he fell down.
HIRSCHLER: Oh? I don't remember that.
HELTAI: You don't remember it, because it was you who hit him.
HIRSCHLER: I did? No kidding! I don't remember hitting him.
HELTAI: You went like so.
HIRSCHLER: Well, I couldn't have hit him very hard. Shall we say it was a glancing blow?
      (UNCLE *falls down, with a thud.*)
HELTAI: You knocked his fucking head off!
HIRSCHLER: I was hungry!

HELTAI: Of course you were hungry. We were all hungry. The knife was taken away to cut up Puffi *(belches)*.

HIRSCHLER: It still upsets you?

HELTAI: No. *(Retches.)*

(Helped by THE KID, UNCLE *crosses to the bunk.)*

HIRSCHLER: What's the matter with you? It's been twenty-five years.

HELTAI: It was me who took the knife away from him and gave it to Weiss. And Weiss sharpened it on the stove.

*(*WEISS *starts sharpening the knife, going* "Kss-Kss.")

HIRSCHLER: Weiss? Weiss? Which one was Weiss?

*(*WEISS *smiles and waves.)*

HELTAI: Weiss was the cook.

HIRSCHLER: I don't know what you're talking about.

HELTAI: You must be sleeping well.

THE OTHERS: Kssss-ksss.

HIRSCHLER *(to the audience):* I had my second stroke the day after Thanksgiving. *(To* HELTAI; *mouth paralyzed.)* Listen, what d'you want me to do, become a vegetarian? Those that have suffered, don't want to suffer any more. I mean, they've been in that country, and their voices are calm.

THE OTHERS: Ksss-ksss.

HIRSCHLER: Okay, I can't stand certain dishes. The other night, in that Spanish joint on MacDougal Street, I had this roast pig. Specialty of the house. Flattened, ridged, appallingly realistic. I mean, it looked like a pig.

THE OTHERS: Ksss-ksss.

HIRSCHLER: I don't mind a porkchop. A porkchop is an abstraction. A porkchop could be anything. A porkchop doesn't remind me of a pig.

*(*PUFFI *has been dragged into a dark corner by the stove.* WEISS *starts carving him up.)*

SCENE 6

The Wager

UNCLE *(To God):*
> What do you want from me?
> Why do you let them torment your servant?
> Why do you lay the burden of these people upon me?
> Have I conceived them that you should say to me:
> "Carry them in your bosom!" I can not carry them alone.
> They are too heavy, and they keep crying out:
> "Who shall give us flesh to eat? We remember the fish
> In Egypt which was free of charge, and the cucumbers,
> And the melons, and the garlic. But now our soul
> Is dried away. There is nothing, nothing at all."

LANG: What's he doing?

KLAUB: Praying, what else?

UNCLE: No, I'm not praying. I'm telling Him. Listen! You! I'm talking to you!

HIRSCHLER *(giggling):* Hey, mister, speak a little louder so we can hear you!

UNCLE:
> You have turned your hand against me
> Again and again all the day. You have worn
> Out my skin. When I call for help, you shut
> Out my voice.

(All the others climb on top of the mountain, forming an enormous God-figure, with KLAUB on top. They let out a deep hum.)

UNCLE:
> We shall die soon. Two more days?
> Let the children shiver and play with our bones.
> The enormity of our grave makes no difference.
> We may be squashed together like lovers
> In perfect union, but when we die, we die alone.
> We rot one by one and drop like leaves

Raked up and burnt as in September.
Some will stay still in the dignity of their silence,
Some will squeal like scalded cats
As they scramble for the exit, scratching
Their little farewells into concrete: I WAS HERE!
Until their fingers break. I'm not complaining.
I'm sick of my lamentations. Our privies
Are already monuments, our bones are world-famous.
So damn your pity, your justice, even your love.
I want none of it. I still have my pride
In this mud, this wilderness, this city of murder, this Ausch-
 witz.
All I want is a little information, no, I insist on it.
I want to know why this ending.

HIRSCHLER: Hey, Uncle, look who's here.
 (KLAUB, *on top of* THE GYPSY, *comes forward.*)
KLAUB *(as God):* All this crazy stuff you're telling to the Lord?
UNCLE: All this and worse to come.
KLAUB: And you expect an answer, *boobele?*[3]
UNCLE: I demand it.
KLAUB: Don't you dare raise your voice in my presence!

 (A deep hum.)
You *meshugene,*[4] get down on your knees!
On your knees, and not a peep out of you!
Excessive talking! Hard and stiff-necked pride!
Down, boy, and beg for mercy, and no interruptions!
I do talk to my chosen children on occasion;
I enjoy a conversation in the afternoon.
Is this a conversation? I can't get a word in edgeways.
If you want help in your darkness, be humble,
Or I'll strike you dead.

 (He makes thunder.)
Now what's your problem?

3. *Boobele:* a Yiddish term of endearment, here used sarcastically.
4. *Meshugene:* Yiddish for a crazy person.

UNCLE: They are waiting for a meal.

KLAUB: What's that to you that you make so much noise?

UNCLE: I don't know, I don't know.

KLAUB: The man is dead; he's been cut up, and is boiling.

UNCLE: It's a horror. I have no name for it, but if they eat, they will be damned.

KLAUB: Who says so?

UNCLE: You said so!

KLAUB: When, on what mountain, from what cloud or bush?

UNCLE: YOU SAID SO! *(Gives a deep hum.)*

KLAUB: Such an idea I've never entertained.

UNCLE: YOU SAID SO!

KLAUB: Listen, I don't like to be misquoted.

UNCLE:

> "Only be steadfast in not eating the blood;
> For the blood is the life; and thou shalt not
> Eat the life with the flesh. Thou shalt not eat it,
> Thou shalt pour it out upon the earth—" [5]

KLAUB: Are you deaf and dumb, boy? I always speak to you loud and clear. And I said to you on a certain day—it was raining—Thou shalt not eat any abominable thing. Haven't I made it perfectly clear. What was meant by abominable? I gave you a list. Where is it now?

(UNCLE hands him a Bible.)

> Ye shall not eat of them that only chew the cud,
> Or of them that only have the hoof cloven.[6]
> The camel, and the hare, and the rock-badger,
> And the swine, and the great vulture, and
> I think, I'm not entirely sure, the bearded
> Vulture, and don't you touch the osprey and the
> Glede, whatever that is, and the kite after its kinds,

5. Uncle quotes Deuteronomy 12:23–24, in which the Jews are prohibited from eating blood.

6. Klaub refers to Deuteronomy 14:7, to prove that the list of animals prohibited for food does not include Puffi.

And I'm pretty sure you'd better lay off
The pelican, the cormorant, the heron and the hoopoe,
And every creeping thing that flieth,
And unless I'm very much mistaken,
The great owl, too, the little owl, and the horned owl.
O.K., have I ever mentioned Mr. Puffi Pinkus?
Have I forbidden you the fat man, the freak,
The selfish gut, who organized some bread three days ago,
And hid it in his armpit, waiting for a chance
To eat it unobserved so he needn't share it
With anyone? Oh, boy, I could give you the plague,
The fever, I could make you big with boils,
But I enjoy a good argument before dinner,
Especially if I can win it, so I'll make you a wager,
I give you five to one that you will join the meal,
And what's worse, you will ask for a second helping.

(UNCLE *starts laughing, tumbles the* GOD-FIGURE. WEISS, *his hands blood-red, is dropping hunks of meat into the pot, humming a waltz to himself, gaily.* UNCLE *stops laughing and runs out of the room.*)

SCENE 7

The Waiting

GHOULOS: Water's boiling.

WEISS: Blob-blob-blob.

THE OTHERS: Blob-blob-blob.

THE LOUDSPEAKERS: Blob-blob-blob.

(PUFFI rises from the dead, addresses the audience.)

PUFFI: How good is your sense of values? What is your first thought when you prepare a meal? Is it of a decorated cake or a fancy salad? Gastronomy and nutrition are not synonymous—so don't confound them. Attempt variety in ingredients, texture and flavors. If you have but little time, choose a menu that may be quickly prepared. Start with the dish that takes the longest time to cook. Set the table in one of the intervals. Keep calm even if your hair straggles and you drip unattractively. Brush up before serving. Your appearance is important, but eating in a quiet atmosphere is even more important to the family's morale and digestion. Your first effort at cooking may result in confusion, but soon you will acquire a skilled routine that will give you confidence and pleasure. You don't believe it? Will it encourage you to know that I was once as ignorant and helpless a bride as was ever foisted on an impecunious young husband? Together we placed many a burnt offering on the altars of matrimony, but I've lived to serve a meal attractively and well. *(Chuckles and leaves.)*

(The others sit at the table, watching WEISS, mesmerized, as he begins to stir the stew. A very long silence.)

KLAUB: How long will it take?

WEISS: Don't rush me.

GHOULOS: He was only asking.

WEISS: A decent meal takes time.

THE GYPSY *(screams):* All right, but how much time?

WEISS: Time.

(Long silence.)

218

KLAUB: One hour? Two hours?

WEISS: If you don't stop nagging me, I'll quit.

LANG: No offence meant, Mr. Weiss.

GHOULOS: No one wants you to quit, Mr. Weiss.

KLAUB: I've asked you a question, you might as well answer it.

HELTAI: Leave him alone, he is an artist. Flaubert took five years
over *Madame Bovary*.

THE GYPSY: Fuck Madame Bovary.

(Long silence.)

HIRSCHLER: Would you be prepared to say that it'll be ready by say
. . . say . . .

HELTAI: To begin with, dear boy, what time is it?

(A frightened silence.)

WEISS: Since when do we know the time or care about it?

GHOULOS: The work siren blew at five-thirty.

KLAUB: The work siren has been out of order the last two weeks.

(A frightened silence.)

GHOULOS *(suddenly)*: It's almost noon.

KLAUB: How can you tell?

GHOULOS: The shadows are darker.

THE GYPSY *(amazed)*: The shadows? What shadows?

HELTAI: There is a sun outside, you know.

HIRSCHLER: A what?

HELTAI: Let's tentatively agree that it's . . . it's . . .

HIRSCHLER: Why should I agree to anything? For all I know it's
four p.m.

LANG: You mean teatime?

HIRSCHLER: Don't interpret me, boy.

HELTAI: The light fades, darkness falls, it's night. So far so good.
The light fades, the darkness fades, it's another day. It's cold,
then it's hot. The leaves are green, the leaves are yellow, the
leaves are gone.

THE GYPSY: I can't wait that long!

HIRSCHLER: On the other hand, to strike a less lyrical note, I always
take a crap when the work siren blows, whether it blows or
not. Some things don't change.

HELTAI: Ah yes, the eternal verities.

(Long silence.)

HIRSCHLER: I must say I've been to some of the finest restaurants in Europe but I never had to wait this long for anything, not even a soufflé.

THE GYPSY: What was that you just said?

PUFFI: Soufflé.

THE GYPSY: What kind of soufflé?

HIRSCHLER: I don't remember.

THE GYPSY *(strangling him):* Remember, you bastard!

HIRSCHLER: I think it was a cheese soufflé.

ALL *(whispering):* Soufflé . . . soufflé . . . soufflé . . .

HIRSCHLER: PEACHES!

(A silence.)

THE GYPSY: Liverwurst!

WEISS: Muffins! Toasted English muffins!

(They giggle in delight.)

GHOULOS *(cries out):* Fettucini con insalata verde!

("Ooohs!" and "Ahhs!")

WEISS: Omelette, the Prince of Denmark!

(Laughter.)

GHOULOS *(playing with himself):* With what?

WEISS: Mushrooms!

GHOULOS: Oh God!

WEISS: And garlic toast!

GHOULOS: Call me Theo!

WEISS: Green peppers!

GHOULOS: I'm coming, I'm coming!

(Applause. THE GYPSY *jumps on top of the table.)*

THE GYPSY: Entertainment! Watch me! Watch the Notorious-Never-To-Be-Solved-Liverwurst-Murder-Case!   Jingle-jangle, forty cents! I sold my yellow shoes this morning. I loved my yellow shoes! So tight and bright, they went Zzz-zzz. *(Struts about.)* Zizzz-zizzz!

You could hear me for miles in the village!

And all the whores went "Ooooh!" and "Aahh!"
And "Here comes Laci Rácz the fifteenth!
In his brand-new yellow kid-leather shoes!"
This is my knife. These are my naked feet.
And this is winter.
(Appoints HIRSCHLER.*)*
This is the snow.
(Appoints HELTAI.*)*
There is the cold wind.
(Appoints HAAS.*)*
This is the city of fat men.
(They look out front.)
And here is the grocer.
(Appoints GHOULOS.*)*
There's the window, and here's the liverwurst.
(Appoints LANG.*)*
I stood outside for hours, looking at it. Hello, liverwurst.

LANG: I don't recall meeting you.
THE GYPSY: You're beautiful.
LANG: I don't converse with strangers.
THE GYPSY: The wind was much louder.
HAAS: Shhhhhhhhhh!
THE GYPSY: Good evening, Mr. Grocer. Got any liverwurst?
GHOULOS: No begging.
THE GYPSY: I've got money. Jingle-jangle.
GHOULOS: In that case I've got liverwurst.
THE GYPSY: That's the way it goes.
GHOULOS: That's the way it goes.
THE GYPSY: Let me see the liverwurst.
GHOULOS: Here you are, boy.
THE GYPSY: It's beautiful.
GHOULOS: You can say that again.
THE GYPSY: How much?
GHOULOS: One-fifty a pound.
THE GYPSY: What's the matter, you want to die rich?

GHOULOS: Listen, you're my first customer today.

THE GYPSY: How much for forty cents?

GHOULOS: About this much.

THE GYPSY: Please, Mr. Grocer, show it to me exact.

GHOULOS: Don't worry, I'll cut you a nice piece for forty cents.

THE GYPSY: I sold my yellow shoes this morning.

GHOULOS: Things are rough for everyone.

THE GYPSY: Not everyone.

GHOULOS: You talk nice and easy, boy, or I'll throw you out on your ass.

THE GYPSY: Watch it, Mr. Grocer. I've been walking up and down this city for two days, and it's winter. Who lives here, tell me? Stones? Now if you're going to be a stone, d'you know what I do to stones? I carve my name in stones.

GHOULOS: If you only have forty cents *(brings* HAAS *forward)*— buy a piece of baloney.

THE GYPSY: I ain't coming through to you, Mr. Grocer. I don't want to play in the Royal Opera House. I don't want to fuck Betty Grable. I don't want baloney. I want liverwurst. Usually my head is full of interesting possibilities—flowers—palaces— tropical storms—ladies with long red hair. But these last two weeks it's got nothing in it except liverwurst.

GHOULOS: Look, I'll cut you a nice piece, a piece like this for forty cents.

THE GYPSY: That all?

GHOULOS: That's all.

THE GYPSY: No, Mr. Grocer, here is where you cut it.

GHOULOS: You must be in a humorous mood.

THE GYPSY: You know what it's like out there without shoes?

GHOULOS: It's winter.

THE GYPSY: The sparrows are dying.

GHOULOS: Then eat sparrows.

*(*THE GYPSY *plunges his knife into* GHOULOS *several times.)*

THE OTHERS: Run! Run!—Murder! Robbery! Police!—It's getting late!—Keep out of this!—Run!—Let him finish! Let him eat! Let him have his liverwurst!

THE GYPSY *(carrying* LANG*):* I was never caught! Vanished mysteri-
ously! Description in all the papers! Tall—black—handsome—
barefoot!—Hid in a freightyard with the liverwurst! *(Raises*
LANG *as if he were the Host.)* Christ has risen! Christ has risen!
(Dumps him on the table.)

THE OTHERS: Go on! Do it! Do it now!

THE GYPSY: My head is usually full of interesting ideas. Flowers—
palaces—tropical storms—ladies with long red hair—but that
time I ate—I ate all night long.
(He pretends to eat LANG*. The others watch him.)*

HIRSCHLER: My God, he eats talented!

HELTAI: One of the most talented eaters I've ever seen!
*(*HAAS *croaks.)*

THE KID: Give me a piece.

THE GYPSY: No.

THE KID: One small piece.

THE GYPSY: Go away.
(The others start grabbing imaginary bits of liverwurst. THE
GYPSY *fends them off. They eat. They stop eating.)*

HELTAI: It's not the same.

HIRSCHLER: Something's missing.

THE GYPSY *(in tears):* It ain't what it used to be.
(Sadly, they start singing "Yes, We Have No Bananas." THE
GYPSY *steps forward, bows to the audience.)*
He was Laci Rácz the fifteenth, why, because there were fourteen other Laci Ráczes. He played before all the crowned
heads of Europe. Titled ladies sat at his feet. He was a great
artist: when he did a glissando not a cunt remained dry. He
didn't know what he was doing among all those fucking—excuse me!—Jews. He didn't care what he ate as long as he ate.
*(*THE LOUDSPEAKERS *pick up the Banana Song. They all dance
the Charleston, demented.)*

SCENE 8

The Return of Uncle

UNCLE *(suddenly re-enters):* I smell soup.
  (A silence. He stands sniffing. They all sniff.)
HIRSCHLER: What kind?
HELTAI: Carrots?
UNCLE: I'm not sure.
  (They stand about, sniffing.)
THE GYPSY: Turnip!
GHOULOS: Definitely not!
LANG: Chicory?
UNCLE: Something—new?
THE GYPSY: It ain't meat.
KLAUB: There hasn't been any meat since October.
HIRSCHLER: Let's not jump to hasty conclusions.
KLAUB: What the hell are you talking about? The kitchens are
  closed, the kitchens have been closed for five weeks. I saw all
  the cooks drive off in a truck.
UNCLE: Look, I didn't mean to mention it before, but Lupowitz
  told me—
KLAUB: What does Lupowitz know?
UNCLE: Admittedly, he's a big mouth, a rumormonger, but last
  night at about one-thirty he heard a sound—
KLAUB: Sounds are penny a dozen.
THE KID: What kind of a sound?
UNCLE: According to Lupowitz—it was like—*(bleating)* Baaaah!
  (They all go "Baaaah!")
KLAUB *(furiously):* There is no soup. There is no Baaaah.
  (They go crawling on their knees like sheep, going "Baaaaah!")
  There is only Puffi!
  *(They flop down exhausted, except for KLAUB and UNCLE
  looking at each other. GLATZ gets up suddenly, trying to think,
  massaging his head. A silence. The wind is heard.)*
UNCLE: It's eleven-thirty.

KLAUB: How would you know?

UNCLE: I have a watch.

KLAUB: Since when?

UNCLE: It's eleven-thirty and twelve seconds. And let me assure you there are shadows outside, all over the compound, lying down, flat on their faces. Shadows from huts, from the watchtower, from the high-voltage fence—now there's a pretty shadow for you!—from the wheelbarrows piled with bodies. I think, I'm not sure, the sky is still there, streaked with smoke. Who is in that smoke today? Let us give thanks for being indoors.

KLAUB: How you talk. *(Goes for* UNCLE's *throat.)*

GLATZ *(massaging his head):* Milk!

KLAUB *(lets go of* UNCLE): What, what, what?

GLATZ: Milk.

HIRSCHLER: What's that?

HELTAI: I forgot.

(HAAS makes an inarticulate sound, bows, mimes a sleeping baby. Mimes a young mother proud of her breasts. Mimes baby waking and crying. Mimes mother watching it in disgust. Mimes baby crying. Mimes mother unbuttoning her blouse.

Now LANG *joins the game. Mimes baby crying.* HAAS *mimes mother changing her mind, buttoning up her blouse.* LANG *mimes baby crying.* HAAS *mimes mother giving baby the bottle.* LANG *mimes baby drinking.* HAAS *mimes mother taking bottle away.* LANG *mimes baby crying.* HAAS *mimes mother putting the bottle out of baby's reach.* LANG *mimes baby trying to reach the bottle. Now all the others join the game [except* UNCLE*], mime babies trying to reach the bottle.* HAAS *mimes mother walking away. The others rush and engulf him.* HAAS *croaks in pain. When they let him go, he is stripped bare, holding his wounded breasts.)*

HAAS *(bows to the audience):* Violets, sparrows and young boys made his eyes water. No one had ever thought him Jewish until those two rather marvelous-looking Gestapo boys asked him to drop his pants and his little thing stood at attention. Gentlemen, he argued, let's not be dogmatic; even the English Royal

Family is in favor of circumcision, but his arguments carried no weight. They told him to cry *Sieg Heil!* and he refused and they beat him until his heart turned to stone. Then they raped him, but he enjoyed it. He was what you might call a Faustian man.

WEISS *(taps him on the shoulder):* May I?

(They dance.)

Laci, play something gay, something irresponsible!

(THE GYPSY pretends to play the violin. They all hum a tango, watching the dancers.)

UNCLE: Orphic tranquillity! The taming of the beasts! I'm not sure I approve of this.

HELTAI: Watch that dame go!

WEISS: Say something dirty.

(HAAS croaks.)

GHOULOS: Earwax.

WEISS: Surely you can do better than that.

LANG: Petroleum jelly.

WEISS: You are a shy one, aren't you?

(HAAS croaks.)

Glad tidings, gentlemen. Mr. Haas is having a gigantic erection.

(Applause. They dance slowly, locked in embrace. Everyone is watching them, mesmerized.)

HIRSCHLER: Culture! Give me culture!

LANG: The *Unfinished Symphony!*

KLAUB: Toilet paper!

UNCLE: If God is dead, everything is permissible.

WEISS *(to HAAS):* I love you. *(Kisses him.)*

SCENE 9

Uncle's Cup Runneth Over

UNCLE *(walking around):* I think that's outrageous behavior.

(HELTAI *hushes him.)*

I have an open mind. Nothing human is alien to me. I'm not averse to light entertainment provided it's balanced with something educational.

(LANG *hushes him.)*

(To HIRSCHLER.) Isn't it a fact that the incidence of sodomy is markedly low among the Hebrews?

(HIRSCHLER *kisses him.)*

What are they doing now?

(GHOULOS *hushes him.)*

(To the dancers.) Piss off, you two!

(Shocked "Ooohs!")

Amazing! I've never in my life uttered an obscenity. We were decent people. My wife played the harpsichord. We might occasionally defecate, urinate, copulate, we had six children, but let me assure you I've never fucked anyone in my life. I think I'm going insane. Fuck, shit, piss! Fuck, shit, piss!

(The others try to shut him up but he breaks loose.)

Lovely sunshine. Another winter gone by. We are still alive. You call this living? *(Claps his hands.)* Maxie, I want you to bring me in rapid succession, or even simultaneously, five coffees—one mocca Turkish-type, one demitasse with cream, one demitasse without cream, one kaputziner in a glass, and a Viennese folly.

HIRSCHLER: You like coffee?

UNCLE: What's the matter with the sun?

HIRSCHLER: It comes and goes.

UNCLE: That's the matter with this fucking Hungarian sun, it never stays put. I've always taken care of myself. *(Drinking imaginary cups of coffee.)* I've been with my doctor all morning. You know Dr. Schlosser. I like Schlosser. "Cornelius, you don't

227

want to keel over in the middle of a faro game?"—"No, I
don't."—"Or expire on top of your wife?"—"No, she wouldn't
fancy that."—"Or drop dead in the middle of a death
scene?"—"It's that serious?"—"Cut out the coffee, Cornelius,
come Monday, and cut it out." *(Drinks.)* Monday is Monday,
and today is what? It's only eleven a.m. I'm going to stay here
till closing time. I'm going to drink 450 cups of coffee.
(Drinks.) A man ought to know how to say goodbye. I trust
Schlosser. You know what he is like, smoking like a chimney
and dying on his feet. I like that about him. *(Drinks.)* It implies
complicity. He is not only a doctor, he is a patient, too. He will
die one day, which is a lot more than you can say about most
doctors. *(Drinks.)*

(HELTAI *and* HIRSCHLER *drink.)*

THAT'S MY COFFEE! *(Drinks.)* If I have to die, I want everybody else to die, too. I don't want any of you bastards sitting
around on my grave. At my funeral I want no mourners, I only
want coffins, I want everybody down there with me. *(Drinks.)*
I've always taken care of myself. For my Gloucester I lost
twenty pounds, for my Faust I gave up smoking. *(To* HAAS,
who drinks.) PUT THAT COFFEE DOWN! I don't want anybody else to drink. I want you to die of thirst, all of you.
(Drinks more rapidly.) Last year it was "Animals fats is a
killer!" Life is a killer; everything is bad for you, but I'm going
to live forever. *(Drinks.)* I know how to say goodbye to
chocolate éclairs. *(Waves to* KLAUB.) Goodbye chocolate
éclairs! I trust Schlosser. He is the only one I trust. I mean, if
you think of it logically, what's a doctor's true vocation? To
make you as sick as possible. Never mind the hippocratic oath.
(Drinks.) They give you a couple of aspirins to show their concern for humanity, but all the time they're waiting for something terrible to happen. What they like best is a tumor with
frequent remission, no use killing you off too fast. Six or seven
operations is what they like, ten years in a wheelchair is what
they like. Not Schlosser. All morning, he smoked like a chimney, he looked like a ghost. With Schlosser you feel it's he who

needs a doctor, not you. *(Drinks again.)* The sun is out again. Another round, Maxie. *(Slurps from coffee to coffee.)* I've always taken care of myself. *(Slurps.)* Goodbye. *(Slurps.)* Goodbye. *(Slurps.)* Goodbye. *(Slurps.)* Goodbye.

KLAUB: That's enough, Uncle.

UNCLE *(having a heart attack):* Watch me suck the sugar out of the mocca!

THE GYPSY: For God's sake, get that pig out of here! Get him out! *(Sweeps an imaginary row of cups off the table.)*

UNCLE: He spilled all the coffee! Call the police! *(Lies on the table, licking coffee off it.)* Goodbye, my darling! Goodbye, my sweetheart!

KLAUB: Uncle, it's all over now.

UNCLE: One more sip from the bottom where it's sweetest.

KLAUB: Uncle, you are going too far.

HIRSCHLER: Get me something to cover him up.

(They cover him with a blanket. HIRSCHLER gives him mouth-to-mouth resuscitation. A pause.)

UNCLE *(sits up suddenly):* Tell me, was his face pale or red?

HIRSCHLER: Oh, very pale.

UNCLE: Had trouble breathing?

HELTAI: Nearly choked.

UNCLE: What was it, asthma or the heart?

HIRSCHLER: The heart.

UNCLE: Always the heart! Why didn't you let him die, you murderers! At 11:45 he was still innocent. *(Pointing at them accusingly.)* Feet—legs—arms—splendid—mechanical—scientific—tits and bits—banished from the stage—my last job—at the War Office Artificial Limb Manufacturing Plant—sitting under a mountain of bones—stacked up—sorted out—filed away—packing jockstraps—playing with knees ... *(THE KID is the last one he points at.)* Where were you in my hour of need?

THE KID: You should never have given up coffee.

UNCLE: You too, my little brute?

THE KID *(shrugs):* The fewer the guests, the bigger the portions. *(UNCLE is about to strike him, but is restrained.)*

SCENE 10

Yellow Roses

HIRSCHLER: May I suggest we change the ambience by some cultural activity?

KLAUB *(drags* THE KID *forward):* Recitation!

(Applause. THE KID *takes a bow.)*

THE KID: "Yellow Roses." By Olga Paul.

*(*UNCLE *groans.)*

"Delicately tinted are my yellow roses
That adorn my window which the moon discloses."

UNCLE: Oh my God!

(Someone hushes him.)

THE KID:

"I inhaled the perfume of the prettiest flower,
Knowing that I'd shortly breathe my final hour."

UNCLE: I don't believe my ears.

(The others hush him.)

THE KID: "Pretty roses tell her though by silence mooted
That my life seems worthless since my love's uprooted."

UNCLE: Do I have to listen to this drivel?

(Hushed again.)

THE KID: D'you mind not interrupting?

UNCLE: I most certainly do mind! What grotesque arrogance has made you get up here, in front of all these people, and perform, actually perform? Get up here all alone and open your mouth, and actually speak! Speak not casually as a civilian so to speak, to say for example: "When's dinner gonna be?" but speak in the special, no, sacred tones of a public performance that turns the word into flesh and, if God happens to be backstage, into gooseflesh as well?

(Noise.)

THE KID: I know I'm not an actor.

UNCLE: You're damn right you're not an actor, so shut your hole and sit down. If I say to you, "Listen, fellows, let's eat some-

230

body!" I speak as a carnivore, a criminal, a wolf, a hippogriff, oh, I don't know. I'm not a zoologist. But if I get up on the mountain or the stage, same thing, and speak out of the whirl-wind to the multitude below—"Thou shalt not eat of thy father's flesh!" then I have spoken as an actor, that is to say, as God. I really must protest—

(Noise.)

The kid may be well-meaning, all amateurs are, but he has assaulted my profession, no, I'd go further, my humanity, no, I'd go even further, he has assaulted my silence. *(Mimicking* THE KID.*)* "Delicately tinted are my yellow ro-ro-ro-roses . . ."

(Laughter.)

THE KID: You're being very unkind.

UNCLE: You reptile! You rapist of the word! You dumb civilian p-p-prick, why should I be kind to you? My ears have heard, my hair stood up, I will not tolerate any further abuse of our holy tongue. I know where such abuse can lead to, I have my cre-dentials, I was there, I heard it happen, I protested, I was ban-ished to the blasted heath for being God's newsboy, I mean a Jew, same thing—

THE OTHERS: Speech! Speech!

UNCLE: —A blasphemy I could only protest by silence, five years of silence. I wouldn't utter a single word for five years, not even to my mirror. I refused to use something that was being abused, I was on strike against these hysterics, these whores, these thieves who plucked the purest words out of our lan-guage—Glory! Honor! Freedom!—when all they meant was— *Kill them!*

THE OTHERS: Bravo! Cheers!

UNCLE: What you don't understand is the threat of separation, of being exiled from the language. When I was born, I did not cry *Oi vey is mir!*[7] I cried AHHHH!

---

7. *Oi vey is mir!*: a Yiddish exclamation here meaning "Oh, my God!" or "Good-ness, gracious!"

KLAUB: Hey, do "To be or not to be."

UNCLE: Kiss my ass! I'm not a performing seal! Besides, you should have asked me before. It's too late now, this p-p-p-place has been contaminated by the child's recital, it's got to be exorcised. You don't appreciate the awful burden of uttering a word at a time like this, a single word as for example— "Please." Or—"Mercy." I haven't worked in five years!

THE OTHERS (chanting and stamping): "To be or not to be!"

UNCLE: What d'you think I am, a string of bowels connecting two holes? Look at my mouth, my glorious mouth! Here, look at my tongue! Have you ever seen such a tongue? I was one of the rare ones, I used no tricks, no shortcuts, my balls didn't clang when I walked across the stage, but my every moment was a work of art, you could have framed my every moment. I did not put on masks, I wasn't afraid to strip down to the bones, to show what man is, and if you scratch a man you'll find a Jew, and naturally that was too much for the little ladies out front. You wouldn't understand but as a child I stammered terribly . . . like this . . . (Tongue writhing, wrist flapping.) I grew out of it—sheer willpower—even so—the master of my impediment—every time I was up there—inside me, down here, where all art begins, here, crouching behind the pubic hairs, there was always a f-l-l-lapping and a writhing.

(Silence)

And shame.

(He covers his face with his hands. The others too cover their faces with their hands, watching him through their fingers. He walks forward, bows to the audience.)

At that point he was suddenly overwhelmed by shame. Quite inexplicable at the time. And explanations are essential when otherwise you are empty. When you're empty you've got to keep your mouth occupied, sorry about that: when you can't eat, you talk. Anyway, he couldn't have explained his shame in January, that Sabbath noon in January, but in the evening— when they were liberated—

(Wild laughter.)

WEISS: Who was liberated?

UNCLE: A heap of bones.

(The others laugh and mime various attitudes of dying.)

Except for Hirschler and Heltai, breathing very slowly, staring into nothing.

(HIRSCHLER and HELTAI breathe very slowly, stare into nothing.)

And my father, curled up like a fetus, trying to explain the shame he felt at noon! How did he explain it?

HIRSCHLER: I couldn't hear what he was saying.

HELTAI: He could barely whisper. *(Whispers something.)*

HIRSCHLER: His jaw dropped and his tongue appeared. *(Imitates it.)*

UNCLE: Yes, but that was at night. He could barely whisper at night, but at noon, that Sabbath noon, he talked quite fluently, his face burning with shame, he got unreasonably mad at the kid, long dead by the end of the day.

(THE KID waves, face covered.)

He carried on, he babbled, he theorized, but all he wanted was attention, I suppose, to use his mouth once again, for the last time before . . . *(To the audience.)* Listen, it's easy for you. You can keep your mouths busy in all kinds of ways—cigars—candy—nipples—GODDAMN YOU! *(He touches his burning face. The others do likewise.)* But for him on that Sabbath noon in January—I mean here and now—waiting for the stew to get ready, all that mattered was to use his mouth again, for the last time, to astonish his b-b-b-brothers. Come, Miranda. No,—Titania? Lavinia?[8]

(He beckons THE KID who comes forward, sits down in front of him.)

"Have I caught thee?

He that parts us shall bring a brand from Heaven,

---

8. The Shakespearean heroine Uncle the actor is trying to remember is Cordelia; the quotataion which follows is from act 5, scene 3 of *King Lear*.

And fire us hence like foxes. Wipe thine eyes;
The good-years shall devour them, flesh and fell,
Ere they shall make us weep. We'll see them starved first."

(Stops and covers his face.) Well, then he stopped, or so I've
been informed. They applauded.
(Applause.)
The shadows grew.
(They do.)
Someone heard the sound.
(They listen. WEISS *is tasting the stew.)*
They turned to the stove. Weiss was slurping. Professionally, I
might add.

WEISS: Slurp. Slurp.

UNCLE: Everything happened rather slowly. Someone said, "Is it
ready?" Weiss said, "Not yet."

LANG: It was me who said, "Is it ready?"

UNCLE: Whoever, what does it matter? Weiss said, "Get off my
back." The kid said, "May we taste it, please?" Weiss said,
"Certainly not." Everyone was driven toward the stove, slowly
driven toward the pot on the stove. Klaub was getting visibly
upset. He didn't want the full effect of the meal to be spoiled
by . . . by . . . any . . .

KLAUB: Precipitate action.
(They move toward the stove, slowly. KLAUB *tries to stop them.)*
Stand back! Stand back there!

WEISS: It's not yet ready! I'll tell you when it's ready! I can't do my
job if you crowd me! Get out of my kitchen!

UNCLE: The kid came tumbling out of the tumult.—Wandered
about.—Fell down. Klaub went to him and removed the knife
from his back.—Passed it to Ghoulos.—It passed from hand
to hand back to Weiss.

WEISS *(screaming):* It's impossible to work under these conditions.
What happened?

UNCLE: An accident.
*(*HAAS *croaks.)*

LANG: He's dead.

HIRSCHLER: Isn't he lucky?

UNCLE: They sat down.—Struck various attitudes of grief.—The Gypsy sang "Ramona" or some other unsuitable lament.

THE GYPSY *(singing):* Ramona . . .

THE KID: Be quiet.

(*A pause.*)

I've always hated school.

UNCLE: Can't blame you for that.

THE KID: But you I respected.

UNCLE: I'm very glad to hear it.

THE KID: I've understood some things.

UNCLE: That is sufficient.

THE KID: Others you'd better explain.

UNCLE: There is never enough time.

THE KID: You must be simple with me.

UNCLE: Yes, yes, I apologize.

THE KID: Everything ought to be clear.

UNCLE: There are mysteries.

THE KID: Your white gloves aren't clear to me.

UNCLE: They are a memory.

THE KID: Now what does that mean?

UNCLE: D'you want me to tell you the story of my life?

THE KID: I want to understand!

UNCLE: I'm not an archeologist.

THE KID: Always these excuses!

UNCLE: Go back to school, boy!

THE KID: Our first day in camp wasn't clear at all.

UNCLE: The sun was shining, wasn't it?

THE KID: Is that important?

UNCLE: No, but it's clear.

THE KID: The sun hid when Jesus died.

UNCLE: Yes, He missed the effect.

(*A silence.*)

THE KID: The day we were arrested you wore something peculiar.

UNCLE: My wedding suit.

THE KID: In jail? With a top hat? Who were you going to marry?

UNCLE: It was a gesture.

THE KID: What's that supposed to signify?

UNCLE: It was a festive occasion.

THE KID: They made you wash the sidewalk.

UNCLE: Yes, that's what I mean.

THE KID *(loudly):* Why didn't you strike them dead?

> (UNCLE *is silent, evades* KLAUB's *grin.)*
> When they dragged you outside, through the great doors, all you said was, "After you, gentlemen!"
> *(Pause.)*
> I wrote down most things you said that day. For instance you said, "The geese have arrived."

UNCLE: Yes.

THE KID: You meant the Nazis?

UNCLE: Yes.

THE KID *(screaming):* Then why didn't you say so, goddammit?!

> (UNCLE *is silent.)*
> You also said, "The only way to resist geese is to stay as un-gooselike as possible." How was I supposed to do that? By wearing white gloves? Cursing a meal? Starving to death?

WEISS *(as if from a great distance):* By cha . . . ri . . . ty!

THE KID: And what the fuck does that mean?

HELTAI *(pushes* THE KID *aside impatiently):* No, no, that's not how it was at all! *(Playing* THE KID.*)* What the fuck does that mean? . . . In our first camp you behaved just as peculiar. Nights when everyone else was asleep on the floor you stood under the naked bulb, reading. And when I asked you, "Uncle," I asked you, "why don't you lie down and sleep like everyone else?" you said, "In certain circumstances it may be necessary to remain standing up." That's bullshit . . . And later, in Csepel Camp where the cold wind blows, a man spat out as we clambered off the truck, and you looked at him severely, but not too severely, and he apologized. Now how did you achieve that? I think I'm entitled to know. And here in this room you said, "I denounce this . . . this . . . "

HIRSCHLER: Abomination.

HELTAI *(cries out):* I'M ONLY TWELVE!

(A pause. HELTAI *walks away.* THE KID *takes his place as before.)*

THE KID: I was going to give you this box.

HELTAI: That's better.

THE KID: I was going to give you this box. There is nothing in it. Still, it's a box. I'm not going to give it to you. I wanted you to get up and strike these men dead. All you do is stand around like a waiter. My God, you love these pigs! I hope they will gas you tonight, I hope they will stuff you in the oven.

(He drops the box and dies.)

UNCLE *(furiously):* Ramaseder, I'm very disappointed in you. I know you're only twelve but that's no excuse. You keep breaking the rules. Look at your jacket! Always sleep with your jacket on! Never leave your bunk with your jacket unbuttoned! And what is that? A rust stain is permitted but a mud stain must be scraped off. And why don't you pad your jacket with paper now that the cold wind blows? And what about your shoes, Ramaseder? Why didn't you wrap a rag around your feet as I told you? Shoes chafe, they pinch, corns grow hard here, shoes can kill you, but don't ever let them out of your sight, or they'll be stolen, carry them wherever you go, hold them between your knees while you wash, put them under your head when you sleep . . . And Ramaseder, is this the way to die? In the middle of the day, at the age of twelve, with no one holding you? Will you never learn? . . .

KLAUB *(to the audience):* He picked him up. Not easy at his age. Carried him outside. They could hear him scratching furiously, like a dog digging for a bone, digging the child's grave.

UNCLE *(to* WEISS, *who touches* THE KID*):* Tomorrow's lunch?

WEISS *(doing a mad Hassidic[9] dance, chanting):*

"Rules for frying fritters:

Fritters may be sauted in butter.

But are better when prepared in deep fat.

9. Hassidic: orthodox Jewish.

Heat a kettle of fat to 390 degrees.
Dip food in batter.
Fry the fritters until they're a delicate brown . . ."

I'm going home. I'm going to climb the high-voltage fence. *(He starts out—they hold him back.)* I'm going to kill one of the dogs. *(To the audience; struggling to get free.)* He was a political. He didn't like to be spat in the face. You could hit him, you could kick him, but you couldn't spit in his face. Well, we all have our little idiosyncrasies. He was a bel canto until they smashed his larynx. *(Starts singing; croaks as if hit in the throat.)*

KLAUB: Slurp. Slurp. Slurp.

EVERYBODY: Slurp. Slurp. Slurp.

WEISS: Excuse me. Excuse me. *(Goes back to the pot.)* Dinner will be ready in half an hour.

GHOULOS: Friends, I insist we make this an occasion, a very festive occasion. Let's sweep the floor and wash the window. Everybody please shave. And let there be music. My own contribution to the festivities is this candle.

("Oohs!" and "Ahhs!" greet the candle as he lights it.)

Yes, we'll dine at candlelight as I've always dined with my parents in the pink light of Heraklion, a sail bobbing on the horizon. Oh, I'm so excited, I haven't been so excited in years. Let's make it a very festive occasion, friends. And Gypsy should say grace.

THE GYPSY: I'd rather bite my tongue off.

GHOULOS: Listen, if you try to spoil it, I'll eat you. *(Falls upon THE GYPSY's neck and bites him. HIRSCHLER pulls him off.)*

HIRSCHLER: Don't play with your food, boys.

KLAUB: All right, men, let's clean up the mess.

(They go down on their knees, with pails and brushes, and scrub the floor, staring at the audience, coming closer and closer until they collapse. UNCLE can be heard scratching outside. WEISS keeps stirring the stew.)

INTERMISSION

SCENE 11

The Dream

They re-enter and sit on the mountain of clothes. The room is festively decorated. UNCLE *returns, with mud in his hands. He slings it at them. They back away, except for* KLAUB.

UNCLE *(raging):* "The Lord shall pursue you until you perish—" [10] *(Stops.)* Excuse me, was his face pale or red?

HIRSCHLER: Oh, very pale.

UNCLE: Were you afraid of him?

HELTAI: Oh, terrified.

UNCLE: A minor point, but his teeth must have been gone by then. He was lisping, wasn't he?

HIRSCHLER: Yes.

UNCLE *(raging, with a lisp):* "And you shall be a horror to all the kingdoms of the earth . . . "

KLAUB: Why d'you make fun of him?

(A silence.)

UNCLE *(without a lisp):* "And your carcasses shall be fed to all the birds of the air, and there shall be no one to frighten them away." Kicked over the table, didn't he?

HELTAI: Yes, he did.

*(*UNCLE *kicks over the table.)*

THE GYPSY: Uncle is back!

HIRSCHLER: Hold it! O.K. we were frightened, but what do you do when you're frightened? *(Strikes various corny attitudes of fear.)*

HELTAI: Not at all.

HIRSCHLER: D'you mind? *(Thumbs his nose, sticks out his tongue, scratches his armpits.)*

HELTAI: That's more like it.

---

10. Uncle refers to Deuteronomy 28:22–26, which lists the punishments to be visited upon the Jews for not heeding the word of God.

HIRSCHLER: We behaved like nasty little boys.

HELTAI: *Hysterica passio!*

HIRSCHLER *(like a six-year-old):* Look who's here!

HELTAI *(ditto):* Uncle is back!

WEISS *(thumb in mouth):* Hello, Uncle!

UNCLE:

> The Kingdom of Children has come, the sons
> Have taken over, swarming down the stairs,
> Messing up the parlor and smashing the crockery.
> And later in the evening they lurk behind the hedge,
> Waiting for the old man—

WEISS: Who? Wha'?

UNCLE:

> And when he comes, they dash out of the shadows
> And cut him down and cut him up and eat him.
> Goodbye the Age of Reason, goodbye certitude,
> Goodbye hard hats and high hopes, goodbye
> Baggy trousers, the pain in the side, and
> The resigned sigh before falling asleep, goodbye
> The fullness of time. The rose dies young.
> They want whatever it is. It's all here and now.
> And now and here, now, now, now, me, me, me me,
> Here and now!

WEISS: Where have you been, Uncle?

UNCLE: Asleep.

THE GYPSY: Uncle had a snooze!

WEISS: A siesta!

THE GYPSY *(mincing):* A brief—afternoon—nap!

LANG *(camping):* So what else is new on the Rialto?

UNCLE: I think I had a dream.

HELTAI *(jumping up and down):* Quiet everybody! Uncle had a drrrream!

HIRSCHLER *(like a moron):* I got a tewible pwemonition he's gonna tell us about it.

> (GLATZ *starts out as if he knew what was coming.)*

THE GYPSY: Where d'you think you're going?

GLATZ *(thinking hard):* I don't know.

THE GYPSY: There is no way out of here except through the great chimney, so sit down.

GLATZ *(salutes):* Yes sir.

THE GYPSY: What did you drrrrrream about, Uncle?

UNCLE: We were home.

(All but KLAUB *stamp their feet and shake their heads as if terrified.)*

KLAUB: Not very original.

UNCLE: No, the usual dream of the inmates.

*(*WEISS *closes his eyes.)*

You are home again.

(They stamp their feet and shake their heads.)

But it's all right. It's safe. They're gone. Nothing bad can happen any more. The sun is warm. You walk down the street.

*(*HAAS *croaks, closes his eyes.)*

GHOULOS *(eyes closed but pointing):* Girl adjusting her stocking.

WEISS *(eyes closed but listening):* Church bells.

HIRSCHLER: Dingdong. Dingdong.

UNCLE: Telephones.

HELTAI *(eyes closed but annoyed):* Yeh, stupid, the phone rings but it's all right.

ALL BUT KLAUB: It's all right. It's all right. It's all right.

WEISS *(eyes closed):* Hello, who's that?—It's me.

(All but KLAUB *smile.)*

GLATZ: Mother, are you there?

UNCLE: The neighbors stop you *(they shake their heads and stamp their feet),* but it's all right. They shake you by the hand. They tell you their problems.

LANG *(eyes closed):* "Where shall we dine tonight?"

HIRSCHLER: "Hey, Bernie, did you turn off the gas?"

HELTAI: "I smoke too much."

THE GYPSY: Incredible! Incredible!

WEISS: "Milk or lemon, sir?"—"Both."

(All but KLAUB *laugh.)*

UNCLE: You walk upstairs lightly, walking on water. A dog barks, but it's all right. You ring the bell, standing there in your striped garb, a stinking skeleton, but it's all right. She opens the door.

GLATZ: Mother!

HIRSCHLER: "Where have you been?"

HELTAI: "Why didn't you call Friday like you promised?"

HIRSCHLER: "What were they feeding you—chickenshit?"

THE GYPSY: "Come in, son."

UNCLE: You walk in. You wash your face. You sit at the table.

(HAAS *is the first one to join the table.*)

You take your shoes off.

THE GYPSY (*violently*): *She* takes your shoes off.

UNCLE: She takes your shoes off. (*Kisses* HAAS' *feet.*) How about a little hot soup to open your stomach?

HIRSCHLER: With matzo balls?

UNCLE: Anything you fancy. No, sorry, that chair is reserved!

(HIRSCHLER *joins the table, his eyes closed,* UNCLE *takes his shoes off.*)

HIRSCHLER: In the camp they called me Three-Feet Hirschler. No one with only two feet could stink that high.

(UNCLE *kisses his feet.*)

HELTAI (*joins the table, eyes closed*): What's for dinner?

UNCLE: I've prepared a roast.

HIRSCHLER: How in hell did you get it?

UNCLE: I sold the bedsheets.

HELTAI: It's not horsemeat, is it?

UNCLE: Not in my kitchen!

HELTAI: Got anything to drink?

UNCLE: Yes, a fine riesling.

HELTAI: Chilled?

UNCLE: Chilled but not too chilled.

HIRSCHLER: Mustn't spoil the bouquet.

HELTAI: I don't give a damn about the bouquet. I've learnt to be modest. I've been drinking my own piss, I've eaten . . .

(HIRSCHLER *hits him.* UNCLE *kisses* HELTAI's *feet.*)

LANG: Mother! *(Eyes closed, joins the table.)* Mother, my ulcer's been acting up again. I fart like a horse. All I can have is yogurt and a little Mozart. Have I changed much?

(UNCLE takes his shoes off.)

You're not looking at me. Look at me. *(Shows his left profile, then his right.)* Look. *(Shows the shriveled skin on his hands.)* Look. *(Shows his gums and tongue.)* Look!

(Tears at his hair to show it's become thin. UNCLE kisses his feet. LANG kicks him away and steps forward.)

(To the audience.) He always tried to scare his mother by— climbing mountains—falling in love—smoking too much— but his goddam mother wouldn't scare. Last time he saw her . . . on the other side of the high-voltage fence . . . she was nibbling a carrot . . . Imagine, they still had carrots in those days . . . he walked close, very close to the fence, he almost touched it. He was taking a grave risk. She didn't bat an eye.

WEISS *(joins the table)*: I've brought a friend along. May he spend the night?

(THE GYPSY joins the table.)

UNCLE: For him I'll make up a bed in the living room.

WEISS: That won't be necessary. We're married.

(UNCLE kisses his feet.)

THE GYPSY: I hope I'm not causing too much trouble.

UNCLE *(takes THE GYPSY's shoes off)*: You're entirely welcome.

THE GYPSY: Madam, I've seen such things. I wish I'd been blind.

GHOULOS: Excuse me, does Mrs. Ghoulos live here?

(Pause.)

UNCLE: I am Mrs. Ghoulos.

GHOULOS: I'm your son.

UNCLE: Who?

(A pause.)

Oh!! *(Kisses his feet.)*

GHOULOS *(steps forward, to the audience)*: He too was a political, utterly convinced that after the revolution girls would have bigger breasts and smaller asses. I'm afraid he was mistaken. One day he said to me, "There are at this moment 35 million women pinched, fondled and mounted, but not by me. Is God just?"

GLATZ *(wandering about):* Mother! Are you there? *(Imitating traffic.)* Grrrr. Grrrr.

UNCLE: What's the matter?

GLATZ *(trying to think):* Lot of traffic tonight. *(Joins the table.)* I'm home, Mother.

UNCLE: The prodigal returns.

GLATZ *(massaging his brows):* No, that's not the way she talks.

UNCLE: How does she talk?

GLATZ *(tormenting his face):* "You shouldn't have come. It's too soon. They're not gone yet. There are fingers all over the city." *(Points at each of them.)*

UNCLE: You look tired. Let me take your shoes off.

GLATZ: No, no, she wasn't nice. *(Beating his head.)* "Did you bring me something? Got any money? Got an apple? You can't just walk in with nothing, after five years." Shit, why do I make her sound like a harpy? She was bad, she wasn't that bad. She kept blowing the hair out of her eyes. *(Beating his eyes.)* Grrr. Grrr.

UNCLE: Grrrr.

GLATZ: Lot of traffic tonight. They're driving up and down the avenue, picking up people—plimp-plim-plim. *Heraus! Heraus!* The ice is breaking on the river. The worst thing is the cold wind. *(Beating his mouth.)* They arrested Uncle Tabori this morning.

UNCLE: Well, that's got nothing to do with you.

GLATZ: That's right, nothing.

UNCLE: So how do you know?

GLATZ: I've heard. *(Listens.)* Grrr. Grrrr. *(Beating his mouth.)* Someone must have denounced him. *(A silence. Prompting:)* "Who would do such a thing?"

UNCLE: "Who would do such a thing?"

GLATZ: You buy a little air to breathe, this much, a little life. Under the circumstances the only moral thing is to keep breathing. It's a matter of logic. You scratch my back, I scratch yours.

There is a certain kind of elegance in the equation of breathing with treason. *(Steps forward, bows to the audience.)* A great mind; a great analytical mind. Something happened; they won't tell me what, except . . . *(Trying to think hard.)* One day he sat in the quarry. A lizard came out, an exquisite little creature. They looked at each other, he and the lizard. Then, a guard passed by and, for no reason at all, crushed it under his heel. The lizard looked up at my father with ancient eyes, as if to say, "What's the matter with you people?" He didn't know what to say, he didn't know what to say, he didn't know what to say . . . You go to them. You bow. You say, "Guten abend." You don't have to say much. "Mr. Weiss? Hmmmmm. Mr. Haas? Oh well . . . Mr. Lang? Ah him? . . .

(WEISS *makes a furious sound and rushes at* GLATZ.)

UNCLE: You move one step closer to my son and I'll split your head.

GLATZ *(beating his mouth):* "Uncle Tabori? Tsk-tsk-tsk."

(UNCLE *hits him.*)

Trouble is you run out of people. You consult the phone book, the tombstones, you start inventing people. Finally you are left with no one to denounce but yourself. "Professor Glatz? Oh him!"

UNCLE: Are they looking for you?

GLATZ: Grrr.

UNCLE: Grrr.

ALL BUT KLAUB: Grrr.

UNCLE: Would you like to eat something?

GLATZ: That's not what she said.

UNCLE: What did she say?

GLATZ: "I hope they will come for you. I hope they will break your bones. I hope they will cut your tongue out. And when they beat your head against the floor, I will say, Beat a little harder."—Let me hear you say that!

UNCLE: "And when they beat your head against the floor, I will say, Beat a little harder."

GLATZ: Oh, but they're not monsters. If you're healthy, they send you to a labor camp. You get a lot of fresh air and exercise. If you are sick, they put you in a hospital. Heltai's mother, for instance, was taken to the Rokus Hospital the day after I'd mentioned his name.

(HELTAI *rises sadly.*)

You will like it there, the nuns are nice. True, there's nothing seriously wrong with you, an occasional fit, not serious enough for hospitalization, but don't worry, I'm going to break your leg. I'll break it so well, it'll take years to heal, and by then the whole thing will be over. Put your leg on that chair.

(UNCLE *obeys.*)

(*Prays.*) "The children ask bread; nobody breaks it for them; they that were brought up in scarlet, embrace the dunghills now." See the leg? See the son? See the hammer? (*Smashes* UNCLE's *leg.*)

(*A silence.*)

UNCLE: Come now, it's time for your supper.

GLATZ: Is the table set?

UNCLE: With a white cloth and a bowl of flowers.

GLATZ: Is everyone present?

UNCLE: Yes, it's a reunion.

GLATZ: Oh, I like this dream. Are you the host?

UNCLE: Yes.

GLATZ: Will they let me sit at the table?

(UNCLE *signals the others.* HAAS *croaks a welcome. The others greet* GLATZ: "We missed you . . . Good to see you . . . How are the kids?—Say, have you heard . . . ? Well, what d'you know? . . . You haven't changed a bit . . . ")

What's my penance?

UNCLE: Life.

ALL BUT KLAUB (*a toast*): To life!

UNCLE: Now the meal is served. Here, a steaming tureen with hands and feet.

(*The others are stamping their feet and shaking their heads in terror.*)

Here, a dish of sweetbread, glazed to a delicate brown. Here, a plate with eyes. Here, a sautéed kidney.

(HAAS *croaks.* THE GYPSY *lets out a scream. But none of them can move.*)

And here, on a great silver platter, the roast itself, swimming in a bloody gravy, a number tattooed on his back.

(GLATZ *covers his mouth.* WEISS *turns away, retching.* LANG *collapses.* HAAS *croaks and runs, leans against the wall.* THE GYPSY *bends in double.* HELTAI *takes deep breaths.* HIRSCHLER *starts out, slumps down by the door.*)

UNCLE *(pursuing them):* No, that's Puffi's chair. Puffi always gets the big chair . . . He is late but he'll be here. D'you think we should wait for him? No, says Hirschler, I don't think we should wait for him. Let's be fair, says Little Lang, he is coming from the country, the trains aren't running on time. Too bad, says Heltai, I'm famished, let's start. Maybe he forgot, says Ghoulos. No, I talked to him on the phone this morning. "I'm taking the 6:30," he said, "I'll be there before you."— Listen! I think I can hear him now. Yes, he is coming upstairs. You know how he walks—with the airy grace of the very fat. There he is. No, it's not him. It's a young man, with an umbrella; it's Puffi's son. Look, he come in.

(PUFFI *comes in.*) His head is shaking, he circles the table. (PUFFI *shakes his head, circles the table.*) "Where is my father?"

PUFFI: Where is my father?

UNCLE: "What have you done to him?"

PUFFI: What have you done to him?

KLAUB: We ate him up and spat him out.

SCENE 12

The Trial

KLAUB *(playing with the knife):* I know what you've been trying to do, but I won't let you spoil my appetite or give me heartburn for all eternity. Meat is meat, and fuck my father in heaven. I'm not an evil man. I wouldn't hurt a lamb in the field; if I saw a man hurting it, I would kill that man; yeh, I might bash in his face, but there are daily murders in every housewife's kitchen: chicken slaughtered, fish decapitated, etcetera, and where do you draw the line? If I'm served a lambchop I would not weep over it, I would not go away hungry. I'm not a fool; there is no goodness in a fool. Meat is meat, and I want to be, to be a witness, a walking exhibition of wounds; and I will show my wounds to my children. No, I will push their faces into my wounds, I will make them kiss my running sores, I will make them drink of my pus: let them learn not to find virtue in suffering. And if there be two men here, one victim and one murderer, I would not be the victim. I don't care where my next meal is coming from, from what butcher shop, by what accident. I care about one thing: How did I get here? Was there no other place to go? No other way to spend this evening? Do you see this knife?

UNCLE: I see a knife.

KLAUB: Remember the other knife, the knife that was passed around in the cattle car?

UNCLE: Vaguely.

KLAUB: Let me refresh your memory. *(To the others.)* Come closer. Closer. Much closer! Closer!
(They stand about him like sardines in a box.)
The cattle car was big enough for forty men or six cows. There were a hundred and eighty of us in it, facing the door. The door closed, squeezing the light out of our eyes. The train began to move. We stood jogging like puppets in the dark. Where were you, Uncle?

248

UNCLE: I was standing next to you.

KLAUB: How would you describe the atmosphere of the cattle car?

UNCLE: Terror.

KLAUB: As for instance?

UNCLE: Mauer had a fit and choked to death.

KLAUB: Very good. Anything else?

UNCLE: Boredom.

KLAUB: Go on.

UNCLE: Humor.

KLAUB: Could you be more specific?

UNCLE: I'd rather not.

HIRSCHLER: "Say, where d'you think we're going?"

HELTAI: "California."

HIRSCHLER: "Isn't that too far?"

HELTAI: "To far from what?"

(All laugh.)

KLAUB: Who had the knife?

(HAAS croaks. KLAUB hits him.)

I was asking him. What kind of a knife was it?

UNCLE: I believe it was a penknife.

HIRSCHLER: No, no, it was one of those Swiss hunting knives, you know, with several blades and a corkscrew.

KLAUB: What did Weiss do with the knife?

(A silence. KLAUB hits UNCLE.)

What did he do with it?

UNCLE: He passed it around.

KLAUB: For what purpose?

UNCLE: For us to consider . . .

KLAUB: Consider what?

UNCLE: To kill the guard at Sopron and escape.

KLAUB: What was Sopron?

UNCLE: The last but one stop.

KLAUB: How would you define as briefly as possible, the idea of killing the guard at Sopron?

UNCLE: "I will not go like sheep to my slaughter."

KLAUB: Am I correct in assuming that the idea of killing the guard

at Sopron while the train made a brief stop did not appear as
particularly inhuman? absurd? violent?

LANG: No.

KLAUB *(hits him):* I was asking him. Could we have escaped?

UNCLE: Perhaps.

KLAUB: What was the alternative?

UNCLE: Nothing.

KLAUB: Meaning?

UNCLE: This.

KLAUB: Here?

UNCLE: Yes.

KLAUB: Were the practical considerations fully discussed?

UNCLE: Yes.

KLAUB: The technical details worked out?

UNCLE: Yes.

KLAUB: How did I summarize the plan?

UNCLE: "The train stops. The door is opened. They let us out. The
bucket is emptied, the dead removed. The fields . . ."

KLAUB: Go on.

(UNCLE *is silent.* KLAUB *hits him.)*

"The fields are over there. The swamps are over here."

THE GYPSY *(getting hysterical):* Give me the knife! Who's going to
stand behind the guard? Who's going to strike? Who's going
to engage the guard in conversation? Who's going to smile at
him? Who's going to run? Who's going to live?

KLAUB: Very good. What happened to the knife?

UNCLE: Nothing.

KLAUB: Was it ever used?

UNCLE: No.

KLAUB: Where did it end up?

UNCLE: In the bucket.

KLAUB: Who put it there?

UNCLE: I did.

KLAUB: You mean I gave it to you?

UNCLE: Yes.

KLAUB: How would you explain this extraordinary change of heart?

UNCLE: I was in rather good form that night.

KLAUB: You were magnificent. I accuse him of magnificence. He pleaded, he reasoned, he roared. How come the Lord never roars at his adversaries? Why is it always the family that takes the rap? He spoke with a tongue of fire in the cattle car *(mockingly)*, God's own pimp, hustling the same old pox:

"Resist not evil. Turn the other cheek.

Blessed are those that men revile, those that

Wash the sidewalk, blessed, blessed the dead.

And damn the living that want to eat.

Honor thy father, so he may go on lying to you.

Thou shalt not bear false witness, lest you protect your brothers.

Thou shalt not kill, why complicate matters for the pigs?

Those that live by the sword shall perish by the sword."

And those that don't? How will they die, Uncle? Tell us, Uncle, you who brought us here.

UNCLE: I did not bring you here. What d'you want from me, immortality? To live without pain? How dare you take me to account? What is it you are afraid of? What are you hanging on to with such desperation? A little warmth in your belly? Was there a promise made? I promised you nothing. I told you the weather would be cold. What do you want from me now, a benediction on your murders?

KLAUB: That's when the train was slowing down.

UNCLE: I tell you now as I told you in the cattle car: When murder meets murder, they fuck like skunks and multiply.

KLAUB *(pursuing him)*: The train stopped; it was in the middle of the night. The door opened; they let us out for ten minutes. We emptied the bucket. There was no moon, but we could see the fields. The guards came closer. Plump little men, no longer young.

(The others play guards now.)

UNCLE *(praying):* "I am a worm and no man; a reproach of men and despised of the people."

KLAUB: They mocked his singsong prayer.

(They do.)

UNCLE: "He trusted in the Lord that He would deliver him."

KLAUB: A crowd gathered. Women and children, too.

HIRSCHLER: Yes, I remember a girl in a *babooshka.*[11] She never stopped giggling *(giggles like a little girl).*

UNCLE: "I am cast upon Thee from the womb."

THE GYPSY: Wash the floor, yid. *(Pulls* UNCLE's *beard.)*

HIRSCHLER *(tweaks his nose):* Do some pushups.

*(*UNCLE *obeys.)*

HELTAI: Run up and down the platform.

*(*UNCLE *obeys.)*

KLAUB: They called us the usual names—*Saujud! Arschloch! Scheisskerl!* Meaning—freely translated *(kisses* LANG*)*—Jew-pig! *(Hugs* GHOULOS.*)* Asshole! *(Embraces* THE GYPSY.*)* Shit-head.

UNCLE: "Thou art my God from my mother's belly."

WEISS *(as a woman, dashes forward, hits* UNCLE*):* Jewpig!

THE GYPSY *(dashes forward as a child, kicks* UNCLE*):* Asshole!

GLATZ *(another woman, dashes forward, knocks* UNCLE *down):* Shithead.

*(*HAAS *croaks, dashes forward, spits in* UNCLE's *face.)*

UNCLE: "Be not far from me, for trouble is near."

ALL TOGETHER *(chanting, stomping, approaching* UNCLE *in a tight group):* Jew—pig—ass—hole—shit—head!

UNCLE: "I am poured out like water and all my bones are out of joint."

ALL TOGETHER *(chanting):* Saujud! Sau . . . jud! Sau . . . jud!

LANG *(horrified):* Stop it! Stop!

UNCLE: "Deliver me from the sword; my darling from the power of the dog."

---

11. *Babooshka:* a scarf worn over the head.

(ALL *but* LANG *surge about him, lift him high as if to lynch him.*)

KLAUB *(egging them on):* It was getting late; they got bored.

GHOULOS: So they put us back on the train.

KLAUB *(pointing at* UNCLE*):* HE PUT US BACK ON THE TRAIN!

PUFFI: They stripped us naked!

KLAUB: HE STRIPPED US NAKED!

THE GYPSY: They will lead us into the shower room.

KLAUB: HE WILL LEAD US INTO THE SHOWER ROOM!

(All the others let out a grunt.)

With a prayer, without a knife!

(They fall upon UNCLE *and strip him naked. An improvised fight, as if the actors were out of control. A ram's horn is heard. Exhausted, they step back, revealing his nakedness. He is on the floor, shivering. They carry him on to the mountain and huddle close to warm him.)*

UNCLE: What are you doing? I'm not him. I'm me, his son. I can't figure him out. I try, I try, I've tried for twenty-five years. True, he was always a small eater. Flesh made him shy. Veal or women. But he wouldn't be seen dead in a synagogue. In his last note—found miraculously on his body—forwarded to me on 72nd Street—he says to me—"I wish you were here. I'm surrounded by realists. I cannot blame them. For the past three weeks they have eaten nothing but chicory leaves. And now they have enormous teeth. They look at each other like gourmets. I am trying to behave well. Forgive me, I shall probably fail as all the others have failed, including God. Everything has gone wrong for Him from the very first day: the weather, the lights, the people, and now this appalling breakdown. He ought to throw away the whole mess and start from the scratch. I feel very close to Him today. I call upon His name, and wait for Him in the latrine, where all the gossipers meet; perhaps He will come, and we shall sit side by side, two born losers comparing notes." Oh, I'm cold, I'm cold. He was such an ordinary man; but one day the city becomes as a widow;

the heathen have entered her gates, and he is made to wash the sidewalk. He feels the mighty hand and the great terror; he joins the fraternity of those whose teeth are broken with gravel. In other words: he becomes a Jew. No, you don't become a Jew. You are merely reminded that you are one.—I'm cold, I'm so cold.

(They surround him, pressing against him, to give him warmth, and they dress him, gently.)

WEISS *(banging on the pot):* Dinner's ready.

(A silence.)

KLAUB: I'm not hungry.

(A silence.)

Make sure the pot is poured out, and poor Puffi decently buried; and a prayer spoken for his soul.

SCENE 13

The Raid

HAAS *gives an inarticulate warning. They start growling and barking like dogs.*

GHOULOS: There's a raid going on.
THE GYPSY: A selection.
　(They bark.)
LANG: Last night they took everyone over fifty from Block 11.
　(They freeze, petrified. HAAS *brings a bowl of water. They go to wash their faces.)*
WEISS *(as if crying from a great distance):* You can have my shoes . . . Tell my wife . . .
　(They freeze, listening.)
HIRSCHLER: Isn't it amazing? In Block 11 they still have the strength to cry.
　(They are galvanized into action.)
GHOULOS: Item: face washing and hair-wetting with snow.
THE GYPSY: Item: rehearsal of youthful posture.
LANG: Item: rehearsal of heel-clicking and smiling.
　(They wet their hair, they click their heels, they smile, they giggle, they try to look young.)
HELTAI: Hirschler raised the main youth-maker: a lipstick!
　(They line up. HIRSCHLER *raises the lipstick, walks down the line, marks every face with the lipstick.)*
HIRSCHLER: They hoped to look young.
　(The dogs of SCHREKINGER *can be heard outside.)*
KLAUB: Sing something.
　(They line up for inspection, sing something jolly.)
　At which point, Schrekinger came in, the angel of death.
　(SCHREKINGER *comes in with* KAPO, *who has an imaginary camera.)*
SCHREKINGER *(fast and mechanical):* How old are you?
HIRSCHLER *(with a dopey grin):* Twenty-five.

255

SCHREKINGER: How old are you?

GLATZ (*thinking hard*): Twenty—twenty—twenty—

SCHREKINGER: How old are you?

HELTAI: Twenty-four, sir.

SCHREKINGER: How old are you?

(LANG *has fainted.*)

HIRSCHLER: A mere youth.

SCHREKINGER (*pays no attention*): How old are you?

HIRSCHLER: Thirty-six. Er—thirty-seven.

SCHREKINGER: He was lying. At which point an enemy plane roared overhead.

(WEISS *imitates roar, raises hand, longingly.*)

There were three possibilities: to be nice to these wretches, to kill them off at once, or both. I put my arm around the liar's shoulder. Little Moe asks his Mom, "Is it true that Hitler is dying of throat cancer?"—"Shut up and keep learning Russian."

(HIRSCHLER *gives a forced laugh.*)

KAPO (*taking picture*): Click.

SCHREKINGER: "Sharing a joke with some of the old-timers."

KAPO: Click.

SCHREKINGER: How old are you?

THE GYPSY: I'm not supposed to be here at all, sir.

SCHREKINGER: Oh?

THE GYPSY: I don't know how I got in with these Jewish gentlemen.

SCHREKINGER: Drop your pants.

THE GYPSY (*obeying*): I'm an indispensable member of the Camp Orchestra. I can raise and lower my balls at will.

SCHREKINGER (*without looking*): Let me see. Very disappointing.

(*Looking at* GHOULOS' *pin-up nude.*) Who is she?

GHOULOS: It doesn't say, sir.

SCHREKINGER: We stood there, looking at the pin-up.—You could eat that, couldn't you?

GHOULOS: Yes, sir.

SCHREKINGER: Yum-yum-yummy?

GHOULOS: Yes, sir!

SCHREKINGER: He slapped him on the back of his head and tore up the pin-up.

(GHOULOS *reels as if hit in the back of his head.*)

—How old are you?

WEISS: Twenty-odd.

SCHREKINGER: He offered the prisoner a miniature chess set. He made a move. He resigned. He shook him by the hand.

KAPO: Click.

SCHREKINGER: "The Good Loser." *(Sees* LANG.) What have we here?

(UNCLE *moves to help* LANG *up.*)

Don't touch him, he's mine.

KAPO: Click.

SCHREKINGER: "Paying respect to the fallen."—How old are you?

LANG *(gets up):* Fifteen, sir.

SCHREKINGER: Turn around. Oh, it's you.

UNCLE: I was born in 1874.

SCHREKINGER: Never mind.

UNCLE: I'm seventy-one, sir.

SCHREKINGER: Is that your idea of a Jewish joke?

UNCLE: No, sir.

SCHREKINGER: Let me see you do fifty kneebends.

(UNCLE *starts doing kneebends. The others do the same, out of solidarity.*)

I offered a sugarcube to the boy.

KAPO: Click.

SCHREKINGER: "Charity never faileth." *(To* LANG.) Come to my office.

UNCLE: He is only fifteen.

SCHREKINGER: What did you say?

UNCLE: He is only fifteen.

SCHREKINGER: WHAT DID YOU SAY TO ME?

UNCLE: Take me instead. *(Collapses.)*

SCHREKINGER: I couldn't fuck you, could I? Where is the fat man? Where is my favorite subject?

(A silence. They stop doing kneebends.)

KAPO *(yelling):* Where is the fat man?

SCHREKINGER: Listen, if there'll be any yelling around here, it's going to be from me. How old are you?

KAPO: Thirty-one.

SCHREKINGER: You look terrible. *(Sniffs.)* What's cooking?

(A silence. The KAPO *brings the pot to him.* SCHREKINGER *looks into it. He smiles.)* Set the table.

SCENE 14

The Meal

The table is set. The Camp orchestra is heard at a distance, playing a jolly polka.

SCHREKINGER: Start serving.
   (The KAPO *starts serving.)*
   Bon appétit.
   (No ones moves.)
   The camp orchestra is giving a concert.
   (No one moves.)
   I'm taking pictures.
   (No one moves.)
   Eat.
   (No one moves.)
   Eat.
   *(*HAAS *shakes his head and croaks.)*
   Into the showers.
   *(*HAAS *starts stripping.)*
   EAT.
EVERYONE *(imitating the showers):* Sssssssss.
   *(*GHOULOS *rises.)*
SCHREKINGER: Into the showers!
EVERYONE: Ssssssss.
   *(*GHOULOS *starts stripping.)*
SCHREKINGER: Eat.
   *(*LANG *starts stripping.)*
EVERYONE: Sssssssss.
SCHREKINGER: Eat.
   *(*GLATZ *hesitates, massaging his head.)*
   Eat.
   *(*GLATZ *starts stripping.)*
EVERYONE: Sssssss.

259

Serving the meal, from the 1968 production at the American Place Theatre, New York. Photograph by Martha Holmes.

SCHREKINGER: Eat.

 (WEISS *starts stripping.*)

EVERYONE: Sssssss.

SCHREKINGER: Eat.

 (THE GYPSY *starts stripping.*)

EVERYONE: Ssssssss.

SCHREKINGER: Eat.

 (KLAUB *starts stripping.*)

EVERYONE: Ssssssss.

SCHREKINGER: Eat.

 (UNCLE *starts stripping.*)

EVERYONE: Sssssss.

THE LOUDSPEAKERS: Sssssssss.

SCHREKINGER: Eat.

HIRSCHLER: I'm eating.

KAPO: Click.

SCHREKINGER: Eat.

HELTAI: I've always found it difficult to decline an invitation.

KAPO: Click.

THE LOUDSPEAKERS: Sssssssss.

 (*Huddling close for warmth, the naked ones go out.*)

SCENE 15

The Survivors

HELTAI *and* HIRSCHLER *are eating.* SCHREKINGER *joins them, sitting at the other end of the table.*

SCHREKINGER: Nowadays he runs a restaurant in Dusseldorf.
HIRSCHLER: Oh yeh?
SCHREKINGER: Calls it "Schrekinger's Hideaway."
HELTAI: Say, that's clever.
SCHREKINGER: Specializes in Southern Fried Chicken.
HIRSCHLER: Hm-hmmm.
SCHREKINGER: Daddy, what did you do in the war?

(*A silence . . . As the* FATHER.) Oh, I've always had this fantasy about virtue, a sort of admiration; and a terror. On the other hand, evil is the only authentic thing, isn't it? I mean, you read about a man who has killed his wife and you say, "Uh-huh!" But read about a man who hasn't killed his wife, and you say, "What's the matter with the son of a bitch?"

(*As the* SON.) Daddy, what did you do in the war, Daddy?

(*As the* FATHER.) I was obeying orders. Everyone was obeying orders. There is a Fuehrer in the asshole of the best of us. Those wretches, too, were only obeying orders. Whose orders, what orders, you figure that out, but, my God, they had more discipline than the whole fucking Wehrmacht. Oh, I was terrified of them, and mind you, I'd been in Dresden Town[12] when the bombs began to fall. I didn't mind that, it was a conversation between murderers, evil chatting with evil. I looked at the rubble

---

12. Dresden Town: Schrekinger refers to the Allied bombing of Dresden in 1945, which virtually destroyed the city.

and the roasted children, and I cried out to the bombers, "You dumb shits, you're no better than me." Yes, sir, in Dresden Town I felt—comfortable.

(As the SON.) Yes, but what did you do in the war, Daddy?

(As the FATHER, interrupting.) But these hairy, bugeyed, stinking skeletons gave me gooseflesh. It's fashionable to say that they didn't fight back, didn't resist; you don't know what resistance is; I know what resistance is. I knew it way back in '33 when I had told this whiskered old fart to wash the sidewalk, and he did, and I was waiting for a sign, a sign of contact, something recognizable, a gesture, anything, to show that he too was was playing the human game, that we were brothers under the skin, sharing a certain civilized concern for accommodation. There was no sign. He washed the sidewalk. He remained absolutely pure, no, intact, in his otherness.

(As the SON; with some impatience.) Daddy, you haven't answered my question.

(As the FATHER.) Oh, it's not that they were kindly or brave, no, they stole, they cheated, they betrayed one another, they stank, they hungered, they murdered, that's easy, anyone can do that, but there was always this otherness with which they let themselves be butchered so that they can define the nature of butchery. They did not suffer evil, they pointed at it, you know that rather vulgar way of theirs of pointing a finger at you and you and you.

(As the SON.) Daddy, don't give me any more philosophical bullshit, just tell me plain and simple (screaming) what did you do in the war?

Last time I saw him he was playing with his cash register. I threw a chair at him. (Throws a chair. A silence. He starts eating.)

HIRSCHLER *(to the audience; his mouth paralyzed):* Last night I was with my shrink on Park and 94th. He is 200 years old, comes from Vienna, can't speak a word of English, and as far as I can tell, is totally deaf. The moment I lie down, he turns off his hearing aid. I have to holler my banalities, the whole block knows what's my thing, and when I'm in good form I wake him up.

HELTAI *(as the* ANALYST*):* Now then . . . about your sister . . .

HIRSCHLER: Sister? What sister? I've been coming to you for five years, you bastard; for fifty bucks a throw. You should goddam well know I ain't got a sister. Okay, there I am, flat on my back and eating Almond Joy and telling him about this dream.

HELTAI *(as the* ANALYST*):* A dream? What do you mean a dream?

HIRSCHLER *(bellowing as if to a deaf man):* I dreamt I saw this child in a rice paddy. Had a gaping hole in one eye, a nose burnt off, his tongue cut out, but . . . and that's where the fascinating part comes in . . . I was happy.

HELTAI: Why was you unhappy?

HIRSCHLER: Not unhappy, you idiot, happy, I was happy, because I realized that everybody is a murderer, not only me, everybody, d'you hear?

HELTAI: Not everybody.

(A silence.)

HIRSCHLER: I hit him. It was a real breakthrough.

*(*SCHREKINGER *climbs on top of the table, wolfing, gulping, licking each bowl clean. The camp orchestra is heard playing.)*

THE LOUDSPEAKERS:

Herodotus and Strabo
Tell of the Scythian Massagetae
Who killed old people and ate them.[13]

---

13. See the end of the first book (chap. 216) of Herodotus' *The Histories* and book 2, chaps. 6 and 8, of Strabo's *Geography*. Herodotus, an historian of the fifth century, B.C., is discussing the customs of primitive societies; Strabo was a geographer who lived in the first and second centuries, A.D.

Sporadic cannibalism occurs among civilized people
As records of shipwrecks and sieges show.
The practice of devouring dead kinsfolk
As the most respectful method of disposing
Of their remains is combined with the custom
Of killing the old and the sick.
But some savages eagerly desire the body of a murdered man
So that his ghost may not trouble them,
For which reason I recommend, dear brethren in Christ,
The Jew's heart, in aspic or with sauce vinaigrette,
So soft it will melt in your mouth.

(SCHREKINGER *eats. The orchestra is playing.*)

THE END

Charlotte Delbo

WHO WILL CARRY THE WORD?

Qui Rapportera Ces Paroles?
translated from the French
by Cynthia Haft

Music for the original production of *Who Will Carry the Word?* was composed by Alain Kremsky.

Author's Note

No sets. The site is suggested by the positions and movements of the characters, and by the lighting. The action takes place in the barracks (there is no need to represent them; the light and text suffice) and on the roll call square outside a barren, snowy place or a barren, dusty place. The following is suggested: an inclined plane, which will serve as the roll call square, and on which the group's movements will take place as they go to roll call, for which they position themselves. The scenes which take place in the barracks will be played in the foreground, in front of the inclined plane. On the edge of the inclined plane the women will lie down for the night; they may exit on the garden side or the court side, but only one or the other, for the barracks have only one exit.

During the first and second acts, everyone except Laure is on stage at all times, and the impression of being in a crowd must be constantly maintained (noises, murmurings, conversations).

No make-up: faces powdered in gray, including eyelids and lips. *The faces do not count.*

Costumes: tunics or smocks or delivery-boy shirts either in ticking or gray, mid-calf length. *Certainly no stripes.* Kerchiefs on the head of the same gray or a variety of muted colors: brown, olive, military green, maroon. In the first and second acts, kerchiefs tightly knotted under the chin, covering the ears (it's cold). In the third act, they are tied at the nape of the neck. Gray slippers, and gray stockings.

The costumes do not count.

In a desolate landscape (nowhere . . . a place that no one can imagine), in a light of unreality, the groups mill about, then move into formation.

The movements will always be slow and voices will never be raised. The action of the play should be continuous and without intermission.

269

CAST OF CHARACTERS
In Order of Appearance

The action takes place in a death camp in which several thousand women of all nationalities are confined. Two hundred French women arrived there. Among them:

CLAIRE.

FRANÇOISE.

MOUNETTE, eighteen years old.

GINA.

YVONNE.

MADELEINE.

RÉINE.

MARIE, sixteen years old.

RENÉE.

AGNÈS.

SYLVIE, twenty years old.

SMALL PEASANT GIRL.

RÉGINE.

ELISABETH.

HORTENSE.

DENISE, seventeen years old.

MONIQUE, Denise's sister, twenty years old.

BERTHE.

DÉDÉE, Bertha's sister, twenty years old.

HÉLÈNE'S MOTHER, forty years old.

HÉLÈNE, eighteen years old.

LINA.

LAURE.

All those for whom no age is indicated are between twenty-five and thirty years of age.

WHO WILL CARRY
THE WORD?

Prologue

Music.

FRANÇOISE:
> Because I have returned from where there was no return
> You think I know everything
> And you crowd me
> Bursting with your questions
> Questions you cannot even formulate.
> You think that I know the answers
> All I know are facts
> Life
> Death
> Truth
> I return for truth.
> For there everything was true.
> Everything was stamped with truth, a mortal truth
> Clear and sharp, without nuance or measure.
> Pure cruelty, pure horror.
> Who could bear to face
> The truth in that cruelty?
> Close eyes forever,
> Or look on wide-eyed,
> Wild-eyed
> The only choice, the only chance.
> The light seared the eyes that dared to seek.
> So why should I speak?
> For the things I would say
> Could not be of any use to you.

ACT 1

Scene 1

In the barracks. In an aisle between the boxes which serve as beds, that is to say, in front of the inclined plane, in the foreground. Some groups chat. On one side, a group composed of FRANÇOISE, MOU-NETTE, YVONNE, GINA, MADELEINE. *Coming from another group,* CLAIRE, *who will be followed by* RÉINE. *Some standing up, the others lying down. It is late afternoon in winter. Hazy light inside. Outside, the light is hard and cutting on the snow.*

CLAIRE: Come here. I want to talk to you.

FRANÇOISE: Who, me?

CLAIRE: Yes, you.

FRANÇOISE: And who are you?

CLAIRE: Claire. Don't you recognize me?

FRANÇOISE: Now I recognize your voice. Voices are difficult to recognize. Even the voices have changed. Are they muffled or is it my ears?

MOUNETTE: It's the air here. It's the air that changes the sounds, the snow that blots out sounds.

FRANÇOISE: It's even more strange when you don't recognize those who are close to you. The hair, the walk, the silhouette. Is it enough to have your hair shorn to no longer be yourself?

YVONNE: If the men who loved us could see what has become of us . . . Let's be happy that on the morning of their death they could say goodbye to us when still we had the faces they loved.

GINA: We'll soon get used to these others that we have become and we'll recognize each other.

MOUNETTE: When is soon?

GINA: A few days.

YVONNE: A few days, that's too long. Days are slow, death is quick.

FRANÇOISE: And what did you want with me, Claire?

CLAIRE: Come over here.

FRANÇOISE: Talk. Here, we think out loud.

275

CLAIRE: What have I heard?

FRANÇOISE: What have you heard?

CLAIRE: That you wanted to commit suicide.

FRANÇOISE: Yes, so what?

CLAIRE: You have no right to.

FRANÇOISE: Oh, that'll do, Claire. Forget your formulas; here they aren't worth anything. It's the only right I have left, the only choice. The last free act.

CLAIRE: There are no free acts here. No choices like that.

FRANÇOISE: Oh yes. I have a choice. I have a choice, between becoming a cadaver which will have suffered for only eight days, which will still be clean enough to look at, and one which will have suffered fifteen days, which will be horrible to look at.

CLAIRE: You have nothing left. No such choices, nothing. You are not free to do it. You don't have the right to take your life.

FRANÇOISE: And why don't I have the right?

CLAIRE: A fighter doesn't commit suicide.

FRANÇOISE: Claire, please. Forget your affirmations, forget your certitudes. None of them fit here. Don't you see that truth has changed, that truth is no longer the same?

CLAIRE: I am asking you why you decided to commit suicide.

FRANÇOISE: You ask me! . . . Ask those who are lying rigid in the snow; ask their faces which are no longer faces; ask the sockets of their eyes which the rats have widened; ask their limbs which resemble dead wood; ask their skin which is a color no one has ever seen before. Don't you know all that a human being can withstand before dying? Don't you believe that to become so scrawny, so ugly, so convulsed, so trapped in what remains of skin and flesh, you have to have suffered to the limit, a limit which no one reached before us? I don't want to suffer to that limit.

CLAIRE: Can't you see further than yourself and your own death? Can't you see . . .

FRANÇOISE: I see. I am lucid. I am logical. I've never been more reasonable.

CLAIRE: You don't want to fight.

FRANÇOISE: I'm willing to fight, to try, but with a chance, even a little one, however small, but a chance. And I don't see any. No one will survive. If it's to be death for death's sake, then better right away, before having suffered that suffering you see written on the dead there in the snow, over there on the pile where the ravens and the rats get together, those naked dead bodies, entangled in a pile, even on top of those still alive, who arrived a week before us. I prefer to die before becoming a corpse as ugly as those.

CLAIRE: Coquetry is out of place here.

FRANÇOISE: I have no gift for lost courage.

CLAIRE: Will you listen to me?

FRANÇOISE: You must wait until my eyes do not see what they see, for my ears to listen to you.

CLAIRE: My eyes see as well as yours. You're afraid. You're a coward.

FRANÇOISE: Afraid to suffer, yes. A coward—another word that is meaningless here.

CLAIRE: I'll tell you again that you don't have the right to take your life. You don't have the right because you're not alone. There are the others. And above all, there are the little ones, Mounette, Denise, and her sister, Rosette, big Hélène and little Hélène. Aurore, Rosie who isn't even sixteen, all the little ones whom you taught to recite poetry, whom you had perform in plays before we left, when we invented pastimes while we waited for the departure. They admired you because you were grown up. They listen to you, they follow you. If you commit suicide, they may imitate you. Suppose that among them, there is one who has a chance to come back, just one, and that because of you, she loses that chance. Even if you were to die in fifteen days and become as tortured a cadaver as those, you have to stand it.

FRANÇOISE: What good will it do? None of us has a chance. No one knows we're here. We're fighters off the battlefield, useless. If we fight to get out, it's no use to anyone, not even to ourselves. We are cut off from everything, cut off from ourselves.

CLAIRE: There must be one who returns, you or another, it doesn't matter. Each of us expects to die here. She is ready. She knows her life doesn't matter any more. Every one of us looks to the others. There must be one who comes back, one who will tell. Would you want millions of people to have been destroyed here and all those cadavers to remain mute for all eternity, all those lives to have been sacrificed for nothing?

FRANÇOISE: It's exactly that. For nothing. To die here, in this place, whose name we don't even know—perhaps it has no name?

CLAIRE: There must be one who comes back, who will give it its name.

FRANÇOISE: Here, at the frontiers of the inhabited world, yes, it's to die for nothing. It's already as if we were dead.

CLAIRE: If the world never knows anything about it. But there will be one who will return and who will talk and who will tell, and who will make known, because it is no longer we who are at stake, it's history—and people want to know their history. Haven't you heard them, the dying, who all say, "If you return, you'll tell"? Why do they say that? They say that because none of us is alone and each must render an account to all the others.

FRANÇOISE: The others . . . Other people in other places. To us, here, *they* have lost their reality. Everything has lost its shape, its depth, its sense, its color. All that is left is the amount of time we must suffer before dying.

CLAIRE: Yes, the others, the people you know, your friends—this one or that particular one—have lost their reality. But I speak of men, of the men of the whole world, those who are now and those who will come afterwards. To them you must render an account.

FRANÇOISE: Why me? One more, one less . . . Choose someone else for your mission.

CLAIRE: We arrived two hundred, 200 women from all the provinces, from all classes, who were thrown here into this population of 15,000 women. 15,000 women who are never the same. They die by the hundreds each day, they arrive by the hundreds each day. Of these 15,000 women from all countries of all the languages of Europe, how many will survive? 15,000 women more or less, 200 women more or less, what difference does it make? You, me; it doesn't matter who—no one matters. They will only matter if there is one who returns.

FRANÇOISE: It won't be me.

CLAIRE: Don't you really want to understand anything? Even if you hold out for only fifteen days . . .

FRANÇOISE: I won't hold out for fifteen days because I don't want to, because I don't believe it matters, because I prefer to finish it off right away and skip those fifteen days.

CLAIRE: Suppose you hold out fifteen days during which you will have helped others to hold out? Even if you give up then, fifteen days will have been gained. Another will take your place, then another, then another, so that there will be one who makes it until the end.

FRANÇOISE: Until the end . . . When do you see it arriving?

CLAIRE: I don't see it any more than you. Even if there is no hope, even if all is lost, you still have to try.

GINA: I'm ready to hold out for as long as it takes. Who knows the future? There may be a surprise, something may happen which would change all the calculations.

FRANÇOISE: The Allies will drop from the sky suddenly, tear out the barbed wire, pull down the watchtowers, and we'll be free? Do you believe in miracles?

GINA: Whatever way we get out, getting out of here will be a miracle.

MADELEINE: You have to believe in miracles. My father used to say that in all battles, in all shipwrecks, there's always one survivor.

YVONNE: Is it a rule? No rules stand here. I know we'll win, but the war will last another two years and I won't last two months.

CLAIRE: You'll last two months if you want to.

YVONNE: No, Claire. Until we came here, I believed that a man, a woman, could be stripped of everything, could lose everything, but could still keep her pride. When I joined my resistance group, I thought of torture; I thought of it a lot, so as not to be caught unaware, to get used to resisting it, and I acquired a certain strength, the certainty of resisting torture. Before, I was afraid. I was especially afraid of myself, afraid of weakness. That's why until we came here, I believed that nothing could divest a human being of his pride. Nothing except dysentery. You can no longer look at yourself when you gradually dissolve, turning into dirty water, when diarrhea is dripping from you night and day without being able to do anything to stop it, to hide yourself, to wash. I am turning into dirty water. My strength is ebbing, stinking, it flows, right here, right now, while I stand still because if I move it will be worse. My strength and my will are going. I am emptying. It is normal for life to expire through the lips. When it goes through the intestines—that's complete humiliation.

FRANÇOISE: We've been here for eight days. We've already lost ten of our group.

MOUNETTE: What did they die from, so quickly?

FRANÇOISE: What their eyes saw made their hearts burst.

CLAIRE: The old ones. You're young. You too, Yvonne.

YVONNE: Death will be coming more and more quickly. There are some who no longer have the strength to stand on their feet. Every morning, at roll call, they fall. We help them stand up again. Today. Tomorrow, we won't have the strength to help them.

FRANÇOISE: You see, Claire, I'm not rambling.

(Enter RÉINE, who listens.)

CLAIRE: Since you've decided to die, a little sooner or a little later doesn't matter. Make it a little later, for the sake of the one who has to return.

FRANÇOISE: None of us shall return.

CLAIRE: How do you know?

FRANÇOISE: I know. And you know just as well.

CLAIRE: Reasonable knowledge isn't necessarily right. I know it's easier to die than to live. You tear your dress lengthways, you twist it and attach it to a beam in the roof. You tie the knot and jump into the middle of the aisle between the bunks.

FRANÇOISE: Or you run into the barbed wire, you touch the wire . . .

MOUNETTE: Electrocuted . . . I wouldn't choose that, it's horrible.

FRANÇOISE: Here, there are only horrible versions of death.

CLAIRE: And you think you can do that? You aren't free. Even if you are nothing but the smallest link, you are part of a chain that links all men—that links them far into the future. No matter what you do, you are part of the human chain. You cannot exclude yourself.

RÉINE: Claire is right. If there is only one chance to get out of here and for only one of us, we must force that chance and help the one among us who will have it. There must be one who returns.

FRANÇOISE: You're lucky, Claire, and you too Réine, to always know what ought to be done.

(CLAIRE *and* RÉINE *move away to return to their group.*)

Scene 2

The same place. Another group, also standing, composed of RENÉE, AGNÈS, BERTHE *and her sister* DÉDÉE, *holding onto her.* MARIE *joins them.*

MARIE: My name is Marie. I am sixteen. Can I come with you? I mean, can you take me with you? Because I'm all alone now.

RENÉE: Did you arrive all alone?

MARIE: No, with my parents. My father, my mother, my grandmother and the little ones: my little brother, my little sister. In a big transport.

RENÉE: Where did you come from?

MARIE: Paris.

RENÉE *(looks at her number):* You haven't been here very long.

MARIE: Oh yes. Ten days. Years of a single season, years of winter and of night. It was a big transport. Almost the whole train went to the gas. There were many old men and many children. My parents weren't old, but they didn't want to leave grandmother and the little ones. Me, I wanted to stay in the same column. They said that it was a column for the health camp, a special camp for the aged and for the children. An officer took me out and put me in the other column. A very small column. The only person I knew was a girl of my own age who had traveled in the same freight car. Her parents had been taken too, so we stayed together—until this morning.

RENÉE: What did she die of?

MARIE: I don't know. Her face was all swollen, all red, and this morning she was dead at my side.

RENÉE: You can stay with Denise and her sister. They have a box at the end with five other little ones. They'll make room for you, you're not very fat. *(Calling.)* Denise! Monique! Would you take this little one with you? She's all alone. *(To* DENISE, *who enters.)* Her name is Marie. She's sixteen, like you.

MARIE: She was beautiful, my little sister. You can't imagine how beautiful she was. They couldn't have looked at her. If they had looked at her, they wouldn't have killed her. They wouldn't have been able to.

(Siren for evening roll call. The women leave the barracks in disordered groups, going towards the roll call square, form ranks, at first chaotically, each looking for her friends, then making themselves into rows of five. In the meantime, the lights have dimmed. Now it is night, violently lit up by the spotlights from the back of the theater).

Scene 3

In ranks for roll call. FRANÇOISE *in front,* GINA *behind her, three more in back of them. And so on by rows of five. Since each speaks only to her neighbors, it must be arranged that those who speak to each other be next to each other. During the roll call, the women change places so as not to be always at the end of the rows, because of the cold. They all rub their arms, rub each other's backs, huddle close to one another, etc.*

FRANÇOISE: There are only two options: life or death. It's simple. There is only one penalty: death. Death if you break rank, death if you drag your feet, death if you don't run fast enough, death if you don't understand an order or an insult, death if you can't stand still for five hours in the cold, in the night. Death if you catch cold. Catch cold . . . What an expression. Funny, isn't it? We are in the cold, we are cold, blocks of cold. Before we didn't know what cold was. Yet in the freight cars it was cold. The bread froze; we couldn't eat. Here, blades, needles of cold pierce you straight through. Jaws of cold crush you. Cold contracts the fibers of your flesh, even those on the tongue, even those of the heart. Cold feet is nothing. Cold in the heart, cold veins, cold drafts in the lungs, as though they were hanging in the wind naked. A thorn of cold stuck into every vertebra. It's as though the cold peels you and strips you inside of you. Here, you don't wait for death, you expect it. Why struggle?

GINA: It's what I wonder. Why do we still want to live? It seems to me that it's not I that makes the decision. It must be that which is still alive wants to keep on living, for no reason.

FRANÇOISE: Always the only question: life or death?

MOUNETTE *(in the adjoining row):* When we entered the camp, when we passed through the gate and we saw all the naked cadavers on the snow, we tried to walk around, to sidestep cadavers, and they came with their sticks to make us walk

A roll call, from the 1974 production at the Cyrano Theatre, Paris, France.

straight . . . I had never seen a dead body. And you, had you ever seen any?

FRANÇOISE: No. For me too they were the first.

MOUNETTE: You remember how we jumped over them running? I tried not to look, to look only at where I was putting my feet. If, at that moment, they had told us: "This way to be shot," we would not have walked, we would have run. And now that all we have to do is let ourselves fall down in the snow, we're clinging to life. I think the way you do, Françoise, and if it were for nothing . . .

FRANÇOISE: You have to make a bet with yourself, Mounette.

MOUNETTE: Is that what you're doing?

FRANÇOISE: Yes, right now.

MOUNETTE: Claire convinced you?

FRANÇOISE: No, you did. You would have preferred to have been shot when we arrived, and now you want to live. I won't leave you.

Scene 4

AGNÈS: Something is happening over there.

GINA: What is it?

AGNÈS: Claire left her place. I don't know why. Where is she going? I don't see her.

YVONNE (at the end of the row from where she sees better): Sylvie broke ranks to use the ditch. A kapo[1] with a stick started beating her and Claire ran to pull Sylvie away from her, to bring her back to the row. The kapo left Sylvie and turned on Claire. She's striking her on the head, on the chest, on the eyes. Oh . . . Claire is furious. She's giving it back to the kapo blow for blow, with her fists, with her feet. But the other one won't stop

---

1. Kapo: a prison guard often recruited from the inmates and having a reputation for extreme cruelty.

either. I can't believe that Claire is so strong. There's another one coming.

(The ranks waver; several would like to help CLAIRE. *The shadow of an S.S. guard in a cape passes in front of the row keeping them in place and mute. The shadow moves away.)* Claire is on the ground. The two furies are trampling her. *(A cry.)* It's Claire. They smashed her skull. Now they're leaving. It's finished.

RÉINE: We must go and get Claire.

(The shadow of the S.S. passes.)

YVONNE: They're giving the order to pick her up to put her back in her place. Two are going.

(Two prisoners bring CLAIRE *back and place her in front of the row she belonged to. She does not move.)*

HÉLÈNE'S MOTHER *(crossing herself):* My God, do not let me become evil in this place.

SYLVIE *(to hide she goes from row to row until she is standing next to* GINA *and* FRANÇOISE*):* Claire died for me. The two furies wouldn't have left me alive if Claire hadn't diverted their blows.

FRANÇOISE: All those who die here die for the others. You could say that death must take its toll: it attacks the group. If the group is large enough, some will be left. But the number keeps diminishing. The screen that the others form between death and each of us tears more each day, and soon there will be nothing between us and death.

GINA: And soon it will be our turn. My turn.

AGNÈS: You mustn't say it. Words become irrevocable once they are pronounced. It's only through blindness that we can hope. It's not courage that we need, it's blindness or madness. Our only chance is for each to say to herself: "If there is one who returns, it must be I." And it's madness to say that to yourself. And none knows why she must return.

RÉINE: Oh yes, Agnès. To tell how the others died.

AGNÈS: Do you think that is a sufficient reason?

RÉINE: The only one.

AGNÈS: If there is only one who returns, I don't want to be her. What can she do, that one who returns, to start life again? Do you think you could start again, Gina?

GINA: I don't know. But if you think of the resources within ourselves and each other that we find to draw upon, to help us come out alive, you realize that we will find other resources to live again if we return.

AGNÈS: No, Gina. We'll have left all our energy here. Nothing will remain. If we return, we will live without life.

(A whistle is heard. The women come to attention. By the way in which suddenly, row by row, they stand tall, look straight ahead, perfectly still, by the way that silence prevails, one "sees" that the S.S. are passing to count. As soon as the S.S. are at a certain distance, the conversations resume, at first quietly. At the end of the rows, a woman breaks rank.)

GINA: Why is she breaking rank?

MADELEINE *(whispering):* He called her.

GINA: Why?

AGNÈS: Hush, Gina. We are all thinking it!

MADELEINE: Her feet are swollen. Oh! Enormous. It must be because of that.

(All the women look at their legs. Some go rapidly from the first row towards the middle, to hide. "You go to the back," "Don't stay in front," is heard. And they pull each other, fearing that the S.S. may return and choose some more.)

MADELEINE: It's for Block 25.

FRANÇOISE: Block 25 is the prison within the prison. Those who can no longer walk, those who don't die quickly enough within our ranks, are locked up there. They have almost nothing to eat, nothing to drink. The yard of Block 25 is walled in. Our box has a windowpane which looks out on the yard. We see. The yard is covered with bodies. Every second or third day, a truck empties Block 25 to make more room. Those who aren't dead yet are taken to be gassed. Two prisoners, strong ones—they are chosen by their build, and they are fed well for that work—grab them by the waist or by the arms and throw them onto the truck. They work fast and well. They are watched. Why do they do that work? They are called the Heaven Kommando. They know that they have three months' reprieve, and after that, they in turn will be gassed. Why do they accept that work? Because three months here is a long time; it's as long as all the future. No one here can see for more than three weeks ahead; they are assured of three months. They say to themselves that in three months the war will be over, that they will be free. But how will they live after having done that work? I wonder if they don't wonder. I wouldn't do that. How dearly a man must cling to life to accept that work. How dearly a woman must cling to life to kill Claire. How dearly I must cling to life to see it happen and stay there without moving. But here, no one clings to life. It's life that clings to us.

We saw some of them leaving on the truck. There are some who cry out and their cries do not come from human throats. But most don't cry out. They don't have the strength any more. You would think that they had given up if you did not see their eyes. You've never seen such terror in the eyes. *(Aloud.)* Whom did they take?

MADELEINE: Someone I don't know, a young one. I think it's one of our peasant girls. They took three from the next row, from the Polish women.

THE SMALL PEASANT *(shouting as she disappears in the back)*: Comrades! I leave you my son.

FRANÇOISE: Who will carry her words back to the world?

(The S.S. are still walking through—but we never see them. Shadows; sudden immobility in the rows, total and sudden silence tell us they're there. Whistle blast. The ranks break. The women slowly return to the barracks in small disordered groups. They walk painfully, giving each other assistance, often two by two.)

GINA *(looking at the dead CLAIRE who is left there)*: I cried so much when they shot my husband. Today I envy him. At least he died a clean death.

Scene 5

GINA, FRANÇOISE *and* RÉINE *walk together towards the barracks.*

FRANÇOISE: You're strong, Gina, you'll return.

GINA: You too, Françoise, you're stronger than you think.

RÉINE: We're all stronger than we think. Even before we were arrested. Who would have thought that a little secretary like Mounette would leave her typewriter, her shopping trips, her hairdresser, and her appointments with her boyfriend under the Opera clock, to carry grenades, to throw them into the window of a café full of enemy soldiers? Who would have said that Yvonne would leave her parents, the high school where she taught Greek, to join a band of snipers? That Marie-Thérèse would give her children to a nursemaid to devote herself completely to the fight? For months on end, they lived as shadows among shadows, without money, without eating on time or when they were hungry, without any support but that of their comrades whom they met secretly on a subway platform or in some badly lit station to make liaisons, to carry papers, carry plans, carry orders, carry explosives. Who would have thought that Marguerite would leave her farm to join the partisans?

GINA: Or that I, whose day was spoiled by a run in my stocking, would take an oath to get out of here?

FRANÇOISE: No one really expected that.

RÉINE: Mounette, Yvonne, Marie-Thérèse chose to be ready for anything. We were all ready for anything, without imagining what awaited us; because it was unimaginable, we were protected against surprise.

FRANÇOISE: And indeed, it's not surprise that strikes us down. It is not from that horror beyond measure that we are dying. There were some who, at the start, had their throats so constricted that they could not swallow, who had their eyes opened so wide with horror that they could not close them, and who died of having neither eaten nor slept. We are dying of cold, of fatigue, of dysentery, of fever. What defense do we have against cold, against contagion, against lice, against filth, against thirst, against hunger, against fatigue, that overwhelming fatigue?

RÉINE: We are fighters. We must fight. Here, we fight against death.

FRANÇOISE: With bare hands, with bare heart, with bare skin. From where can we draw strength?

GINA: We must not give in. I want to return. I swear I will and if I do not return—hear me well Françoise—if I do not return you'll tell my father that at no time did I give in, at no moment. I'll never give in.

FRANÇOISE: You'll never give in! I wish I could say that. How can you say that?

GINA: You can't give them the thing that they want. By deciding that we will get out, we're defying them. Harden yourself, Françoise. We must not permit them to triumph over our corpses. They will have many of them, they must not have all. Those who return will have won. I don't like to lose. I'll win.

FRANÇOISE: You'll win what?

GINA: It does not matter what. You're in a battle, it's hand-to-hand combat and you don't want the enemy to win.

FRANÇOISE: It isn't there that we will prevent them.

GINA: No, unfortunately.

RÉINE: The real battle is not taking place here. It's taking place in the woods, in Stalingrad, in London, in Athens, in Belgrade, in Paris, in Warsaw. Those who are fighting, outside, are fighting for us. But were they not to see us again, their victory would taste of defeat. They would have the feeling that they had fought for nothing.

FRANÇOISE: No, not for nothing, for freedom, as we fought.

RÉINE: We wanted more than freedom, more than a graveyard.

FRANÇOISE: It will be so vast, this graveyard . . . It won't leave space for the survivors.

GINA: The children who will be born will make room for themselves, don't worry.

FRANÇOISE: Whose children? All the husbands, all the lovers, all the fiancés have been shot. /

GINA: All humanity will not perish here. There will still be children. I want to return to tell them.

FRANÇOISE: You will return, Gina.

GINA: I'd like to be sure of it. I want to talk myself into it. If you stop believing in your return, you're lost. I believe in it in spite of everything, but, swear to me, if you return, if you return without me, tell my father the truth. Don't hide anything. You'll have to tell the truth, even to the mothers.

FRANÇOISE: Would you be able to tell Claire's mother how she died?

RÉINE: I will do it; I will because it has to be done, because it is in order that the truth be known that we want to return. We will have had the strength to live it, why would the others not have the strength to hear it?

FRANÇOISE: I wonder if we will have the strength to tell it. And they won't believe us. They'll think that since we have returned, it was not as terrible as we say. By returning we will deny our own story.

(They have returned to the barracks.)

Scene 6

In the barracks. Most of the women are already stretched out, in regular and compact groups, on the side of the inclined plane which represents a row of "boxes" where they sleep. GINA, FRANÇOISE *and* RÉINE *settle down for the night, without undressing, near their friends who are already stretched out, also clothed. One hears the death-rattle which comes from the end of the aisle.*

FRANÇOISE: Do you hear? What is it?

GINA: Who is it? One who can't take it any more. One who is dying. Another one. How many will remain? How many of us will remain?

FRANÇOISE: None. It's not possible.

Scene 7

The same. MOUNETTE *joins them.*

MOUNETTE: You're not sleeping yet?

FRANÇOISE: We're going right to sleep. The nights are so short and we waste them chatting.

MOUNETTE: Talking is as important as sleeping. It helps as much. If I did not talk, it would seem to me as if I was no longer alive. I say anything; we say anything. But we never speak of more than one thing.

GINA: Oh no! We make plans, too. If I return, I'll open a tea shop. The cakes will be exquisite, especially the éclairs, and I'll make a chocolate that will be the sensation of Paris. Paris has never known one like it: creamy, thick, with a touch of coffee. Have you tried coffee-flavored chocolate? You make very strong coffee, a real coffee extract, and you put a drop in the chocolate. It's delicious! It gives a tiny bitterness which enhances the taste of the chocolate.

MOUNETTE: With chocolate, I like toast, very crusty, crunchy, and in the middle it's soft, soaked in warm butter put on the hot toast and that spreads while melting. *(The death-rattle.)* You think it's someone dying?

FRANÇOISE: Who's dying?

GINA: Do you think it is one of us?

(A voice screams, "Quiet!" They stretch out and huddle one against the others to sleep. The death-rattle punctuates the silence.)

Scene 8

In the next box, the women from Touraine are not sleeping yet.

RÉGINE: When we heard they were in Paris, my husband went to
get cement and bricks at my brother's; he is a builder at Saint-
Martin. It's a mile away so he took the cart. I was in the garden. I was gathering chives for salad when I saw him come
back, put the cart away and start mixing the cement. "What
are you doing? Bricklaying at this hour? It's lunch time." "Pay
no attention," he answered. And he went down to the cellar
with his hod. He came up for a quick snack and he sent me to
call our nephew to help him carry the bricks down. In the
evening, my Steven came back up with a bottle. "I chose one
of the best. Left over from the kid's communion. It's the last
we will drink until the end of the war." We invited the neighbors. It was our own white wine. We have a little vineyard, not
far from the house. There are years for which it's famous.
"Touraine wine is not for the Prussians to drink." My husband
had walled up the cellar. Lovely work he did. Really, you
would not suspect anything. He even made water stains. When
will we return to drink it?

ELISABETH: Never.

HORTENSE: How can you say that, Elisabeth?

ELISABETH: Look at my legs. I press down and the indentation remains, all white. With swollen legs, I have got only three days
to go.

RÉGINE: And mine? are they swollen?

(Shot outside, some distance away.)

Did you hear? What is it?

ELISABETH: A prisoner going toward the electric barbed wire to end
it all. The guard shot before she could touch it. With the spotlights covering the camp, the guards always see them first. Attempted escape, they say.

HORTENSE: Why do legs swell up so fast? At night, there's nothing.
The next day . . .

RÉGINE: It's the heart.

HORTENSE: Do you think we'll drink it again, Régine, some of that Touraine wine?

ELISABETH: None of us will ever drink that little wine of Touraine. *(Death-rattle. It's the last sound heard.)*

Scene 9

MOUNETTE *(sitting up in the box where* GINA *and* FRANÇOISE *are; everyone is sleeping or seems to be):* I'm afraid to sleep because I'm afraid to dream. Night is more frightening than day because at night, as soon as I fall asleep, I'm alone. During the day, I talk. Gina and Françoise or someone answers. At night, in my dreams, no one answers. I'm always alone and I'm afraid. While I'm falling asleep, I already know what I will dream. I'm afraid. If we've carried bricks during the day, I carry bricks and they are colder against my breasts, heavier to my hands than during the day. Frozen bricks. In our house, Mother used to give us a warm brick in winter to heat our bed. I burnt my sheet once. There was a smell of burning in the bed. Mother scolded me. At night, the bricks are covered with ice, ice which cuts even more deeply than during the day, and the skin on the inside of my hands is burnt by the ice. I still carry bricks, on an interminable road, and the bricks are heavier and heavier, colder and colder. During the day, while carrying the bricks, we chat. Gina tells us about the great restaurants where she used to eat with her husband and her friends. She would put on a dinner dress. A dinner dress! . . . black, with just one jewel. She must have been elegant, Gina. She must have been beautiful, dressed up with her hair done. Françoise tells about her trips. At night, there are just the bricks. And when it's not the bricks, it's the dogs. I try to make detours. I cheat. I figure out how to get away from the dogs, but they leap far and in one single jump cover the entire dis-

tance that I've succeeded in putting between them and me.
They throw themselves on me—they're enormous dogs. And
I feel their warm and repugnant breath, their panting on my
face. I am petrified with fear. It's impossible to escape from
those dirty beasts. Their breath on my cheek is so strong that
it awakens me and then I understand that it's the breathing of
Renée or Agnès who sleep next to me. I reassure myself and I
tell myself that I have to go back to sleep; otherwise I won't
make it through the next day. But I'm afraid. I'm afraid that
this time it will be the mud. The black mud, sticky and icy
when the ice melts as the day progresses and the swamp turns
to muck. A lake of mire that extends as far as the other end of
the horizon. I swirl in the mud, I go in deeper and deeper and
I can't get hold anywhere; there's nothing to hold onto. I'm
afraid to have it in my mouth. I want to cry out for help. I
hold myself back. I close my mouth tightly because the mud is
at level with my lips. I'm too scared; I scream. The mud goes
down my throat through my mouth and my nostrils, fills my
stomach with a stinking gurgling and suffocates me. Probably
I really screamed. My neighbor shakes me awake. The most
atrocious dream is the one when I come home. I come in
through the kitchen. My mother is doing dishes or she's ironing. I come close: "Mother, it's me. You see, I've come back.
O Mother! I still don't believe it. I was so afraid I wouldn't
come back. But it's true. This time it's true." Mother doesn't
turn her head towards me. "It was hard, you know, mother."
She continues her washing or her ironing. She doesn't hear me.
She doesn't turn towards me. "Mother, it's me. Your Mounette. If you knew, Mother, how many times I dreamt I was
coming back! But this time it's true, it's true, it's true because
I'm touching you, I'm touching your hand. Your hand is a little
rough—a little hard—you should wear gloves to do dishes."
Happiness flows through me to the tips of my fingers. I feel
warm and sweet all over and I awake with Renée's or Agnès'
hand in mine. It's the dream that frightens me most. At night,
you're afraid. In the morning, you want to die.
(*Darkness. Siren for morning roll call. Music.*)

ACT 2

Scene 1

At the siren, the women wake up, pull themselves together, straighten their dresses, retie their kerchiefs. They leave the barracks where it is still dark to go to roll call. Spotlights: the effect of violent electric light upon the snow. It's 3:00 a.m. in winter. Pitch black night. Daylight will come slowly. At the end of the act, the spots will be out; it will be early morning in winter.

DENISE, MONIQUE, AGNÈS *(still in the barracks, in their box):* Renée! Renée! Come help us. Marie doesn't want to get up. She doesn't want to go out for roll call.

(RENÉE had begun to leave, but retraces her steps.)

ELISABETH: Did you hear the shot during the night?

RÉINE: Everyone heard it. There's no point in talking about it.

ELISABETH: Now I understand the one who commits suicide. For me it's not worth the trouble any more. My legs are more swollen than yesterday.

RENÉE *(returns, holding up* MARIE*):* Come on, Marie. Come, my little one. Hold your breath when you go out. The air is cold. There, slowly, you see you can walk.

(They all move towards the roll call square. The columns begin to form unevenly, slowly, painfully. RENÉE, *holding up* MARIE, *comes last.)*

RENÉE: Look, it's Berthe. *(We do not see* BERTHE.*)* Her sister died during the night. Didn't you hear her? She groaned almost all night. She groaned feebly, leaning against Berthe's chest. For a long time. Then she was quiet and Berthe held her tight to keep her from turning cold too fast, to keep her warm near her. She would have wanted to keep her warm and near her forever. This morning, we had to pull apart her arms to take Dédée away. Madeleine was near her. Then Madeleine helped Berthe wrap Dédée in a blanket and take her down. Now, Berthe is carrying Dédée outside. She is laying her down along

296

the wall of the barracks, there where the snow makes a bank. The snow is clean there, thick, soft and almost gentle. She lays her sister down softly in the soft snow. Go help her, Agnès. I'll stay with Marie. Take her hand so that she comes to roll call. She won't want to leave Dédée. Go get her. Drag her. *(MARIE is falling down.)* Get up, Marie. You have to be ready for roll call. Get up, my little one.

MARIE: I can't anymore.

RENÉE: Yes, you can. I'm telling you that you can. You have to.

MARIE: Why do I have to? Let me alone. Please let me alone.

RENÉE: No. I won't leave you. You have to. Get up. Hold onto me. There, take my arm. *(She rubs her cheeks, her hands, blows on her face.)* You see that you can. Let's go. Stand up!
(They walk towards the ranks that are forming and take their places.)

AGNÈS *(entering; she is holding up* BERTHE*)*: Make a place in the middle for Berthe; she's frozen.

FRANÇOISE: Come here, Berthe. Come between me and Gina.

GINA: You're cold. Rub her other arm, Françoise.

BERTHE: No, leave me alone. Let me die of the cold. Dédée is much colder than I. She's cold forever. She's in the snow forever. No. They're going to take her away, and put her on the pile. Oh Dédée! My little one.

GINA: Don't think about it, Berthe. Don't think about it like that. Think about how she was before.

BERTHE: How can I go back without Dédée? How do you want me to do it? My father will never understand.

AGNÈS: Yes, he will. He'll understand. As long as you yourself return. We'll all go with you to tell him. Let him at least find one of you again.
(During this time the rows of five are forming.)

BERTHE: Dédée was my little sister and she was my daughter, my child. I brought her up. I was the big sister and the little mother. I brought her up. I was ten when our mother died giving birth to her. She was strong, though, Dédée. She wanted to return with all her heart. At twenty . . . she cheered me up when I weakened. If only you knew how cheerful she was even in prison, before we left. She knew a thousand songs. You could hear her voice all over Montluc.[2] And last night, she said to me: "Don't leave me, Berthe. I need to know you're next to me. Put your hand on my heart. Do you feel it beating?" "Yes, Dédée, I feel it, it's beating strong." Then she didn't speak any more. Her mouth was all dried out. I had kept some tea; I dipped my finger into the mug and I wet her lips and her gums. She couldn't swallow any more; her throat was swollen. I passed my wet finger over her lips and I felt her lips grow cold during the night. And now, I've left her.

AGNÈS: Cry, Berthine. Try to cry. The dead here should not be deprived of our tears. Cry, even if the tears freeze on your cheeks and you don't feel their salt. Cry. It'll help you pull yourself together. You must help us now. We need you.

BERTHE: No one needs me anymore.

AGNÈS: Yes, we do now. Your father will, later.

BERTHE: What will I tell my father? Here I am but Dédée stayed behind. She was taken for a work team. She spent the whole day under the hail of melting snow. She was soaked and her dress never dried again. I couldn't change dresses with her; mine was soaked too. She ran a fever for three days. I knew what she had; I heard the whistling in her chest. I had nothing to care for her with, nothing but my hands to rub her with, my breath to warm her, my arm to make her walk to work in spite of everything, to make her stand in spite of everything at roll call. She ran a fever for three days and she's dead. Pneumonia. Why her? Why her and not me?

MONIQUE (holding her sister DENISE to her): You won't leave me, Nizou, my little darling. I won't let you leave me.

DENISE: No, Monique, no Niquette. We will never leave each other. We were taken together; we'll return together.

FRANÇOISE: Be brave, Berthine.

BERTHE: Why brave? How will I be able to live without Dédée, after having abandoned her in the snow, in the night?

---

2. Montluc: a Nazi prison for political opponents and resistance fighters.

GINA: Hold on, Berthe, hold on for another hour, another minute. It's not from day to day that you have to hold on, it's from minute to minute. One minute at a time. Don't give up.
(The rows are formed.)

Scene 2

YVONNE: That's why the days are so long; all these minutes one by one, these minutes one at a time. Have you ever observed a moment of silence in a ceremony? A minute is long. First you think of the person you are honoring. Then you think of lots of things: I have to buy nail polish; I have to go the bookstore, my order must be ready; I have to call Susie. And when the chairman looks at his watch and you sit down again, you're as relieved as if you had been standing for a long time. Here, each day is broken down into all its minutes. And during each of these minutes, you have to be on the alert, without any respite; to sidestep a blow and not to fall, to force yourself to move your toes in your clogs or they'll freeze, to keep your head, to keep your memory. I'm afraid to lose my memory, my certainty that I am still myself. We must stay on the alert to remain conscious of ourselves and order our hearts to keep beating. But in vain. My heart no longer obeys my command. Dysentery also drains the blood. If only there were a little water to wash. I tried with snow. Snow isn't good for washing and it's icy on the belly. I gave up trying. I don't care any more.

MOUNETTE: What don't you care about, Yvonne?

YVONNE: Whether I die now, this morning, right away.

MOUNETTE: Oh yes, right away. Right away, no one would care. But since it isn't right away, you have to hold on. And what of the others? Look at Berthe, she's more unhappy than any of us.

YVONNE: She'll force herself to overcome her pain because she has courage, and she'll suffer longer for it.

MOUNETTE: You're exhausted, Yvonne. Don't talk any more. With daybreak, you'll find yourself again and you'll tell me about the Acropolis and what you see from there.

YVONNE: Finding yourself is an illusion, a trick. I need not find myself because I am not lost. It's only my body that's losing life. I have become myself and another at the same time: another who is detached, clairvoyant, gifted with a sharpened sense of observation, who looks at the first "me" who is disappearing. I look at my body disappearing and I don't care. I only wish it didn't take so long. All that I'm dreading is dragging on. It takes so long to die of exhaustion. What I dread most is dragging on. I hope that when I'm a little more worn out, my mind will grow dark and I won't see myself any more.

MOUNETTE: You're logical, Yvonne. It's frightening how logical you are. No one can answer you back.

HÉLÈNE'S MOTHER: You have to pray for her.

MOUNETTE: Pray for us all, that the Good Lord prepare Himself to receive us one after the other.

HÉLÈNE: Oh, Mother, do you think that God hears our prayers from here?

HÉLÈNE'S MOTHER: Yes, my daughter. God hears everything, especially the call of those who are suffering.

HÉLÈNE *(aside):* Poor mother, she talks like the priest. *(To her mother.)* God is deaf, blind, and serene in his egotistical perfection.

HÉLÈNE'S MOTHER: Don't be blasphemous, Hélène, my darling. God, forgive her.

MOUNETTE: Let your mother pray, Hélène. Her praying is one more moment won.

HÉLÈNE: I don't believe in God anymore. And for the time that's left to me to believe . . .

RENÉE *(to* MARIE *who is fainting):* Don't try to slip through my fingers, little one. I'll hold you tight. *(She slaps her.)* Marie! Marie! Marie! Do you hear me?

MARIE: Yes, Mother. I hear you.

RENÉE: Then come back.

MARIE: Yes, Mother, what were you telling me?

RENÉE: I was telling you: Courage! Up! Don't let yourself fall into the snow; it's cold.

MARIE: No, the snow is soft. It's like a great coat. I'm so cold, cold all through me. Let me lie down.

RENÉE: No, stand up! Up! Otherwise I'll give you a real spanking. Up! Day is breaking. You see, the sky is becoming light. Look at the sky, those great red patches that are starting to set the sky on fire.

MARIE: It's colder than it was just a little while ago.

RENÉE: Put your hand over your mouth and blow your breath up towards your nose. Like this. It warms you to have the tip of your nose less cold. Try, you'll see.

FRANÇOISE: One day. One day more. Another day. It lights up faces. I can distinguish one from the other. There are some I can't recognize. They've changed during the night. Oh Yvonne! She's going to die. This time, it's for sure. She's marked. Death touched her during the night. She is wearing the look of death. Yvonne?

YVONNE (*in the next row*): Is it you, Françoise?

FRANÇOISE: Yvonne?

MOUNETTE: Berthe's sister died during the night.

YVONNE: I know. For me, death will come before night. By gauging my strength I might last until evening, not tomorrow.

FRANÇOISE: Don't gauge so closely.

YVONNE: And that's with the benefit of the doubt.

Scene 3

SYLVIE (*from a row behind*): Make a place for me in front, I want to see.

FRANÇOISE: What is there to see?

SYLVIE: As soon as day breaks, they take the dead out of the sick bay[3] to carry them to the morgue. You know, that wooden hut behind Block 25. That's where they pile them up to wait for the truck to the crematorium. I want to see if they carry out my mother. She went into the sick bay the other day.

(The projectors go out in one stroke. Natural light of daybreak on the snow.)

RÉINE: What will it do for you to see her pass?

RENÉE: Don't be so hard, Réine.

SYLVIE: I have to see her pass to know the date of her death. What date is today?

YVONNE: The twentieth: The twentieth of February.

FRANÇOISE: You won't recognize her under the little cover.

SYLVIE: The legs stick out. Mother had deformed feet. I would recognize her feet.

FRANÇOISE: There's the funeral procession advancing. *(We do not see the stretchers.)* The funeral procession of those who died during the night, on little stretchers of poorly attached branches too short for the bodies, with the blanket that covers the middle in shreds. Their legs stick out between the front handles; the shaved head hangs between the back handles. You don't see the faces, upside down, rattling between the ends of the branches. The legs are enough. Skeletons' legs which hang between the handles. Every morning I want to die, but when I see the little stretchers passing I don't want to anymore. I don't want to go out that way with my head hanging and my legs dangling. Don't look, Yvonne. Why are you looking?

YVONNE: Today, it's them. Tomorrow, us.

SYLVIE: There are a lot of them today. Young ones.

YVONNE: How can you tell?

SYLVIE: By their tender feet. They didn't last very long here. The skin of their feet is still soft.

FRANÇOISE: I would rather die outside than in the sick bay. No! Not in the sick bay. Better standing up.

---

3. Sick bay: literally "lazaretto" (*lazaret* in French), the wretched place to which the incapacitated and those close to death were taken to die; the medical attention provided was worthless.

YVONNE: Me, no. I prefer lying down.

FRANÇOISE: You don't want to go to sick bay?

YVONNE: Yes, in a moment. After roll call, I'll join the column for the sick. To die here or there, better there. I can't stand up any longer.

FRANÇOISE: Stay with us, Yvonne. Stay another day. Tomorrow, maybe you'll be better.

YVONNE: You're sweet, Françoise. But it's not worth the trouble. I know what lies ahead.

GINA: It's true that you go feet first. It's always in that direction that they carry them.

HÉLÈNE'S MOTHER: My God, grant that this day does not separate my Hélène and me. Make it not be harder than yesterday. Grant us that we both live through it.

(Whistle blasts. Silence. Attention. The S.S. approach to count. They are not seen. Not a breath is heard.)

GINA *(letting go of* BERTHE, *murmurs):* Stand straight, Berthine.

RENÉE *(letting go of* MARIE*):* Stand on your own while they pass, Marie.

(You know that the S.S. stop at each row by the position that the women immediately take when they are in front of them: head straight, no facial expression, hands at attention, one row after the other. As soon as the S.S. are a little way off, the conversations start again, at first murmured, then in a normal tone of voice. The women put their hands in the armpits of those in front of them or rub each other, beginning to change places inside each row, stamping their feet. Stamping feet in the snow doesn't make any noise.)

Scene 4

AGNÈS: It wasn't too long today.

RÉINE: Monday, they rush it. They're hung over on Mondays.

GINA: Today is not Monday, it's Wednesday.

FRANÇOISE: No, it's Monday.

RENÉE: I'd love to have a hangover and have every hair on my head hurt. If we had hair on our head, we'd feel less cold. It's the temples that ache. I feel as if my head were caught in a big nutcracker, and that my skull is splitting apart.

YVONNE: They're calling for the sick bay. Goodbye, everybody. *(She goes towards the end of the formation where a column of invalids is forming. She walks with difficulty but with pride.)*

MARIE *(trying to break lose from* RENÉE's *arms)*: Renée . . .

RENÉE: Stay here, Marie. You hear me. You wanted to come with us; you will stay with us.

MARIE: Please, let me go. I can't take it anymore. If I could just lie down, I think my strength would come back.

RENÉE: Strength doesn't come back when you're lying down. On the contrary. The bed weakens you. Especially that bed. Strength is in your mind. Be strong, Marie. You have to return, you too.

MARIE: No one is waiting for me. I'll have no one at home anymore. Let me go, please.

MOUNETTE: Let her go, Renée. There are some who come out of sick bay.

RENÉE: They come out feet first. Mind your own business, Mounette. Don't you know that in the sick bay you catch all kinds of disease? You are with the dying ones, with the stinking ones, with the delirious ones, with the ones who are burning up one day and frozen the next day, right next to you, and that makes you cold. Marie can still hold out. Can't you, Marie? Maybe tomorrow it will thaw a bit.

MOUNETTE: And me, you would prevent me from going to sick bay?

RENÉE: Think of your mother, Mounette.

MOUNETTE: Oh! My mother. I don't see her anymore. Tonight I dreamed that I returned home and that my mother didn't look at me. Or rather I didn't recognize her face.

RENÉE: Our mothers too must have changed since we left, since they don't know where we are.

MOUNETTE: It's not that I didn't recognize her face: it's more like I didn't see it. Or rather, no. I did see a shape. I knew it was my mother. I squinted, I wanted to see her face. I tried until my eyelids ached. I didn't see her. My mother's face is disappearing.

RENÉE: A mother's face doesn't disappear, ever. And since when are you so upset by a dream? As if there weren't enough in each day to upset us . . .

MOUNETTE: I've lost my mother's face.

RENÉE: Stop saying stupid things, Mounette. Take your place, the lines are moving.

(The ranks begin to move. Each one takes her place again. Some movements. Then stop. Stamping. Then the ranks break again slowly. Some use the opportunity to slip from one group to the other.)

RENÉE: Get hold of yourself, Mounette. You had more spirit before. You were supporting Yvonne and now you're letting yourself go.

MOUNETTE: Yvonne was courageous. And you see . . .

AGNÈS *(who is holding up* BERTHE, *comes to take her place in the row where* RENÉE, MARIE *and* MOUNETTE *are):* What's Mounette saying?

RENÉE: Stupid things. That she lost her mother's face during the night.

AGNÈS: It's a bad dream that the day will erase. Look at the daybreak, Mounette.

MOUNETTE: Another day. One more day. A day is so long, especially when you're not sure to see it through.

AGNÈS: We've made it to the end of the others so far.

MOUNETTE: My strength decreases at each new dawn. Until now I was sure to see mother again. Since last night, I know that I won't see her again.

AGNÈS: Be reasonable, Mounette. It would be much worse if you could see your mother, if she were here with you. Look at Hélène, who's with her mother. Each one suffers doubly, for herself and for the other. For the mother, it's worse yet because a mother always thinks she can protect her child. And here, she can't do anything. She sees her daughter being beaten, and she lowers her head. And for the daughter! To see her mother beaten, naked, tattooed, shaven, dirty. Then one soon thinks that she is a burden on the other. And look at Sylvie, who really lost her mother and who is looking for her among the dead whose feet dangle from the little stretchers. Next to them, you're lucky. Think of your mother to give you courage, Mounette, to give you confidence. Think of her in real life, not in the hallucinations of the night. I think of my son. He's at his grandmother's. If he could think of me as I think of him, at each second, he would never forget my face. But he was too young when I left him.

MOUNETTE: How old is he?

AGNÈS: Six. He's been going to school since the fall. My mother-in-law told me in the last letter I got before we left the prison. When I see the children arrive here to go into the gas chambers . . .

ELISABETH: Or to be thrown alive into the fire . . .

AGNÈS: What are you talking about, Elisabeth?

ELISABETH: They came upon that idea to make more room in the gas chambers. They put the children aside and they throw them alive into an enormous ditch filled with branches and set fire to it. Children don't struggle.

MOUNETTE: How do you know that?

ELISABETH: Yesterday I talked with a girl who works in the Children's Kommando. You saw it, it's the Kommando that comes back after the others at night. They all wear white kerchiefs on their heads. They're cleanly dressed. They're called the White Kerchiefs. There's a girl who speaks French rather well. She lived in Paris before the war.

GINA: Keep your news to yourself, Elisabeth. Don't you think we know enough?

MADELEINE: But Gina, we must know everything.

AGNÈS: When I see the children here, I tell myself that I'll never love my son enough. I have to love him for all the little ones here.

RENÉE: Don't get soft, Agnès. It hurts.

Scene 5

LINA *(coming from the end of the row, looking, asking in all the groups, making a path for herself)*: Is Françoise around here? Is Françoise with you? Where is Françoise?

FRANÇOISE: Who's looking for me?

LINA: Me, Lina. Françoise, I have a secret to tell you.

FRANÇOISE: There are no secrets here. There are only lost secrets, my poor Lina.

LINA: Yes, but listen.

(She wants to get FRANÇOISE *aside. Whistle blasts. The ranks break formation.* LINA, *shoved aside, takes her place again, quickly.)*

Scene 6

RENÉE: This time, we're moving.

(We see LAURE *coming closer, shaking, ready to fall down—a phantom—staying outside of the row which started moving at the blast of the whistle, trying to slide in, with such feeble movements that she doesn't make it.)*

FRANÇOISE: Who is it? Is she from our group . . . ?

MOUNETTE: Isn't it Laure?

LAURE *(her voice exhausted)*: I just came out of the sick bay. I left because a nurse said to get out no matter what. There must be a selection for the gas chamber today.

FRANÇOISE: Oh! Yvonne . . .

(MADELEINE and RÉINE *come forward to hold up* LAURE.*)*

MADELEINE: What are we going to do? What can we do with her? She can't walk. *(LAURE faints in their arms.)* Laure? What are we going to do? Laure?

RÉINE: Laure, Laure, what can we do? Laure?

RENÉE: We're going now. Look straight ahead of you, Marie.

MADELEINE: What are we going to do? Laure? Laure is dead.

RÉINE: We have to leave her.

(They lay LAURE *down on the ground. The whole row will then pass without recognizing her, without seeing her.)*

RENÉE: The first rows are going through the gate. Let go of my arm, Mounette. Hands at your sides.

AGNÈS *(to* BERTHE*):* Can you walk, Berthe?

(She lets go of her arm. They must go through the gate in order, arms at sides, because the S.S., whom we don't see, count them as they pass).

RENÉE: I think it's to the left that they're going today. That would be for demolition work. So much the better, maybe we'll be inside for the soup. Stand up straight, Marie. If we find a little dry corner to sit down during the break, we'll ask Françoise to take us to the theatre. What program will we ask her for? She tells it so well and she does all the voices. You would think you were hearing the actors.

(The stage empties, the rows go by, slowly and heavily. When the stage is empty, Françoise retraces her steps. Normal walk and voice, as in the Prologue.)

Scene 7

FRANÇOISE: I didn't take them to the theatre. I couldn't talk. It was too cold in that lifeless expanse of snow where we stayed all day. After we went through the gate, they made us form squares in the big field opposite. The snow was hard, a crust of ice. Gina said: "It's not snow for skiing." That's all she said. Afterwards, we didn't speak any more, nor did anyone else. A wind was blowing from the plain, which froze the words when they were scarcely formed on our lips. We stood motionless in the wind, in the cold, until the light dimmed. Several of us fell. Elisabeth . . . How could she have stood on her legs that kept on swelling even as we watched? We left them on the dirtied snow. Marie . . . Renée couldn't force her to breathe. The air clawed at our lungs. When they blew the whistle for us to go back into formation and return to camp, they commanded us to run. The extraordinary thing is that we ran. We ran when we were stiff to the point where we couldn't bend either our knees or our ankles, I am still wondering how. From the gate, we had to run between a double row of monsters and furies, all armed with sticks, whips, and canes, who whipped, beat, thrashed all who passed through. The blows rained from all sides. Those who didn't run fast enough, who stumbled, who lost their heads and didn't know in what direction to run, who lost their clogs and limped, were seized by the collars of their dresses and pulled aside. They were thrown into Block 25. Fourteen of us were taken that day. Hélène's mother was among them. Réine, who tried to drag her away, was almost caught. She lasted a long time; Hélène didn't. They both died of typhus. And Lina? I will never know her secret.

When Mounette died, Mounette for whom I stayed, Mounette whom I would have carried until the return because her life was so promising that it broke my heart to see such a waste, when Mounette died, I was violently tempted again to give up. But Denise was alone. There were hardly any among those who could still stand who could have helped her. I stayed for her. It's true I leaned on Gina. And maybe also because after having lasted for weeks, I didn't want to lose my investment.

And now, how many are left? Can we act a play where the characters die before you've had time to know them? I didn't have time to get to know them either.
(*Music.*)

ACT 3

Scene 1

Late afternoon, outside. It's a clear day. There is no more snow, only dust, as gray as the dresses.

DENISE *(sitting on the ground):* We've been here for seventy days. More than two months. It's so long that I don't believe our reckoning. At the beginning we would never have thought it possible to last so long a time. Seventy days and "we" no longer means the same thing. Now "we" is Gina, Françoise and myself. My sister is dead. The others are dead. All of them, all the others. Dead before our eyes, like Juliette from Bordeaux who fell one morning at the swamp. How did she manage to walk there that morning? She didn't know what she was doing any more, where she was, who she was. It was because when she arrived here she took such a strong vow: to hold out, to hold out at any price, at any cost, that her will held up until she fell. Under our eyes, by the swamps. None of us could come close to her to touch her hand, or say a word or read a name on her lips. They put a dog next to her, right on the edge of the swamp where they ordered that she be placed. She stayed there until night. At night, she was carried back to the camp. She had been counted at roll call in the morning, so she had to be counted at roll call in the evening. Four of our group carried her, each taking a limb, and at every step of the way they wondered how they would make it back to camp. It's probably the only time they looked forward to seeing the watchtowers at the fork in the road, the only time they were encouraged when they smelled the odor of the camp. Extraordinary, how far the odor spreads. It's an odor that . . . There are many things I didn't know, like how cadavers are soft and difficult to manipulate long after death. . . . She was heavy, so heavy, Juliette, with nothing left of her at the end of her life, emaciated in a way we had never seen before. Those who carried her were at the end of life too.

There was one who was bitten by a dog. She wanted to break ranks to gather dandelions on the edge of the road, one morning while we were on our way to work. We pick up dandelions each time we can. Stealthily—you have to be quick, it's forbidden, but since everything is forbidden . . . We tear the leaves into little pieces and we mix them into the soup. It's for the vitamins. Since we started eating it we don't get scurvy any more. She was on the outside row and she was preparing herself, already bent over, to leave the row. She didn't look around carefully enough, the dog jumped her and put his fangs into her throat. She let out a cry, a single brief cry. The dog dragged her by the throat. It even dropped her for a second on the road because it was tired, then took her up in its mouth again. That time she didn't cry. It dragged her like that to the swamp. She panted for many hours, at long intervals. At each interval, we hoped it was over. We listened to hear how long she would hang on. To remember, too. It was long, so very long. Then someone said: "She's not breathing any more." Suddenly everything was motionless and silent in the swamp. The screaming of the guards did not break the silence. We had to carry her at night too, to bring her back to the camp. And it was unbearable to look at, that throat. We couldn't take our eyes away from it and at every second we said over and over: "Don't look. Look straight ahead. Look far away." We're almost all used to looking far away since we've been here, those of us who remain. Far away in space, of course; in time, not seventy days. We kept count of the days so as not to feel a break in time between what we were before and what we have become. Until now, we haven't gotten confused, or at least I think not. It has happened that we'd discuss a whole day imagining we'd made a mistake in the count. But there's no mistake. Seventy days. And now, it's spring. The spring of this place. Here spring is not shown by trees or leaves: there are none in camp. The snow melted and the mud has replaced it. Mud is worse than snow. It's colder. It's dirtier. We lose our clogs, which get stuck in it. We have to go in with two hands to pull them out. Mud retains odors. It smells of diarrhea.

With the coming of spring, it's less cold. Well, that's one way of putting things. In the middle of the night, when we go out for roll call, we stand for hours on end. I say hours because they are real hours, not minutes that seem like hours to us. From three in the morning until seven in the morning, that's really hours. Standing for hours, motionless, with the wind lashing us or an icy rain pelting us. The nights in April are cold, particularly at daybreak. A coat of humid cold falls upon our shoulders, envelops them and weighs heavily upon them for a long time. Since we must leave for work at daybreak, roll call is not as long as in winter.

Then the mud changed to dust. All those feet going over the same spot, the same roll call square, stir up a cloud of dust; and not a blade of grass grows in the camp, nothing, not even a nettle on the garbage heap. But at least you can sit in the dust. Spring also came to the swamp so that we don't carry clods of frozen earth, we carry wet earth. It's less difficult to dig up but it's heavier to carry. Spring thawed the ditches, and at noon, during the break, we can wash ourselves. It's the only water we have. You mustn't drink it, it smells rotten. Some did try to drink it, but they're dead. They would have died in any case. Once I wanted to stop my sister from drinking it. She told me: "Let me drink: death is already hovering over me."

And there are those who will still ask: "But what did they die from, all of them? All of them didn't drink the water, all of them weren't strangled by dogs, all of them weren't beaten to death the way Claire was?" Well, it's true. There are those who died of thirst. Little Aurore. Her lips were all chapped. She couldn't talk any more because she had no more saliva in her mouth. She lasted a long time. She was enclosed in solitude because she couldn't talk. She must have been so afraid! Her eyes had grown bigger than her face. She had mauve eyes, yes mauve, and with thirst they became discolored, like her lips which were no more than torn pieces of gray skin. I don't know when or where she died, or if someone was near her. In any case, she wouldn't have been able to say anything. Her lips wanted to talk but no sound came out.

There are those who were taken in the race, the day of the great roll call in the field of snow, and who died in Block 25. There are those who died of typhus. That's the best death here. You're delirious almost immediately and soon fall into a coma.

"But the others?" The others, all the others, they died of the life here. Why them and not I? Impossible to know. I was neither among the strongest nor among the bravest. Of the young ones, of those who were less than twenty, I am the only one left. There are so many questions without answers. Impossible to know.

How many of us will remain? How long will we stay together, the three of us? Three is very few. Not even a row. In the beginning, when we were still together, the camp seemed less hostile. Day and night, everywhere we heard our own speech. Today our very language has vanished with its accents. We were Tourangelles, Charentaises, Bordelaises, two from Marseilles. Now we are not more than three, and we speak constantly to hear our own voices, to hear words we understand and perhaps to make ourselves believe that we are still many. I say that because I'm trying to understand myself. We can't deceive ourselves. Here, you have nightmares at night. During the day, there is nowhere to take refuge. You cannot escape into the imaginary. To think of other things is impossible. To look elsewhere is impossible. To pretend is impossible. Impossible to live as if it were not you that were there.

They will also ask "When did they die?" I don't know. The days are all the same. I don't know anything anymore. My sister died in the sick bay. She decided to go in when the boils on her legs became infected. We didn't have a piece of rag, a drop of water. The swamps were still iced over. We three that remain, we went two months without washing, without washing at all, not even our fingertips. At night, after the roll call, I sometimes succeeded in slipping over to the sick bay. When I told Gina that a rat had eaten Monique's ear and that Monique wasn't even dead, Gina forbade me to go back to see her again.

Scene 2

Enter GINA.

DENISE *(getting up):* Tell me, Gina, why did you forbid me to go to see Monique? Do you think that she went quickly or that she lingered on with those rats that she no longer had the strength to brush away? The last time I saw her, she couldn't even raise her hand to place it in mine.

GINA: Stop taking the roll call of the dead. You have to defend yourself against the dead. You must wait until we're back home to remember.

DENISE: Do you think that each day I can wait for another tomorrow without thinking once of my sister?

GINA: You have to, or give up thinking about her forever.

DENISE: You think I can postpone what comes into my head?

GINA: You have to, or give up any hope of living.

DENISE: You have become hard, Gina.

GINA: Hard . . . We'll have to keep on being that way for a long time.

DENISE: How will we live afterwards, if we come back so hardened?

GINA: I think of that too, but I tell myself that if I could cry on my mother's shoulder, tenderness and weakness and pity would come back to me.

DENISE: You have a mother. Me, my father . . .

GINA: If we come back, I'll share my mother with you.

DENISE: All our sentences start with: "if we come back."

GINA: We must say: "When we come back."

Scene 3

FRANÇOISE *(entering):* What will we do, when we come back? I see myself coming back—well, there are days when I see myself coming back—but I can't see beyond that. I can't see myself getting back into the routines of before.

GINA: It would be easy if we found what we left, if we could just take up where we left off, like when you come home after a long trip. But my home will be missing my husband . . . No, I don't know what I'll do. We mustn't think about it. Let's return first, then we'll see.

FRANÇOISE: I can't see myself for the rest of my life without my husband.

GINA: And yet we weren't married for a long time. Me, three years, you, four. For me, it's as if I never lived before my marriage. Everything begins with Henri. But here we never evoke anything but our childhood. I never think of Henri; and you of Paul?

FRANÇOISE: No, never. But I know why: it's because it's too painful to remember love and happiness here, and to know they'll never be found again. We assumed the task, so as to preserve our energy, of thinking only of our childhood years, which are past, when everything was simple and unshadowed. It is in the order of things that they should pass. I think of my mother.

DENISE: So do I. And I even forget very often that she's dead. She died when Monique and I were in prison, last summer. Last summer . . . We could say a century ago, a world ago, a life ago . . .

GINA: You, Denise, you'll take up again quickly, you'll see. Your life hasn't started yet. When you return, you'll begin life. You left as a child, you'll return grown up.

DENISE: No, Gina. It will be harder for me than for you. You learned how to live. When you were arrested, you knew. I was going to school and I won't be able to go back. I'd know too many things to go back to studying, even if we returned right now. I'd be old next to the other schoolgirls. And I'll miss what I haven't learned in school for the rest of my life.

FRANÇOISE: But you can study in other ways; there are books . . . I say that the way people say things, without weighing what they say. Will we be able to get interested in stories in books? We'll have to learn to live all over again, if we come back.

GINA: When we come back.

FRANÇOISE: To stay motionless, alone, sitting with a book . . . I wonder.

DENISE: You know, Françoise, I told myself often: "If I come back—when I come back, I'll read all the books Françoise told me about." But it's not enough to read books. You also have to have a career, to do something to earn a living. Earn a living! it's strange to say that here. I don't know what I'll do, what I can do. I have no idea. I envy you. At the worst moments, when all our comrades were falling, when several fell every day, I envied you: Gina and Françoise, if they die now I thought, they will have lived. They will have had something. They traveled, they went to the theatre, they were married, were loved. They loved. They loved. I will have had nothing.

FRANÇOISE: When you come back, you'll start to live whereas we'll have trouble starting anew.

GINA: And everything you've learned since . . .

DENISE: Do you think that what we've learned here is useful in life?

GINA: Everything a person knows is useful.

FRANÇOISE: You think so, Gina? What use is there in knowing how to read death sitting on a face at the very minute when it pinches the nostrils, clings to the cheek bones and tints the eyelids purple? In life, those who are going to die are in a hospital, or at home in a room, with little bottles on a night table, flowers, tea, a slice of lemon that floats on the top. What use is it ever to read truth in a face? In life who needs to see through people, to know in one split second if they'll share their bread or help others to walk? This is a gift we have acquired here which we'll have to get rid of because it will be terrible to see everything in that light.

Here everything is true. In a hard way. Without shadows.
The executioners are executioners. They have the costume, the
marks, the traits. They don't try to conceal it, to pass for human beings. They are executioners without hypocrisy. They
never try to flatter, they never try to fake a smile. They don't
see us although we see them and how different they are from
us. The victims are victims, brutalized, defeated, humiliated,
disgusting, lice-ridden. And those among the victims who suc-
ceed in crossing over to the other side, they immediately take
on the badges that distinguish their new office: armbands,
sticks or whips, and the faces to go with them.

We have seen, side by side, the worst cruelty and the greatest
beauty. I mean those who practically carried me in their arms
when I couldn't walk, those who gave me their tea when I was
choking from thirst when my tongue was like a piece of rough
wood in my mouth, those who touched my hand and managed
to form a smile on their chapped lips when I was desperate,
those who picked me up when I fell in the mud when they were
so weak themselves, those who took my feet in their hands at
night when we were going to sleep, and who blew on them
when I felt they had begun to freeze. And here I am. They all
died for me. No one dies for anyone else in life.

GINA: All the same we learned something from them. Courage, the
simplicity of courage.

FRANÇOISE: You don't need so much courage in life. You don't need
that kind of courage.

DENISE: Life will be much harder for us after. We've gotten into the
habit of showing our naked faces. Can you go without a mask
in life? Can you take the masks off others? Others will turn
away so as not to let us see the faces that only our eyes discern.
They'll be afraid of us. Then what will we say to them who
will never understand that we're unlike anyone else, different
even from them? What can we do to be as if we had never
been here?

GINA: We'll have to find a way to get along, to readjust.

DENISE: The gap will be too big, Gina. I don't see how it's possible.

FRANÇOISE: We'll explain and no one will understand. We'll never be able to make them see what we have seen. We'll bore people, the way those from the First World War bored us. They never stopped talking about Verdun and we didn't understand.

GINA: That's because there was nothing else in their lives except the moment when they were at one with history. It's not so for us. When we come back, we won't live without knowing why, we won't have fought just to come back just to survive. When we come back we'll do something . . .

FRANÇOISE: You forget all that was, all that we saw.

GINA: If we do something afterwards, something exciting, something exalting, those memories will take their place in our lives which will go on and will be a single moment but not the only moment.

FRANÇOISE: What will be exciting to us afterwards? I think often of what Agnès said: we will have left our energy here, our desire to live.

GINA: No, Françoise. The desire to live would have already left us were we going to lose it here. Here, that's easy.

FRANÇOISE: I don't know. Maybe we fight here because the fight is superhuman, excessive. It's a challenge. There is no other goal: to survive, to get back. When there is no longer a challenge, what will we live for?

GINA: It will be worthwhile if only to communicate this knowledge we have gained.

DENISE: It's an incommunicable knowledge as Françoise said, useless.

GINA: With our comrades dead we should say that we're lucky to have lasted so long.

FRANÇOISE: It's not over. The moment hasn't come to walk through the gate for the last time.

GINA: In any case, you can be sure that I won't look back that time.

FRANÇOISE: What of all those we'll leave behind?

GINA: We won't leave them, we'll take them away with us, in us.

DENISE: You mean, Gina, that we won't ever forget them? There are some of them whose names I didn't even know.

GINA: Even without a name they'll be in us. We will restore them with a look, a gesture. Maybe in our dreams.

DENISE: If I have to return to relive all of this in my dreams . . . Oh no!

FRANÇOISE: Don't be afraid, Denise. Dreams fade.

GINA: Me, I'm not afraid to dream. I'll touch my clean sheets, fine and crispy, my nightgown. I love crepe de Chine nightgowns. They're like another skin, softer than your own. I'll caress my sheets and I'll know that I'm dreaming.

DENISE: You've had so many things in your life.

GINA: You'll have them, Denise. Just to get undressed to go to sleep, to sleep in a bed, with sheets, with slippers when you get off the bed, that alone . . .

DENISE: Seventy days during which we haven't taken our dresses off . . . They must stink, but we don't notice because our nostrils are full of the smell of the crematoria. If we could smell . . .

GINA: Oh! And perfume! It's so nice. It's something that you touch and that you don't touch, opaque and transparent, real and unreal. I love perfume.

DENISE: You see you'll be able to live again. There are so many things that you love. I don't know anything about perfumes. My mother never bought any. She never bought much of anything.

GINA: Yes, Denise, you'll have everything to love.

FRANÇOISE: What does that one want from us? *(There is someone that we don't see; GINA turns away.)* It looks as though she's calling us. Me? The three of us? She's signaling you, Gina.

GINA *(looking):* All right, I'm going.

(Exit GINA.)

Scene 4

FRANÇOISE: What can she want from Gina? Do you know her, the big kapo?

DENISE: By sight. It's the kapo of the White Kerchiefs.

FRANÇOISE: What can she have to do with Gina?

DENISE: It looks as if Gina is arguing with her.

(FRANÇOISE *and* DENISE *walk together, passing other prisoners who are also walking, with whom they exchange glances etc., at the same time they watch the scene between the kapo and* GINA, *who are offstage.*)

Scene 5

FRANÇOISE *(to* GINA *who returns):* What did she want?

GINA: Oh, nothing, to ask if I knew some Lydia, a French girl *(gives a hidden sign to* FRANÇOISE). Later.

FRANÇOISE: It's almost nice today. While we were taking a little walk, Denise and I, I was thinking that a night like this, I mean a spring evening, would be marvelous for a walk in a park. Green lawns, maybe tulips. The chestnut trees must be in bloom now in Paris.

GINA: From my window, I used to see the Buttes-Chaumont. I think it was the most beautiful park in all Paris.

FRANÇOISE: I don't know the place. It's not my neighborhood. I'd go to the Luxembourg, sit on a bench with a book, and the noise of the water in the basin of the fountain . . .

DENISE: At home, we walked on the mall. It's a big street, with green walks, under the plane trees. They're very tall. They're really beautiful, especially in the spring when the leaves are like fine lace. They probably don't have their leaves yet; they become green much later than the chestnut trees. We had chestnut trees in the schoolyard.

(Curfew siren. They return to the barracks.)

Scene 6

They reach their box, as do the other occupants of the barracks, but the other boxes disappear into the darkness leaving only FRANÇOISE, GINA *and* DENISE *in view.*

DENISE *(unfolding the blanket):* We have privileges, now that we've been here for a long time. Two inches of hair gets us as much respect as a venerable beard. We've got a bunk for the three of us and no one dares to bother us. Maybe it's also because we've become shrewd. We know how to escape from the clippers and the disinfection. You remember the last time? When we stood naked outside from morning roll call until evening roll call? How cold it was! And they gave us back our dresses all wet. The lice were still there. They just got sluggish from the soaking and when our dresses got warm on us, they came alive again. What a day! And it was Renée who said: "Cabbage soup, margarine or naked women, I don't want to see any more of them ever again, for the rest of my life. You won't find me at the Folies Bergère" . . . Cabbage soup, the way we used to have it at home, with bacon and ham and a piece of goose with some of its fat . . . I'd eat a whole potful . . . She was funny, Renée. That day, we had less hope of getting out of here than today. Just because we're not so cold.

FRANÇOISE: Spring without the taste of spring . . . How I'd like to have a taste in my mouth.

DENISE: After roll call, I saw a Russian woman, one who works in the garden who was selling onions. Two onions for a ration of bread. I had already exchanged my ration of bread for a pair of underpants, the way you told me. If I had known, I would have waited until tomorrow for the underpants.

FRANÇOISE: I'd like to bite into an onion; but when I think of a taste, I mean something good, really good. A fruit . . .

DENISE: A fish . . . Gina, give us your recipe for sole in whiskey. I like sole in whiskey the way you make it. I don't know how it is, I've never had any whiskey. I've never even seen any. You cut the filets . . .

GINA: Another time. It's too late. We have to sleep.

DENISE *(rolls herself in her blanket):* Well, goodnight! Sleep well.

(FRANÇOISE and GINA, *sitting in their places, remain silent until* DENISE *falls asleep.)*

Scene 7

FRANÇOISE: What did she want from you?

GINA: I have to join her Kommando.

FRANÇOISE: But that's impossible. You told her that you didn't want to, that . . .

GINA: She took my number. My name is already on her list. It's an order.

FRANÇOISE: The White Kerchief Kommando?

GINA: Yes.

FRANÇOISE: What can you do? What can we do?

GINA: What is there to do? It's impossible to do what she wants, in any case. Undress children to throw them into a ditch full of kindling wood that they sprinkle with gasoline and then set fire to, never. To undress the children, throw them into the bonfire and fold their little clothes into near square piles while they burn, no.

FRANÇOISE: What can you do?

GINA: There's always a choice. We've often talked about it together.

FRANÇOISE: But Gina, you argued, you told her . . .

GINA: It's useless, Françoise. You know I tried.

FRANÇOISE: What are you going to do?

GINA: When it's completely dark, I'll go towards the barbed wire.

FRANÇOISE: I'm going with you.

GINA *(of* DENISE*):* No, you must stay with her.

(They hold hands. A long silence.)

FRANÇOISE *(pointing to* DENISE *who is sleeping):* What will I tell her?

GINA: You'll explain. Wait as long as possible.

FRANÇOISE: As long as possible? That will be when she gets up, in a little while, at the siren, and you won't be next to us. *(Silence.)* I want to talk to you. It seems to me that I have so much to tell you before we part.

GINA: Words are lost on the one who is going to die. It's I who should talk to you. Let's admit that we've told each other everything during these days and nights we've spent together. Speaking cuts into resolution. Our husbands could still write a name on the walls of the cells where they spent their last night before Mont Valerien.[4] I'll only write on your memory.

FRANÇOISE: Memory is fragile here.

GINA: You'll hold out . . . The worst is over. *(Pause.)* Remember what I told you, for my father.

FRANÇOISE: I remember. I will remember. I'll try to carry back the memory. I'll do everything I can, I give you my word.

GINA: It's the darkest part of the night. I'm going.

FRANÇOISE: You still have time before the siren. Give yourself a minute. Give me a minute.

GINA: You can't give yourself the luxury of a night watch when it's your own. Goodbye, Françoise.

FRANÇOISE: Goodbye, Gina. Thank you. Without you I would not have lasted.

GINA: Bring back Denise. It would be a shame not to after having kept her till now. Goodbye Françoise.

(They embrace. GINA, *who was sitting on her heels, like* FRANÇOISE—*because this entire scene takes place in the box where they sleep together—gently kisses* DENISE's *forehead. She does not awaken.* GINA *jumps to the ground, disappears into the night.)*

---

4. Mont Valerien: a fortress near Paris, where the Germans executed men from the Underground.

Scene 8

FRANÇOISE *remains motionless, sitting in her place. You could say that she is counting* GINA's *steps, perhaps fifty; a shot.*

FRANÇOISE: The guard saw her from the watchtower as soon as she was caught in the spotlight, before she got to the barbed wire. She was dead before she could die. Goodbye, Gina.
DENISE *(in her sleep):* What is it? A shot?
FRANÇOISE: Yes, you're right. Sleep.
DENISE *(sleepily):* Attempted escape. Another unfortunate one who couldn't bear it any longer.
(She turns over and goes back to sleep. The stage goes to black.)

Epilogue

To audience.

DENISE: We have come back
FRANÇOISE: We have come back to tell you and now we are standing here ill at ease not knowing what to say, how to say it . . .
DENISE: Because we came from a place where words had a different meaning.
FRANÇOISE: Words to say simple things:
to be cold
to be thirsty
to be hungry
to be tired
to need sleep, to be afraid
to live, to die.

DENISE: If you don't understand us
it's because we can no longer give those words
the meaning they had there.
FRANÇOISE: We wanted to be heard
we wanted to be understood
DENISE: Don't think we resent it
we knew you wouldn't understand
that you wouldn't believe
because it has even become unbelievable to us
FRANÇOISE: Why should you believe
those stories of ghosts
ghosts who came back and who are not able to explain how?

(Music.)

THE END

Selected Bibliography

The following bibliography is not intended to be exhaustive of the materials on the subject of the Holocaust; rather, it seeks to guide the reader to the major works in each of several areas of inquiry which are discussed, from a theatrical perspective, in the editor's introduction. Additional bibliographic information may be found in the volumes listed below.

HISTORY

Dawidowicz, Lucy S. *The War Against the Jews: 1933–1945*. New York: Holt, Reinhart and Winston, 1975.

Hilberg, Raul. *The Destruction of the European Jews*. New York: Quadrangle Books, 1961.

Levin, Nora. *The Holocaust: The Destruction of European Jewry*. New York: Schocken Books, 1973.

Rubenstein, Richard L. *The Cunning of History*. New York: Harper and Row, 1975.

PHILOSOPHY, SOCIOLOGY, AND THEOLOGY

Arendt, Hannah. *Eichmann in Jerusalem*. New York: Viking Press, 1964 rev. ed.

Bettelheim, Bruno. *Surviving and Other Essays*. New York: Knopf, 1979.

Des Pres, Terence. *The Survivor: An Anatomy of Life in the Death Camps*. New York: Oxford University Press, 1976.

Fackenheim, Emil L. *God's Presence in History: Jewish Affirmations and Philosophical Reflections*. New York: New York University Press, 1970.

GHETTO AND CAMP LIFE

Delbo, Charlotte. *None of Us Will Return*. Translated by John Githens. Boston: Beacon Press, 1978.

Donat, Alexander. *The Holocaust Kingdom.* New York: Holt, Reinhart and Winston, 1965.

Kaplan, Chaim A. *The Warsaw Diary of Chaim A. Kaplan.* Translated and edited by Abraham I. Katch. New York: Collier Books, 1973 rev. ed.

Levi, Primo. *Survival in Auschwitz.* Translated by Stuart Woolf. New York: Collier Books, 1971. Also translated by Stuart Woolf as *If This Is a Man* (New York: Orion Press, 1959).

Ringelblum, Emmanuel. *Notes from the Warsaw Ghetto.* Edited and translated by Jacob Sloan. New York: Schocken Books, 1974.

Steiner, Jean-Francois. *Treblinka.* Translated by Helen Weaver. New York: Simon and Schuster, 1967.

LITERARY CRITICISM

Alexander, Edward. *The Resonance of Dust.* Columbus: Ohio State University Press, 1979.

Ezrahi, Sidra DeKoven. *By Words Alone: The Holocaust in Literature.* Chicago: University of Chicago Press, 1980.

Langer, Lawrence. *The Holocaust and the Literary Imagination.* New Haven: Yale University Press, 1975.

Rosenfeld, Alvin S. *A Double Dying: Reflections on Holocaust Literature.* Bloomington: Indiana University Press, 1980

Photograph by Lawrence A. Pike

SHIMON WINCELBERG (*Resort 76*) is a prize-winning playwright whose work has been produced on and off Broadway and throughout Europe. His short stories, satire, and criticism have appeared in numerous magazines and anthologies, and his work in television has earned him three Writers Guild of America Awards and a "Special Award" from the Mystery Writers of America. His previous produced plays include *Kataki* and *The King of the Schnorrers* (music: Bernard Hermann; lyrics: Diane Lampert). In collaboration with his wife Anita, he recently published the biography *The Samurai of Vishogrod*.

RACHMIL BRYKS, who was born in Poland in 1912 and died in 1974, was a writer of poems, short stories, and novels. His career was interrupted by the Holocaust; he spent those years in the ghetto in Lodz and in the Auschwitz concentration camp. His work, originally in Yiddish, has been translated into several languages; *A Cat in the Ghetto* is his novella upon which *Resort 76* is based.

Los Angeles Herald Examiner photograph by Michael Haering

HAROLD LIEBERMAN (*Throne of Straw*), a native New Yorker, grew up during the Depression and spent his early years as a labor organizer. Since moving to California, he has worked closely with the Los Angeles Art Theatre. His works include *The Ghandi Play* (with D. Freed); *Brother John Faustus; Hogs Run Wild* (with D. Freed), a musical about the robber barons; *Pierre*, an opera libretto based on Melville's novel; and, most recently, *Last Leavings*, a play about the change in a family as one of its members dies of cancer. EDITH L. LIEBERMAN (*Throne of Straw*) was a Yiddishist and author of a cancer resource book. She died in 1975.

Photograph by Elke Grevel

GEORGE TABORI (*The Cannibals*) is a playwright, novelist, film writer, and adapter, who was born in Budapest, Hungary, in 1914. His plays include *Flight into Egypt, The Emperor's Clothes, Brouhaha,* and *Pinkville.* Mr. Tabori has adapted Strindberg's *Miss Julie,* Brecht's *Arturo Ui,* and Max Frisch's *Andorra* into English and created *Brecht on Brecht.* His films include *Young Lovers, I Confess, The Journey,* and the screen adaptation of Sartre's *No Exit.* He is also the author of a number of novels: *Beneath the Stone, Companions of the Left Hand, Original Sin, The Caravan Passes,* and *The Good One.* Currently, he lives and works in West Germany.

CHARLOTTE DELBO (*Who Will Carry the Word?*) was born in 1913. In 1941, while serving as Louis Jouvet's secretary, she interrupted a tour of South America to return to France and join the Underground to fight the Nazis. Arrested in March, 1942, she spent a year in prison before being deported to Auschwitz. She was liberated more than two years later from Ravensbruck. After the war she turned to writing; besides *Who Will Carry the Word?* (*Qui rapportera ces paroles?*), her plays include *La sentence* (1972), *Maria Lusitania* (1975), and *Le coup d'Etat* (1975). Mme. Delbo's essays and articles have appeared widely. The first volume of her poetic trilogy, *Aucun de nous ne reviendra* (1970) has been reprinted in English as *None of Us Will Return* (1978). Mme. Delbo resides in Paris.

CYNTHIA HAFT (translator, *Who Will Carry The Word?*) is on the research staff of Yad Vashem (Heroes' and Martyrs' Remembrance Authority) in Jerusalem. She has published many works in the area of her special interest: the effect of the Holocaust on the Jews of France.

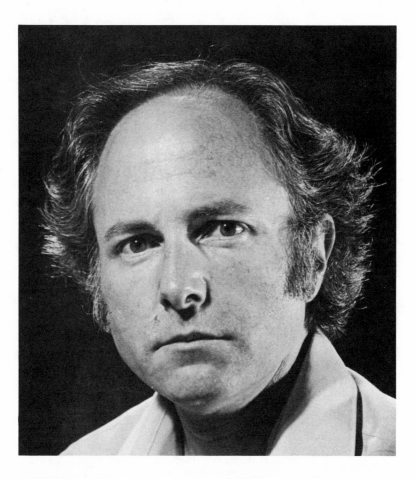

ROBERT SKLOOT is Professor of Theatre and Drama at the University of Wisconsin-Madison, where he teaches and directs plays. He has published widely on a variety of modern playwrights and current dramatic themes. In 1980–81 he was Fulbright Professor of Theatre and Drama at the Hebrew University, Jerusalem, and Tel Aviv University, Israel.

DESIGNED BY IRVING PERKINS ASSOCIATES
COMPOSED BY GRAPHIC COMPOSITION, INC., ATHENS, GEORGIA
MANUFACTURED BY CUSHING-MALLOY, INC., ANN ARBOR, MICHIGAN
TEXT IS SET IN SABON, DISPLAY LINES IN SABON AND WINDSOR

ᐽ

Library of Congress Cataloging in Publication Data
Main entry under title:
The Theatre of the Holocaust.
Bibliography: pp. 327–328.
Contents: Resort 76 / Shimon Wincelberg—Throne of
straw / Harold and Edith Lieberman—The cannibals /
George Tabori—[etc.]
1. Holocaust, Jewish (1939–1945)—Drama. 2. Drama—
20th century. I. Skloot, Robert. II. Wincelberg, Shimon.
PN6120.J4T4   1982   809.2′93458   81–69829
ISBN 0–299–09070–1
ISBN 0–299–09074–4 (pbk.)

ISBN 0–299–09070–1 cloth; 0–299–09074–4 paper

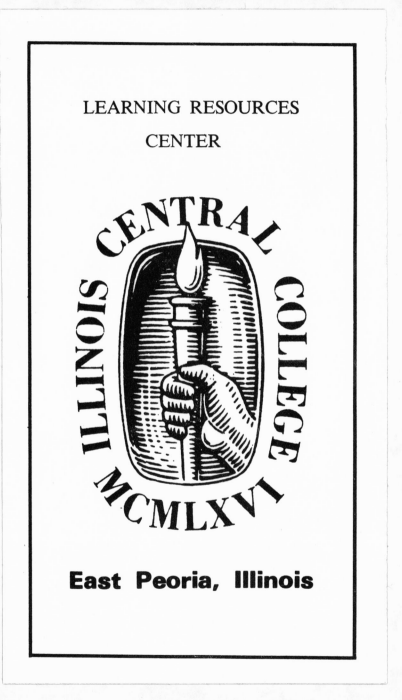

LEARNING RESOURCES
CENTER

ILLINOIS CENTRAL COLLEGE

MCMLXVI

East Peoria, Illinois